WESTERNIZING THE THIRD WORLD

Westernizing the Third World identifies the mainstream economic theories which have been employed in developing countries and reveals why Eurocentric concepts are not suitable for the developing world. The second edition of this successful and popular text has been updated and revised to incorporate recent issues in development economics. Significant new additions include:

- Asian values and development
- democracy, human rights and good governance
- globalization and development
- boxed summaries of key arguments

Ozay Mehmet is Professor of International Affairs at Carleton University, Canada. He is the author of *Islamic Identity and Development: Studies of the Islamic Periphery*, also published by Routledge.

WESTERNIZING THE THIRD WORLD

The Eurocentricity of economic development theories

Second edition

Ozay Mehmet

London and New York

First published 1995, reprinted 1997
This edition first published 1999
by Routledge
11 New Fetter Lane, London EC4P 4EE

Simultaneously published in the USA and Canada
by Routledge
29 West 35th Street, New York, NY 110001

Routledge is an imprint of the Taylor and Francis Group

© 1999 Ozay Mehmet

Typeset in Garamond by
BC Typesetting, Bristol
Printed and bound in Great Britain by
Biddles Ltd, Guildford and King's Lynn

British Library Cataloguing in Publicatino Data
A catalogue record for this book is available from the British Library

Library of Congress Cataloging in Publication Data
Mehmet, Ozay.
Westernizing the Third World: the eurocentricity of economic
development theories/Ozay Mehmet. – 2nd ed.
p.   cm.
Includes bibliographical references and index.
1. Economic development.   2. Mercantile system.   3. Ethnocentrism.
I. Title.
HD75.M43   1999
338.9′009172′4–dc21   98-31890
                                                                        CIP

ISBN 0–415–20573–5 (hbk)
ISBN 0–415–20574–3 (pbk)

CONTENTS

CONTENTS

FIGURES

BOXES

PREFACE TO THE SECOND EDITION

About two hundred years ago, two apparently independent events laid the foundation for Western prosperity: the publication of Adam Smith's *The Wealth of Nations* in 1776 and the onset of the Industrial Revolution. In fact, the two events were causally interconnected. The first was an intellectual achievement, the defining moment of modern capitalism. The Industrial Revolution opened the age of aggressive entrepreneurship, legitimized not only by Smith, but by such European thinkers as Weber – an enterprise guided by the new ethics of capitalism, shaped by the profit motive. Capitalism has served the West well, aided as much by the religion of economics as by aggressive penetration and exploitation on a global scale.

Indeed, the last two centuries have been Western centuries, during which the rest of the world has been Westernized through a market-driven process that operates for the benefit of a privileged minority of humankind. The Westernization of the world began with colonialism and the settlement of the New World. The inner logic of this Westernization, directed from Europe until 1914 (and subsequently from the USA), has been a remarkable, systemic drive for the globalization of Western capitalism. The intellectual origin of this drive has been mainstream economics which has capitalized technology, labour, environment and other productive resources; in practice, these resources have been harnessed by aggressive capitalists (originally called adventurers, forerunners of today's multinational corporations: MNCs) in a worldwide search for profits. This drive has enriched the West but not the vast majority of humanity.

Two hundred years is a relatively short period in history. Despite neo-conservative and neo-liberal voices to the contrary (Fukuyama 1989, 1992; Huntington 1993, 1996), now Western capitalism, like a person approaching old age, is reaching internal and external limits. Within high-income countries, average income per capita has reached a plateau at which a more conserving society is slowly emerging; in the process, *consumer sovereignty*, the core foundation of consumer behaviour in mainstream economics, is eroding away at the edges of 'consumerism'. Social philosophers (Saul 1992, 1995) and social scientists are now seriously questioning the ideology of 'the growth paradigm' (Ayres 1997). Increasingly, the economists themselves are realizing the 'delusions' of Western capitalism (Gray 1998) and leading voices in the profession see the future of capitalism in a globalized context in terms of 'social volcanoes' owing to the system's inherent forces of 'instability, rising inequality and a lumpen proletariat' (Thurow 1996: 325).

Clearly not all is well with the dismal science, Adam Smith's religion of economics, the ideology of Western capitalism. If less is better in a 'greener society', then Western capitalism stands at a turning point: effective demand for goods and services, the engine that drives the system, must henceforth slow down. In fact, the Western profit-driven marketplace is running out of goods; instead 'evils' such as gambling, crime, drugs and pornography are emerging and providing the most profitable opportunities, as these are, one by one, being decriminalized. Externally, too, global markets are changing: shifting comparative advantage is moving the economic centre of gravity from the West to new, and more competitive centres of growth in what used to be the Third World, while the collapse of the Second World has placed the borders, values and prospects of the First into serious doubt.

The decline of Western capitalism would not, of itself, be surprising. After all, its ultimate collapse, 'when (industrial) progress ceases' (Mill 1917: 746) due to vanishing profits in an stationary state, was fully acknowledged by the great theorists of the profit-driven market ideology well before Marx. What is more surprising is the durability of the mystique of an idealized Western worldview: namely, Eurocentricity, the subject of this study.

THE ORGANIZATION OF THE STUDY

The study is organized in seven chapters. The introduction in Chapter 1 sets the stage by defining the problem in terms of a deliberate Western attempt, by analytical and policy means, to Westernize *the Third World*, a value-loaded stereotyping of the vast majority of humanity, with long colonial roots. This is followed in Chapter 2 with a survey of major classical theories, i.e. theories formulated in the pre-1914 world dominated by colonialism and in the aftermath of the Industrial Revolution. In this part of the study what is particularly noteworthy is the contradiction on which the 'old economic order' was built: namely, while free trade theories of development dominated mainstream Western theory promising universal benefits, mercantilist pursuit of surplus value in colonies for the benefit of the mother country was, in fact, the systemic, single-purpose aim of development strategy in the field.

The rest of the study is focused on the 'new economic order' which began to be constructed after World War II. Chapter 3 examines the paradigm debate in the postwar period. These paradigms share a common neo-classical foundation and an optimism growing out of the European reconstruction experience under the Marshall Plan, and then increasingly coloured by the political economy of the Cold War and the challenges of nation-building in the new Third World undergoing decolonization. Chapter 4 is concerned with the more technocratic design of Third World economic development in the postwar period, highlighting the rise and fall of the mystique of (Western) planning.

By the end of the 1960s optimism waned, giving way to rising concerns about the adverse impact of Western developmentalism such as inappropriate technology transfers and MNC–host country conflicts over employment and retained income. But paradigm debate continues. Chapter 5 begins with a discussion of the short-lived New Economic International Order (NEIO) debate after the OPEC crisis of October 1973 and its implications for North–South relations. Of greater importance for theory is the autonomous development experience of the Far Eastern NICs – newly industrialized countries, largely shaped by endogenous factors, in part cultural, but primarily as a result of pragmatic, problem-solving policies of development-minded states, looking East to Japan, rather than to the West. This development experience, however, was based as much on capitalist exploitation of natural and labour resources as on creativity, and, as a result in 1997–8, the Asian NICs suffered a deep currency collapse. This, too, has some important theoretical lessons which will be highlighted in the relevant parts of the book.

Then, in Chapter 6 there is an overview of the most recent paradigms in development studies, including new institutionalism, IMF–WB structural adjustment, globalization, endogenous growth based on human capital, sustainable development, and civil society reforms. Chapter 7 concludes with a look at the future research agenda for development studies.

A NOTE ON REVISIONS

I have welcomed the invitation from Alison Kirk, my editor at Routledge, to undertake this revision of *Westernizing the Third World*. However, it is fitting to note that revisions in the second edition have been kept to a minimum in order to preserve the original argument contained in the first edition.

Two criteria, in particular, have guided the revision work: (1) making the text more 'reader friendly', by adding 'boxes' to explain key concepts, keeping in mind that the book appears to have found a wide readership amongst students not only of economic development, but in other related disciplines such as sociology, geography, politics and administration; and (2) updating some of the material in the light of more recent developments, such as, for example, the Asian currency crisis of 1997–8.

But no attempt has been made to incorporate the large volume of literature on development studies. To have done so would have required writing a new book. Accordingly, *Westernizing the Third World*, second edition, must stand alone as a contribution on its own original merit.

Several people, especially students and academic colleagues, have commented on the first edition of the book and I would like to take this opportunity to thank them collectively and anonymously for their contributions in improving this present one.

1

WESTERNIZING THE THIRD WORLD

A Western worldview is the distinctive feature of the mainstream theories of economic development, old and new (Meier ed. 1976, 1984, 1989; Herrick and Kindleberger 1988; Chenery and Srinivasan eds 1988; Gillis *et al*. 1992). This worldview rests on a utopian presumption of 'economics as value-free science' (Heilbroner 1973), rational, analytical and technical (Yutopoulos and Nugent 1976), concerned with ranking investment priorities and choosing amongst alternative allocations of scarce resources to promote economic development. Allocation decisions are then thought to be optimal, 'objectively' determined in markets; the ideal market, known in economics textbooks as 'perfect competition', rests on rational behaviour and *laissez-faire* laws of supply and demand going back to the 'invisible hand' of Adam Smith (1776), the father of modern economics.

The laws of supply and demand, or market forces, are credited as the causal factors behind the rise of capitalism in the West. And, Western capitalism is generally regarded as the point of departure in economic development theorizing, demonstrating 'how it (i.e. modern economy) all began' (Rostow 1975). In a larger sense, Westernization, encompassing both economic and political development, is taken as the 'universal reference' (Eisenstadt 1987), an example for others to follow.

In the post-World War II period, both economic development and modernization theories have been utilized for Westernizing the Third World (See Box 1). In this period, textbooks summarily dismissed local cultures as 'barriers' or 'obstacles' to economic development (Zuvekas 1979: chaps 2 and 3). Highly technocratic and ahistorical, this was the 'golden age' of economic development theorizing (Meier and Seers eds 1984), producing an incredible harvest of Western theories and paradigms to guide Third World

Box 1

What is Westernization?

Westernization is reconstructing or shaping the rest of the world on Western norms and institutions. Central in Westernization is the idea of economic development as 'progress' determined according to the market forces of supply and demand which emerged in the West. Westernizing seeks to universalize markets, reducing what is worthwhile and valuable to market-determined value. In markets, individuals and households everywhere become buyers and sellers. A buyer's worth is directly proportional to purchasing power or 'ability to pay'. Selling, anything and everything for which someone else is willing to pay, is the standard method of generating value. In the process, ethics are increasingly being subordinated to the supremacy of market forces. As for the Western political process, in theory resting on the democratic principle of one-person-one-vote, it is being undermined by the neo-liberal ideology of ennobling the market which in fact empowers the big corporations that dominate those markets.

countries on the fast track to promised prosperity, helped by Western aid and technical assistance. The United Nations took a major leading role in this venture declaring successive Development Decades and popularizing Western models and blueprints (UN ECAFE 1955; UN 1989).

But, the harvest has been disappointing. After almost half a century of Western-guided economic development what is the end result? The gap between the 'haves and have nots' – to use the original terminology of the debate then – has not diminished (Rosenstein-Rodan in Bhagwati ed. 1970); in many parts of the Third World, in particular in Africa, South Asia and in Central and Latin America, real incomes have declined sharply and there is more poverty today than in 1970 in an increasingly unsustainable world due to ecological limits to growth. According to World Bank statistics, 23 countries had *negative* per capita GNP growth between 1965 and 1990; between 1980 and 1991 the number of countries in this category had risen to 43. As at 1995, according to the United Nations High Commissioner for Refugees (UNHCR), there were a total of 27.4 million refugees, internally displaced persons and other persons of concern as a result of conflict and strife in the Third World, often caused by poverty and underdevelopment (UN High Commissioner for Refugees 1995: 247). Clearly, development, as a field of study, faces 'dilemmas' of Hegelian proportions (Toye 1993), or it is simply in 'crisis' (Hettne 1990), though the nature of the crisis itself is far from certain. We lack clear and convincing theories and explanations for persistent underdevelopment and mass poverty in the Third World.

This study aims at putting much of the blame for persistent Third World underdevelopment where it surely belongs – not on the patient but on the doctor and his prescriptions. This means the source of the blame for failed postwar development lies in the faulty prescriptions derived from Western mainstream (i.e. positive) economic theorizing itself. More specifically, the study is centred on the following three arguments: First, mainstream economics has produced flawed theories of economic development for the Third World. Second, these flawed theories imported from the West have lacked fit resulting in distorted and biased Third World development. Third, for reasons to be analysed below in relation to Eurocentricity, Western theorists have stubbornly ignored the basic flaws in their theories, hiding these behind idealized constructions of perfect competition or rational (i.e. Western) behaviour. Overall, mainstream economists have failed to realize that underdevelopment may be casually linked to: (1) monopoly profits, externalities, transaction costs and other 'market failures' (Bradhan *et al.* 1990), and above all, (2) hidden subjective values embedded in these theories themselves. It is this failure that is primarily responsible for growth without development (Clower *et al.* 1966) or equity (Adelman and Morris 1973; Chenery *et al.* 1974) or social justice (Mehmet 1978).

In fairness to Western theorists, it must also be stated at the outset that, the argument here is not that the theorists themselves were part of some conspiracy or that they were unaware of the inherent flaws of mainstream market theory; indeed, leading figures were men of goodwill, and such key theorists as Kaldor and Rosenstein-Rodan were indeed aware of the deficiencies of equilibrium market theory (Meier ed. 1989: 513–23). Many of them subsequently 'confessed' or abandoned their early optimism derived from rationalist premises (Meier and Seers eds 1984). Kaldor, for example, rebelled against neo-classical idealist theorizing time and again, denouncing such an approach as having 'led to a cul-de-sac' (1985: 57).

But, in the early postwar period, such premises dominated and prevailed, despite solid empirical works documenting imperfect markets and monopoly-monopsony practices in the Third World (Bauer 1948). Also, voices of dissent (Seers 1963; Bauer 1971) on mainstream theorizing were expressed. Accordingly, no amount of good intent can hide the failure of Western theories because, in the end, nothing seemed to influence the rationalist Western mindset idealizing Western capitalism and its dogged determination to apply equilibrium economics to developing countries. When these idealized (i.e. stylized) theories failed in the Third World, the typical reaction of the mainstream economist was to simply rearrange the underlying assumptions of the theory, always preserving its Western rationalist roots, never conceiving the possibility of culture-specific conceptions of rationalism. This has been well put by Harry Johnson's critique of rationality: 'if it [i.e. the rational market model] does not seem to work rationally by my standards, my understanding of how it *ought to work* is probably defective; and I must work harder at the theory of rational maximizing behaviour and the empirical consequences of it' (quoted in Kindleberger 1989: 29, italics added); and hence, the everlasting confidence in the universality of mainstream market theory and of Western rationalism. Therein lie the roots of biased and misguided prescriptions for Third World economic development policy and planning.

The wide gulf between theory and reality (Lall and Stewart eds 1986) lies at the very heart of 'the rise and decline of development economics' (Hirschman 1981). While idealizing theory, in practice the Eurocentric mind is inherently mercantilist, aggressively pursuing private interest, as surplus value, in an adversarial relationship in trade or economic transactions. A few examples of this Eurocentric mercantilism may be cited. Under the 'triangular trade' African slave trade is a historical event that produced great wealth for Europe (Stavrianos 1981: esp. chap. 10). Slavery, combined with Eli Whitney's cotton gin technology, also helped create the wealth of the American South:

> Slaves made fortunes for those who owned and skillfully exploited them . . . Southern slavery . . . was a product of the Industrial Revolution, high technology, and the commercial spirit for mass markets of hundreds of millions worldwide. It was very much part of the new modern world.
> (Johnson 1997: 311–12)

Similarly, in North America, Australia and New Zealand, land originally occupied by native populations, enabled European settlement and colonization. While these events produced wealth for the Europeans and their descendants, it impoverished non-European populations. This unequal outcome is justified with appeal to a remarkable moralistic worldview in which economics and ethics are divorced: 'It is a horrible fact that modern economics and high technology do not always work in favour of justice or freedom' (Johnson 1997: 311).

This is a worldview projected from a zero-sum game framework. In this framework, action in market relations is not guided, in some ethical sense, by the ideals of theory, nor is it subject to voluntary restraint to exercise moderation as in non-Western ethics; idealization of theory merely serves as a negotiating strategy, as in strategic trade policy, to rationalize or justify a private gain in order to win, or to score, at the expense of the other party.

The gulf between idealized market theory of mainstream economics and the practice of economic development is still with us because economic development theories have been Western, made in the West and based on experience far removed from Third World realities. In a word, and with one important exception, these theories lacked *fit* essential for social and cultural soundness. The sole exception has been the Far Eastern model, initially evolved in post-Meiji Japan, and during 1970–95 reconfirmed in the Far Eastern NICs (see pp. 114–120 below), where successful economic development was based on 'made-at-home' solutions through adaptation, a pragmatic blending of local culture and transferred knowledge, manipulated by an authoritarian developmental state committed to capitalist growth.

Sound theories of economic development need to be grounded in culture-specific reality, just as an infant learning to walk must have its feet on the ground. Such theories need to be constructed endogenously, inductively rather than deductively, with open minds to learn about cross-cultural values, institutions and environments before prescribing policy interventions. In particular, development economists must be willing to learn from past mistakes. This brief study is a contribution towards that end.

DEFINING KEY TERMS AND DELINEATING THE SCOPE OF THE STUDY

'Mainstream theories' in this study refers to classical and neo-classical market theories of Western capitalism known as positive economics as distinct from welfare or normative economics. The intention is to identify internal flaws in these theories, using the assumptions and analytical tools of the theories themselves. Therefore, the approach of the study deliberately excludes the large literature of the dependency and neo-Marxist schools, save for occasional references, since the latter utilize alternative concepts and tools of analysis.

'Flaws' in market theories refer to normative or subjective corrections for deviations, termed 'market failures', from ideal market solutions predicted by theory. For example, in the perfect competition model, profits exist as 'normal profits', but 'normal' is not objectively determined. 'Market failure' arises from a wide range of 'externalities', typically as subjective or 'psychic' values, from lack of 'perfect information' or from 'irrational' behaviour. The ideal market solution guaranteeing convergence of private and social optimal outcomes, uses an elabourate theoretical and abstract general equilibrium framework known as the Pareto Optimum (Mishan 1960; Scitovsky 1952: 177–81). This is derived from utility-maximizing behaviour of individual and independent consumers and producers, each acting rationally with perfect information, with no externalities and zero transaction costs, *ceteris paribus*, i.e. other things being equal. Markets are then said to 'fail' if and when one or more of these conditions is unmet, or when the *ceteris paribus* condition does not apply.

'Mainstream theorists', trained in classical and neo-classical market theory possess a conviction, or a faith, in the supremacy of market economy driven by rationalism and the profit motive. The inherent contradiction between the idealism of rationalism and the mercantilism of the profit motive was simply overlooked or dismissed. The trick utilized by mainstream economists here was simply to equate technical efficiency with value-loaded optimality, declaring that the best market is the ideal of 'perfect competition' functioning invisibly without government intervention and perfect information, and then to proceed to policy formulation as if such ideal markets existed or could possibly exist. The *ceteris paribus* condition is a trick which enables the mainstream economist to construct a hypothetical world of interactions and then apply the results from this construction to the real world. In other words, mainstream economists share a strong presumption that 'imperfect' markets, such as monopolies and cartels, can be reformed and ultimately converted into the ideal perfect competition market – in the undefined long run.

There have been notable critics, Keynesians and socialist theorists (Lange and Taylor 1938; Lerner 1946), who have argued in terms of 'market failure' and the myth of a self-regulated market economy (Polanyi 1944). However, the mainstream theorist has relied on the ideal of perfect competition capable of generating a grand optimal solution known as Pareto Optimum (Bator 1957) ignoring the inherent flaws of the theory (Little 1957). The idealized rationalist market solution has been applied in the design of economic policy as a historical, technocratic magic wand to promote economic development. When state intervention with planning and public enterprise was in vogue during the quarter century after World War II, the inherent contradiction between mainstream market theory and an interventionist state was overlooked. Indeed, state intervention in the service of economic development was actively promoted at first before it fell from grace in the post-1980 neo-conservative offensive of new institutionalism (see pp. 122–125 below) when 'government failure', rather than 'market failure', re-emerged in the forefront of the development debate.

THE CENTRAL ARGUMENT OF THE STUDY

This study's central argument is that mainstream economic development theory is, in reality, a branch of Western economics, and as such, it is European centred, suffering in particular from a pair of culture-specific biases: it rests on strong, though unstated, nationalistic premises, and it is pro-capital biased. The net effect is that the West is always the winner. Let's examine how this comes about.

In terms of its nationalist premises mainstream theory has operated as a tool of Western national interests, from the days of chartered companies to the multinational corporations of today, to enrich the First World at the expense of the Third. The nationalist premises of Western economics are deeply rooted in the mercantilism which Adam Smith sought to replace with universally valid laws of an impersonal market. Both the universality and the scientific attributes of Western economics are myths. In place of universality, meaning here universally shared values and tastes, there is Western cultural specificity whereby European economic history is taken for granted as universally valid for theory construction. Western individualism and utility maximization are projected as rational other modes of human behaviour derived from sharing and cooperation being externalized. As regards the scientific attributes of Western economics, this is simply assumed to be the case by means of the *ceteris paribus* assumption, reductionism and other analytical tricks. As a logical system, Western economics is a closed system (similar to Euclidean geometry) in which assumptions are substituted for reality, and gender, environment and Third World are all equally dismissed as irrelevant except for their exchange values fixed in markets. As abstract, deductive reasoning, mainstream economics is clearly neither value-free (Heilbroner 1973) nor tolerant of non-Western cultures. Consequently, development economics has not been culture-friendly and has effectively denied the cultural diversity that exists in non-Western branches of humanity, where group and community rights are often held in higher esteem than individualism, and cooperation rather than competition is prized.

In terms of its pro-capital bias, mainstream economics is universally damaging, irrespective of nationality. Emerging as it did at a time which coincided with the rise of nation-states in Europe (Hobsbawm 1992), now in decline (Gottlieb 1993), Western economics legitimized capital accumulation as economic growth, viewing international trade as the path to acquisition and expansion of capital stock for further growth. The unique, inner logic of Western civilization has been its single-purpose pursuit of capital for profit. In time the West emerged as the capital-rich centre of the world. Western economics favours capitalism in a more fundamental way than Marx's European-centred theory of surplus value (Marx 1972: chaps 5, 7, 14, 15, 16); it promotes capitalization on a global scale by a systemic process of converting, slowly but surely, not just labour but every productive resource into capital. More specifically, global capitalization monetizes and extracts asset values in all productive resources such as technology, ecology, human and natural resources and converts them into private property to be acquired, owned and controlled by capitalists motivated by individualism above all else. Thus, human capital, intellectual property and ecological assets are all viewed as forms of capital which can be accumulated for profits, much like machinery, equipment or physical infrastructure. Under capitalism, the market process rewards directly those who own and control capital in any form. Thus, development economics, as a subfield of Western economics, has operated as a handmaiden of global capitalization. This is a process which damages Western as well as non-Western cultures, but the roots of the process are clearly Western embedded in the phenomenon of Eurocentricity (see below).

Under the rules of mainstream development economics, growth is capital-biased: capital-rich countries of the First World gain from it, capital-poor but labour-abundant and natural resource-rich countries of the Third World lose. In a dynamic sense, this loss occurs in two principal ways: First, the subjective elements of the market process externalize and underprice the Third World's human and natural resources (e.g. rainforests, oil, mines as well as labour); it then transfers surplus values, directly or indirectly, for wealth concentration in the First World to finance further capital accumulation and consumerism. Second, Western interests, typically enjoying monopoly and oligopoly powers, profit from trade in technology transfers intended to expand the capital base in Third World industries, regardless of how inappropriate such transfers might be. Both of these processes reinforce the unequal market outcome which approximates a zero-sum game of gains and losses. The zero-sum outcome arises not because Western economic man (intent deliberate) is assumed to be rational while his Third World counterpart is not; rather, it is because Western economic development theorizing has been formulated as if Western-style rational behaviour in mainstream market theory is universal whereas, in fact, it is not. There are alternative conceptions of rationality in non-Western cultures (Mehmet 1990) tempered with self-determined moderation in economic and interpersonal relations, which Western theorists have simply ignored, while a myth of superiority of individualism has been created through education, justifying biased Western paradigms promising prosperity via economic growth. This biased, narrow Western theorizing is damaging globally, both for Western and non-Western societies, as the sustainable development debate is increasingly demonstrating.

The above argument will be illustrated through a survey of principal Western theories of economic development before 1914 and since, specifying, case by case, their inherent flaws in explaining their failure to work as predicted. The roots of this failure will be sought in the Western cultural phenomenon of Eurocentricity, with two criteria of Eurocentricity in particular utilized to evaluate theories of economic development: (1) pro-Western nationalistic premises, and (2) pro-capital or capitalist bias.

WHAT IS EUROCENTRICITY?

Eurocentricity is a European-centred worldview in which the interest or advantage of Europeans and their descendants is pursued at the expense of others, while justifying this worldview by paradigms or ethical norms that proclaim universal benefits for all (See Box 2). While enthnocentricity or ethnicism prevails, more or less, in all cultures, what makes Eurocentricity particularly important is the dominant position which the West has occupied globally during the last two hundred years as the underlying drive of mercantilist empire-building, while suggesting, and indeed promising explicitly in the post-World War II period, the prospect of Westernization as the path to universal prosperity. Yet, as this study shows, this promise has, for all practical purposes, been a failure. Eurocentricity, like the emperor without clothes, must be subjected to the naked truth before redress can begin.

As shown by Amin (1989), Eurocentricity is a deep-rooted Western intellectual tradition extending all the way back to Ancient

---

Box 2

What is Eurocentricity in development?

It is a Western worldview which relies on 'positive' economics, which is claimed to be value-free, but which, nevertheless, works to concentrate wealth and income in the West. Euro-centricity protects Western economic interest through market forces which are *pro-capital*. These forces operate to transform everything into a new form of capital.

For historical reasons, the West holds the world's largest stock of capital. The capitalist market forces operate constantly to expand and replenish that capital stock globally. This is *capitalization*, as a result of which all productive resources in the world are gradually transformed into new forms of capital for privatization and ultimate concentration in the West.

The role of economic theorizing is crucial in this process. It idealizes the West while promising undeliverable benefits. For example, 'free trade' theory promises equalization of incomes in the long run, a long run which is actually unattainable. Other theories, such as perfect competition, are merely empty shells.

Greek dualism of a cosmos made up of the rational–irrational, citizen–barbarian dichotomy. Western knowledge, constructed out of the same mindset, has effectively denied the non-Greek and non-Roman (i.e. non-Western) antecedents of human knowledge. In mainstream economics, for example, there is virtually no acknowledgement of Ibn' Khaldun, the Muslim scholar, who had developed most of Adam Smith's ideas some three centuries before (Mehmet 1990: 81–4). More generally, Western arts and sciences, especially social sciences, idealize everything Western out of reality, perceiving 'others' as inferior, constantly struggling to 'catch up' with the superior West by imitating it.

Eurocentricity, as a particular form of ethnocentricity, is closely linked to racist theories, a subject of extensive study by social and cultural anthropology (Harris 1968). As such, it is non-factual narrow-mindedness, vain and misleading, resulting in 'culture shock' even amongst otherwise brilliant Western social scientists, old and new, when confronted with higher technology or greater freedom in so-called 'primitive' or developing societies. Eurocentric economic theorizing is especially objectionable as hypocrisy when contradictions in Western capitalism and flaws of mainstream market theory are ignored, while projecting both as the ideal, as the yardstick against which to identify and judge inferiority, irrationality or inefficiency in others elsewhere. Eurocentricity is therefore a Western problem of deep-seated roots exemplified in such expressions as Edward Long's – a resident of the British West Indies at the height of sugar plantations – who justified slavery by claiming in his *History of Jamaica* that Africans belonged to a different species from Europeans and were 'brutish, ignorant, idle, crafty, treacherous, bloody, thievish, mistrustful, and superstitious' (quoted in Harris 1968: 89). From British India there was Lord Macaulay's judgement to the effect that 'a single shelf of a good European library [is] worth the whole native literature of India and Arabia'. Macaulay, the president of the Committee of Public Instruction in India in 1835 under the British Raj, aspired to create a class that was 'Indian blood and colour, but English in taste, in opinions, in morals, and in intellect' (quoted in Brown 1985: 75).

Education has been the principal vehicle for transmitting the Eurocentric worldview of distorted images of reality, from theory to policy, often rejecting factual truth in the process. For example, as recently as 1965 the French Ministry of Education rejected Braudel's masterful *A History of Civilizations* (repr. 1994) as inappropriate text for secondary schools because its survey of non-European civilizations clashed with the official syllabus, which was limited to French and European content. Over time and successive generations, Eurocentricity accumulates as racist stereotyping, as in *The Myth of the Lazy Native* (Alatas 1977), influencing the education of future policymakers, slanting and distorting in the process popular attitudes and images of non-European ways and cultures. Thus, the label 'Third World' (Harris 1987), like 'Orientalism' (Said 1978), is not only stereotyping peoples and economies in images not much different from those of slavery or Victorian days, it is homogenizing and denying the incredible range, diversity and cultural richness existing in the real world. Such diversity is typically overlooked in standardized national income and production classifications (World Bank 1992), the principal tool-kit in quantitative economic analyses.

The Western capitalist experience, as it has evolved in the last two hundred years, is neither universal, nor unique. As shown by Weber, Tawney and others, it is a culture-specific byproduct of the Protestant work ethic, representing the spirit of Western capitalism as it developed gradually in the rationalist post-Newtonian Europe when '[European] man [and woman were] put in a position to understand, to predict, and to manipulate nature' (Rostow 1975: 151).

What were the European means 'to manipulate nature'? Are the consumerism options available to non-Europeans? For example, should every Indian and Chinese family aspire to becoming a two-car family, matching Rostow's ultimate development in the 'High Consumption' stage? Or, are there more sustainable, ethically better choices (Goodland and Daly 1993)? Answers to these questions may lead to alternative paths of economic development and ethics. But, first, much deconstruction of Western economic theorizing, especially about development economics, is necessary. Thus, the myth of overpopulation of the Third World (Mamdani 1972) needs to be replaced by Northern consumerism as the root cause of underdevelopment; while sound population policies are essential in the former, it would be impossible to achieve international security and stability without correcting the global inequity generated through a mercantilist trading system working to support consumerism in the North.

Eurocentricity is also a method of analysis: it seeks to keep 'the Oriental-coloured to his position of *object studied by the Occidental-white*' (Said 1978: 228, italics in original). As a method it has three parts: (1) It is *a priori* Western reasoning, gounded, if at all, in Western empiricism, that seeks to portray human progress not as holistic, but as linear, male and deterministic replication of Western stages and taxonomy, using reductionism in time and space, dating and classifying events with European eyes (e.g. Marco Polo, the New World, the Indian Mutiny). Yet (2) it demands judging everything non-European by European norms. Thus, in development economics, Western theorists prescribed for the Third World, as we shall see, successive waves of abstract paradigms, to spread Western techniques and values, out of a mindset ready to transform 'them' to be like 'us' or 'we' as in 'white man's burden', 'mission civilisatrice' or 'manifest destiny'. In the words of Cecil Rhodes: 'We are the number one race in the world; the more countries we spread to, the more we will contribute to the salvation of the human race.' But (3), when prescriptions fail to work as predicted, 'we' decline moral responsibility; instead, simply another prescription, another paradigm, is offered – similar to Paris fashions or misleading advertising!

As with misleading advertising which can increase market share of sales at the expense of competitors, so Eurocentricity in economic relations is profitable. It is capable of biasing market outcomes in favour of Western interests, concentrating wealth for capital accumulation in the North at the expense of persistent poverty in the South, capitalizing the natural riches and endownments of the latter through unequal trade. Growing global inequality is the inevitable result, facilitated by Western mainstream theorizing.

THE TRICKLE-DOWN THEORY

By way of illustration, reference may be made to the trickle-down theory or 'tricklism' (Arndt 1983), which is undoubtedly the most famed promise of post-1945 Western economic development theorizing. It states that:

> rapid gains in overall and per capita GNP would either 'trickle down' to the masses in the form of jobs and other economic opportunities or create the necessary conditions for the wider distribution of the economic and social benefits of growth. . . . (In other words) this national income growth will 'trickle down' to improve levels of living for the very poor.
>
> (Todaro 1981: 68, 131)

Significantly, in the fifth edition of Todaro's *Economics of Development*, these optimistic predictions have been deleted (Todaro 1994: 157). A theory should be as good as it delivers. Economists who claim that their theories are 'value-free' should, like physicians, take moral responsibility for their prescriptions. If that were done, much of the blame for growth without social justice (Adelman and Morris 1973; Chenery *et al.* 1974) and adjustment without a human face (Cornia *et al.* 1986; Standing and Tokman 1991) would be attributed to Western theorists and their theories. Economic development in many developing countries is often in the hands of such groups as the 'Berkeley Mafia', the 'Harvard Group', etc. Intellectual integrity compels 'us' to learn lessons from past mistakes. But do we? No; instead 'we' shift the blame on the 'other.'

Here is a quote from a book by D.C. North, a leading exponent of new institutionalism, noteworthy for projecting two worlds, the Western and the Third: one approximating the ideal, the other the perverse:

> [The] modern Western world provides abundant evidence of markets that work and even approximate the neo-classical ideal . . . Third World countries are poor because the institutional constraints define a set of payoffs to political/economic activity that do not encourage productive activity.
>
> (North 1990: 110)

Empirically it is not difficult to furnish supporting evidence for North's argument in some cases, but one can hardly endorse his stereotyping of all Third World countries as poor due to a failure to approximate the Western ideal. That the Western ideal is no more than a myth can easily be observed when one recalls such Western institutions as the Mafia which generate mistrust and underdevelopment (Putnam *et al.* 1993: 146–8) or the glaring socio-economic inequalities in even the most advanced capitalist economies, giving rise to 'drug cultures', black economies and underclasses. Moreover, the graduation of the Far Eastern NICs, largely for endogenous reasons, is important in theory no less than in practice, disproving the uniqueness of the Western way (see pp. 113–120 below).

Of course, the North is by no means an isolated case; many other similar quotations can be cited from mainstream theorists who view and judge the world as a Westernizing process. Only one celebrated case needs to be cited at this time. Francis Fukuyama's article 'The End of History?', celebrating the end of the Cold War argued: 'What we may be witnessing is just not the end of the Cold War, or the passing of a passing of a particular period of postwar history, but the end of history as such: that is, the end point of mankind's ideological evolution and *the universalization of Western liberal democracy as the final form of human government*' (Fukuyama 1989: 3–4, italics added). Fukuyama's Eurocentricity, though tempered by nostalgia for the past and some concern for the boredom *his* future may entail, is astonishing in its total dismissal of Islamic, Confucian or non-Western cultures, which, after all, constitute the great majority of humanity. The reality, however, is different from Fukuyama's 'endism': history goes on. After all, why should these other cultures suddenly disappear, just because Marxist-Leninist and other Eurocentric constructions are being dismantled?

The problem at hand is systemic, for the roots of Eurocentricity are long and deeply entrenched in the Western intellectual tradition, in economics, politics and other fields. North and Fukuyama, in this respect, are hardly different from earlier generations of Western scholars who saw the world as 'the West' and 'the rest' or 'us' and 'them'. Boeke, for example, the Dutch economist of colonial Indonesia, constructed his theory of 'social dualism' on a similar stereotyped, two-world rationalization, namely, 'Eastern economies' and Western 'high capitalism' (see p. 74 below):

> Social dualism is the clashing of an imported social system with an indigenous social system of another style. Most frequently the imported system is high capitalism . . . Where two or more social systems appear, clearly distinct the one from the other, and each dominates a part of the society, there we have to do with a dual or plural society.
>
> (Boeke 1953, reprinted in Meier ed. 1976: 130–1)

Higgins (1956), on the other hand, who had a deep and sympathetic understanding of Indonesia and its history, convincingly demonstrated the intellectual flaws of Boeke's theory of 'social dualism'. But, in a deeper sense, his theory was merely a projection of the 'other' in 'us' as the internalized object. The moral inferiority of the 'other' [meaning 'coloureds, wogs, niggers' (Said 1993: 19)] was the standard norm in Western art and literature in the service of Western imperialism, as for example in Austen, Kipling, Ruskin and others (Said 1993: esp. 97–110), and in the social as well as natural sciences. Slavery, essential in plantation economies, was justified by the pseudo-scientific claims of physicians that in the 'great chain of being . . . Negroes' were closer to the apes than to Caucasians (quoted in Harris 1968: 89). The noted Victorian naturalist, Alfred R. Wallace, a contemporary of Darwin was representative of racial determinism, wherein lies the roots of Third Worldism. After seven long years studying the flora and fauna in the Malay–Indonesian archipelago, at the most oppressive period of Dutch colonialism, and shortly after the Max Havelaar affair, this is what Wallace (Mehmet 1992) had to say on the cultures and peoples of East and West: 'I believe that the Dutch system is the very best that can be adopted, when a European nation conquers or otherwise acquires possession of a country inhabited by an industrious but semi-barbarous people' (Wallace 1989: 105).

Wallace was a paradoxical figure who had a sharp eye for the flora and fauna of the tropics, but he failed miserably in his understanding or appreciation of non-European cultures and ways. A prisoner of linear Eurocentric thinking, these other people – 'the lower races', as he termed them – could only be ranked behind the higher Europeans; yet, Wallace in the final part of his *Archipelago*, cannot avoid making an astonishing confession: upon realizing that the Dayaks, Javanese and Malays of Southeast Asia enjoyed greater liberty than the working classes of mid-nineteenth-century England, he admits that he might have gotten it all wrong! Yet, Wallace's confession had no impact at all on his theories or on the generation of Eurocentric adventurers-cum-visionaries.

Empire-builders from Clive to Cecil Rhodes all carried out what Boeke termed 'the colonial enterprise', paralleling Kipling's 'The Great Game' on a world stage, going beyond spying for the mother country's sake. Here was the Eurocentric mind ready to conquer the 'other' by variously justifying it as a religious, civilizational, moral or imperialistic mission, and then justifying Western superiority in everything as natural or normal. Empires and Victorian days are gone; but the structural division of the world into First and Third, the Second having now vanished, seems still as permanent in Western theorizing still as racial determinism was in Victorian times, although Third Worldism, as ideology, may be declining (Harris 1987).

THE BASIC MAINSTREAM MODEL

So what is the basic Western ideal capitalist model? It is a cumulative, joint intellectual product, the work of many minds: this basic model of economic development is a profit-driven growth model with a dynamic and static version. Conceived in grand, universalistic terms, to be challenged below, it is useful to begin formally with the aid of ten equations to capture the essence of the model.

$$I = dK = f(\pi) \tag{1.1}$$

$$\pi = TR - TC \tag{1.2}$$

$$Q = F(K, N, L) \tag{1.3}$$

Eq. (1.1) highlights the fact that the search for profit was the trigger in Western capitalism. But what exactly was profit? It remains something of a mystery to this day with much confusion even amongst the greatest authorities as illustrated below. Mathematically, profit, π, resulted from capital accumulation, dK, which occurred as investment, I, as a consequence of deliberate decision on the part of the investor. Therefore, the narrowly defined profit rate, π/K, was the investor's return, comparable to labour's or land's return. But, profit was also a reward, justified for risk-taking, initiative and enterprise, and viewed as a residual return.

But what is the relationship of profit to the residual return? How does it differ, if any, from surplus value? How, precisely, is it realized? There is much confusion in mainstream theory on these questions, even though in standard textbooks profit maximization is presented as the overriding objective of the rational entrepreneur, matching the rational consumer's maximization of satisfaction. But apparently, 'it is sufficient to assume that entrepeneurs act *as if* they tried to maximize profits' (Ferguson and Gould 1975: 221, emphasis in original) implying that in reality they need not act as predicted by theory. For the famous English economist, Alfred Marshall who taught at Cambridge around the turn of the twentieth century, profits were 'normal' or 'fair', set by custom in a given industry; and Marshall explicitly recognized the zero-sum relationship of profits and wages, hinting at the phenomenon of capitalization (see pp. 28–32 below): 'The greater part of the apparent profit is real wages disguised in the garb of profit' (Marshall 1962: 506). However, Hicks, another noted British economist of the next generation after Marshall, preferred the term surplus to profit, calling it 'that thing we supposed him [i.e. the entrepreneur] trying to maximize' (Hicks 1965: 197).

In standard textbooks (Henderson and Quandt 1958: 53–4), especially American ones, and written in the Samuelsonian style with elementary calculus, profit is measured as the excess of total revenue, TR, over total cost of production, TC, as shown in eq. (1.2), implying that profit is a residual, surplus value resulting from the entrepreneur's control of production. But mainstream economics generally rejects the idea of surplus value usually associated with Marx. Mathematically, this rejection is derived from the production function depicted in eq. (1.3), which shows that the level of revenue and cost, and hence profit, depend on the volume of production, Q, which, in turn is determined by technical input–output relationship specified in the production function. K, N, and L are capital, land and labour, respectively, the three classic factors of production. These factors of production are all taken to be 'separable' and independent of each other – an unrealistic assumption which is untenable in dynamic terms, giving rise to the phenomenon of capitalization (see pp. 19–21 below). In static terms, however, the 'separability' assumption is crucial for market clearance. But market clearance is achieved at the cost of a remarkable degree of fuzziness surrounding profit in mainstream literature, a fuzziness which facilitates extraction of surplus in the Third World for by mercantilist interests from the First.

There is even more: at the bottom of this fuzziness lies a contradiction. To see it, it is necessary to detail revenues and costs in eq. (1.2) further. Thus,

$$TR = pQ \tag{1.4}$$

and

$$TC = rK + hN + wL \tag{1.5}$$

The price, p, in eq. (1.4) is determined in a competitive market according to Adam Smith's 'invisible hand', and the coefficients r, h and w are the unit prices (or marginal costs) of factors, similarly determined in competitive factor markets. If the system works ideally in accordance with perfect competition, these parameters would also represent marginal productivities of factors. In this competitive framework, with free entry and exit of firms, no profit could arise since total revenue, the value of output priced in eq. (1.4), representing the sum of value added generated by factor productivity, would exactly equal factor payments in eq. (1.5); in other words, no surplus value or residual could result (Henderson and Quandt 1958: 65–6). Hence, the first-order condition of equilibrium in perfect competition found in standard textbooks on economics, namely,

$$\pi = 0 \tag{2.6}$$

The only way an actual, positive profit rate, π/Q, could occur is in a state of disequilibrium when markets fail to clear, or when market imperfections exist in the form of monopoly or monopsony, whereby surplus value matches underpayment of factors of production.

THE FLAWS OF THE MODEL

We can now examine the internal flaws of the model. In fact, three principal axiomatic flaws are highlighted below.

The first is the remarkable result in eq. (1.6). It reflects the fundamental contradiction of the textbook version of the capitalist ideal: that in a system dedicated to its pursuit, no profit, as residual or surplus and distinct from return on K, can be generated, except on such subjective or normative basis as 'supernormal profit' or 'fair rate of return'. Equilibrium prices are then viewed as 'natural' or 'fair' prices, with some profit rate tending to equalize amongst different industries. The ambiguities here are reminiscent of the medieval debate about 'just price'. In short, capitalism, as ideal, is self-defeating on its own rules, unless those rules are violated, as in monopoly and other market imperfections.

Take, for example, the ideal market solution, aggregated from market clearance, known as the Pareto Optimum (Scitovsky 1952; Bator 1957; Mishan 1960). Behaviourally constructed on a rationality assumption, this ideal solution requires general equilibrium in factor and product markets to ensure welfare gain for at least one person with no loss to anyone else.

Heuristically, it is an elegant theory; its basic flaw is that in reality it is impossible to achieve (Arrow 1951; Little 1957; Mishan 1960) due to 'externalities', positive 'transaction costs' and other 'market failures'. Consequently, economic development can only be conducted suboptimally, subject to risks and uncertainties of a 'second best' solution (Lipsey and Lancaster 1957; Killick 1981: 18–20). Moreover, the rational behaviour assumption of the model, based on Western individualism, is a poor fit for the cross-cultural environments in developing countries where sharing, cooperation and moderation rather than individualism prevail. All in all, as a guide

---

Box 3

The Pareto Optimum and the second best

The Pareto Optimum is the 'ideal' of Western 'normative' economics when there is maximum output, full employment and the output mix produced by profit-driven firms exactly matches what rational consumers want as revealed in the marketplace with their purchasing power.

Whenever these conditions do not prevail, there is 'market failure', and 'second-best' solutions, based on corrective policy interventions in the economy, may be the order of the day. However, in view of extensive market failures in developing countries, these interventions may actually worsen, rather than improve economic welfare. In brief, economic prescriptions, derived from Western capitalist economics, may be inappropriate for these economies.

---

for policy and planning, the Pareto Optimum model turns out to be an empty box, quite inappropriate for developing countries (See Box 3).

The above, however, is a static, partial equilibrium analysis. If the model is dynamized, so that change over time in consumer tastes, technologies and factors of production are endogenized, the same result is derived but in a more complex manner. Thus, rewriting eq. (1.2) as

$$\pi_t = TR_t - TC_t \tag{1.7}$$

would imply that profit can only be generated over time as windfall gains due to fluctuations and swings in market cycles caused by unplanned shortages and surplus. In short, profit or surplus value is realized as return on risk and uncertainty, and from such strategic decisions as speculative buying and selling, or from gambling-like dealing, during the adjustment process when markets fail. Keynes was full of contempt of this casino-style speculation on the London Stock Exchange and on Wall Street, calling it '*laissez-faire* capitalism', one of the great 'contemporary evils' (Keynes 1936: 159–60).

Figure 1.1 illustrates the problem. Revenue and cost, in real terms, are shown vertically and time horizontally. If, p^*, some real price index [determined as p in eq. (1.4)] is taken as constant, then the

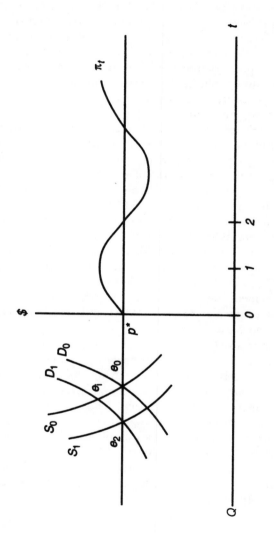

Figure 1.1 Profit realization during market disequilibria

profit function, π_t, is the residual return realized during periods of market disequilibria (shown in standard partial equilibrium terms in the left-hand quadrant). If dynamic equilibrium occurs instantly because markets adjust perfectly along P, then profits, again are 0. If adjustment is subject to time-lag, profits, as a return on risk and uncertainty, converge to 0 when markets ultimately clear. Therefore, as before, so long as the ideal of perfect competition prevails, the possibility of positive profit cannot arise: it would require an explosive, rather than converging profit function; something incompatible with the basic market stability condition of the model.

The conclusion of zero profit under ideal conditions is inescapable. Herein lies the first axiomatic flaw in mainstream theory serving capitalism: classicists and neo-classicists to this day, base their theories on the ideal norm of perfect competition, yet capitalism can only live and thrive in a world of market imperfections. Put differently, under its own axioms of perfect competition, capitalism is destined to remain trapped in a stationary mode, ultimately withering away for lack of new profits. In practice, however, positive, and indeed rising, profits are realized along the transition path of disequilibria, typically as a result of market power by oligopolies and cartels which can determine price and non-price terms of international trade. Typical examples include strategic stockpiling and inventory management and intra-firm transfer pricing long practised by Western oil companies (Yergin 1993) and wheat merchants (Morgan 1980) and MNCs in general.

The second axiomatic flaw of the classical system stems from the ambiguity of short-run and long-run analysis. In theory, there is no (empirically) objective boundary separating the two. Therefore, only subjective or normative attributes are assigned to variability or accumulation of factors of production. Thus, in the undefined short run, classical theorists take capital and land as fixed in supply, while labour is made the sole variable factor of production. Hence the classical labour value theory of production, eq. (1.8), the backbone of such theories as the 'iron law of wages', 'backward-sloping' supply curve, is hopelessly value-loaded, as we shall presently see (p. 43 below).

$$Q = F^*(L) \tag{1.8}$$

$$D_1 = f(\pi) \tag{1.9}$$

$$S_1 = g(w) \tag{1.10}$$

Eqs (1.9) and (1.10) represent the centrepiece of competitive labour market theory, in which labour demand, D_1, is profit-driven, while labour supply, S_1, is determined by the wage-rate or the price of human effort, which is usually the cost of food. If the worker's productivity, the marginal product of labour, in eq. (1.9) is paid in full to the wage-earner in eq. (1.10), no profit arises. Thus, profit necessitates exploitation, i.e. underpayment of labour relative to its productivity. Herein lies the fundamental conflict between labour and capital, the adversarial core of capitalism. Mainstream labour market theories conceal exploitation of labour behind inadequate explanations for wage differentials between occupations or industries such as subjective 'net advantages' or 'psychic benefits' which, in empirical works, are typically ignored. However, in Third World labour markets, from those on industrial estates and export processing zones to those in 'sweatshops', it is these very 'subjective' factors which 'distort' and exploit labour, creating discrimination, inequality and segmentation (Mehmet 1971) or informality (Hart 1973; de Soto 1989). The mainstream market theory has almost entirely ignored labour market performance until very recently (Manning and Fong 1990; Berry and Sobot 1978).

The third axiomatic flaw in the mainstream market theory goes to the root of Eurocentricity. It arises from implicit definitions and meaning of key terms, such as 'cost' and 'benefit' (whose cost or benefit?), 'factor of production' (owned or controlled by whom?), 'surplus value' (generated how? and accruing to whom?) and 'rationality' (whose behaviour?). For classical economists these terms had only European meaning. The excess population in Malthus referred to European overcrowding; 'vacant' lands in colonies were vacant only because they were populated by 'savage' or 'uncivilized nations'. So much for slavery and the destruction of native cultures. Similarly, Ricardian rent applied to land shortage in Europe. Ricardo's rent did not allow for the opportunity cost of native land, i.e. the reservation price for such land was zero, free for the taking and with no thought of compensation. Adam Smith's 'opulence' meant British prosperity. The origins of colonial cheap labour and land policies were legitimized, by subsequent theorists and policy-makers alike, in the name of masters like Adam Smith, Malthus and Ricardo. 'Rational' behaviour, the basic assumption of utility theory, meant behaviour in conformity with the Protestant Ethic; when, for example, supply response in non-European environments collided with Western interests, it was labelled 'irrational' as in the Backward-sloping Curve Hypothesis (see p. 43 below), totally

ignoring cultural determinants of labour supply, e.g. family obligations. In all classical economists' writings non-European peoples
were always projected as 'savage' or 'primitive', without any culture
and unworthy of development. Consequently, their resources (i.e. factors of production) were deemed to be in a kind of Hobbesian 'state of
nature', in which life was not worth much anyway, so land was available
for colonization cost-free. Thus, when non-resident ownership of
resources is allowed in a Ricardian-type growth model, rapid growth
of output, in particular surplus value drained away, may nevertheless
impoverish local populations (Mehmet 1983).

CAPITALIZATION: THE INNER LOGIC OF MERCANTILISM, OLD AND NEW

These flaws of mainstream economic development theorizing conceal
capitalization, the inherent tendency of capitalism to transform non-
capital resources, such as labour and land, over time, into capital.
This is the idea of economic growth as capital accumulation. It is
an ideology driven by the search for profits on a global scale set to
convert every productive resource into capital of some kind: labour
in one period becomes machinery in the next; skills are converted
into human capital; inventions and new knowledge become intellectual property; environment and bio-technology are treated as assets,
potentially capable of generating surplus value. These, and many
other value-creating resources, ranging from professional sports to
rare disease-resistant genes of people in the tropics, are monetized
for surplus value extraction, ultimately augmenting the capital
stock of international corporations, entered in some balance sheet
as a portfolio of assets; each one yielding a specific monetary return,
determined in some market, in proportion to risk and profitability,
where they can be traded or acquired by investors and entrepreneurs.
In short, capitalization is capitalist accumulation, economic growth
traditionally defined, and it must obey the law of compound interest
to avoid decline.

Capitalization arises from the fact that production is not a simple
transformation of inputs into outputs, as described in basic mainstream theory. Rather, as originally shown by Piero Sraffa (1960),
it is a far more complex process of 'production of commodities by
means of commodities', without reference to the simple Ricardian
or Marxian theories of labour value. Production, in fact, occurs
under a variety of conditions involving joint production, multiple

Box 4

What is capitalization?

Capitalization is the inherent tendency of capitalism to expand the capital stock and ensure a rising profit rate. Western technology is capital intensive and its application rewards capital at the expense of other inputs (see the Appendix at the end of Chapter 1). As a process, *capitalization* aims at transforming non-capital resources, such as labour, knowledge, environment and land, into some new form of capital. Examples include human capital, environmental assets, intellectual property, etc. As capital intensity of production increases, the share of value-added accruing to capital rises; conversely, the share of non-capital diminishes.

Capitalization is the cornerstone of the idea of economic growth as capital accumulation. In the postwar period, neo-classical economists constructed the most ambitious formal models (see Chapter 4) for globalizing capital accumulation. This accumulationist ideology ignored local capacities and constraints in developing countries and transferred inappropriate technologies from the West.

In its latest phase, capitalization persists in the global search for profits to privatize, and in owning and controlling resources everywhere under the dominance of MNCs enjoying monopoly–monopsony powers.

products, switching technologies and increasing returns over time. As a result, capital and non-capital resources do not stay 'pure' and fixed over time, but are in fact blended as producers attempt to invest and innovate in the light of changing relative prices and market conditions. A capitalist economy is built on a capital–labour tension, always works in favour of capital accumulation, and rewards capitalists who seek to capture, own and control other productive resources (See Box 4).

Theoretically, capitalization invalidates the separability assumption of the production function in eq. (1.3). In short-run, static equilibrium terms, eq. (1.3) may be fine; it is, however, not so in terms of market dynamics as asset values in natural and human resources are gradually transformed into new capital stock yielding surplus value and windfall profits as described in Figure 1.1 above. In this dynamic market process, capitalization follows monetization, i.e. assigning monetary value to resources including the environment (Gillis *et al.* 1992: 551), a practice favoured by mainstream economists but increasingly rejected by ecologists and environmentalists (van Pelt 1993).

Historically, capitalization is as long as capitalism itself because its inner logic is mercantilism, the pursuit of trade balances by all means necessary. Thus, in the age of colonialism, vacant lands in North America, Australia, New Zealand, mines in South Africa, plantations in Southeast Asia and the Caribbean were capitalized by colonial entrepreneurs as indigenous inhabitants were pushed out or eliminated to make room for European interests, operating as a monopoly or oligopoly and extracting windfall profits. In the process of capitalizing labour, local cultures, family and kinship systems were destroyed, with devastating effect, for example, on female-headed households in the case of the oscillating migration system in Southern Africa (Murray 1980; Chant ed. 1992). Similarly, in the postwar period, technology and knowledge have been capitalized by MNCs through investment in R&D, along with intellectual property created through inventions, copyrights and patents generating windfall, or what Schumpeter would have called 'pioneer', profits for private investors.

The underpricing of Third World resources by Western interests has been the most systemic and widespread technique of capitalization. In colonial times, the North American prairie, the jungles of Southeast Asia and the Australian outback were all regarded by Europeans as 'free goods', in sharp contrast to high-priced European land. Mathematically, this understated costs and overstated profits in terms of eq. (1.7). Over time, these profits financed capital investments in plantations and large-scale agriculture, typically owned by Westerners, so that as agriculture became increasingly capital-intensive, the land itself emerged as a capital asset, and its inherent productivity returned more and more to capital. Labour's share of rising value-added also diminished as a consequence of increasing substitution of capital for labour reflecting yet a further dimension of the dynamics of capitalization. What happened to land, also happened through systemic underpricing of Third World resources in other sectors such as mining, petroleum and manufacturing. In particular, in the postwar period, during the height of Import Substitution Industrialization (ISI), developing countries encouraged capitalization through a great variety of pro-capital subsidies (see the

Appendix at the end of this chapter for a more formal elaboration of this argument). More recently natural resources such as rainforests have been viewed as ecological assets, becoming candidates for capitalization through monetization in the name of economic development.

Who have been the gainers and losers from capitalization? First and foremost, capitalists and those with market power to access and exploit new resources for capitalization have gained. Western MNCs, typically enjoying market power as oligopolies (Hymer 1970; Helleiner ed. 1976) and far removed from the ideal competitive market theory, are prime examples. Hymer's idea of 'uneven development, was shaped less by neo-classical ideal theorizing than by the 'managerialism' of Chandler (1962) derived from extensive study of the emergence of American industrial enterprise.

Why do firms go international? How do MNCs emerge? MNCs expand internationally through investment and trade for a variety of strategic reasons such as 'market-seeking' or 'resource-seeking' (Dunning 1992), but always for profits, a basic motivation with mercantilist roots. These corporations enjoy monopolistic power to underprice Third World resources (see the Appendix at the end of this chapter). They, and their affiliates on industrial estates and export processing zones in labour-surplus economies, can avoid or offset the social security provisions of labour codes to underpay labour. In addition, they exercise transfer pricing and strategic inventory management to shift incomes globally across national boundaries and tax jurisdictions, with a view to maximizing private gains and financing further corporate growth for more profits.

Also benefiting from capitalization are the rich consumers in high-income countries. Consumerism in the North entails a highly capital-intensive lifestyle exemplified by multiple-car-owning families, labour-saving household appliances and personal computers and electronics.

On the other hand, the losers are the Third World masses obliged to live at the brink of subsistence. Higher value-added of modern technology seldom protect or enhance real wages; likewise, rainforests, biodiversity and ecological commons are privatized and depleted for capitalization in a systematic extraction of exchange value for transfer to the North. In brief, capitalization shifts income globally from the poor of low-income countries to the rich of high-income countries.

The end result is not only uneven and unequal international

development at any point in time, but also inequality between the rich and poor which continues to widen. This is neo-mercantilism, with long roots which Adam Smith sought to cure. But these roots are too deeply embedded in the hidden cultural foundations of mainstream economics, which while justifying and legitimizing economic development as the path to prosperity, is, in reality, promoting capitalization and, like a train on a collision course, is heading to global disaster. But this is not inevitable: intelligent and well-meaning human beings, committed to internationalism, can redirect that train towards the goal of peace and security based on shared prosperity in one world.

APPENDIX ON CAPITALIZATION

The purpose of this Appendix is to present a more formal analysis of two important Eurocentric biases of capitalist growth: (1) how capitalization occurs through pro-capital bias in the growth process, and (2) how Third World resources are underpriced by monopolistic interests. The analysis utilizes the standard neo-classical tools of isocosts and isoquants together with the usual assumptions such as profit-maximizing behaviour under perfect competition, foresight, factor mobility and substitution.

How capitalization occurs

In Figure A1.1, a given initial quantity of output, Q_0, is initially produced under profit-maximizing conditions at the tangency point a, with OK_1 amount of capital, K, measured on the vertical axis. K is gross investment inclusive of depreciation and it embodies new innovation. ON_1 is similarly the amount of non-K inputs, NK, measured on the horizontal axis. Most of NK is labour, but it also includes land and environment. At point a, factor proportions are given by the slope of the ray OA reflecting the initial production technique A. Relative factor prices are given by the slope of the isocost curve I. At a standard equilibrium conditions hold as manifested by the equality of the slopes of the isocost and isoquant curves.

Now, let's introduce a pro-capital industrial policy in the course of economic growth such as the ISI strategy. As part of this strategy, relative factor prices are altered by means of low interest rates, overvalued currency, tax-free imports of capital goods and tax holidays; specifically, the relative cost of K declines, pivoting the isocost clock-

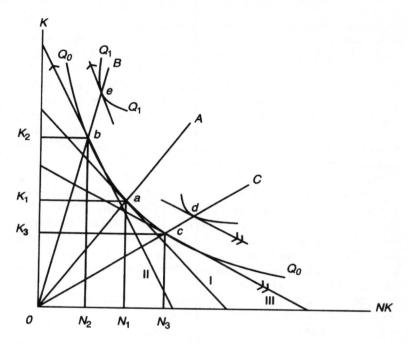

Figure A1.1 The pro-capital bias of Western growth

wise from I to II. The new production at tangency point *b* is achieved
as a result of inter-factor substitution by which process the employment of K increases to K_2 while NK declines to N_2. This substitution
represents capitalization of N_1N_2 amount of NK resources under production technique B: whereas under technique A this amount of non-
capital resources were equally capable of producing the same output,
now they are redundant, displaced by K_1K_2 amount of capital.

The distributive implications of the shift from tangency point *a* to
b are clear: while the same output, Q_0, is produced under both *a* and
b, the factor shares under the latter favours capitalists at the expense
of NK because of higher capital-intensity of production. With a
higher capital stock under *b*, capitalists are well situated to experience a rising share of value-added relative to owners of labour and
other non-capital resources, notwithstanding changed relative
factor prices. This pro-K income redistribution is likely to become
more pronounced over time through successive rounds of capital
accumulation at the expense of NK.

Substitution of K for NK is only one kind of capitalization, i.e.

augmenting the K stock, by simply shifting to more capital-intensive technique to produce a given level of output. It occurs strictly as a result of relative pricing policy inducements in favour of K, *ceteris paribus*. It can be further reinforced by growth-stimulating capitalization as and when corporate investment in the more K-intensive production technique B is financed out of savings or foreign borrowing. A good part of these savings are normally deferred consumption from owners of NK. In other words, over time, NK-productive resources get reallocated, via saving and investment, into further capital accumulation for economic growth.

The case of growth-stimulating capitalization is illustrated along the growth path from b to point e, *ceteris paribus*. This growth is K-augmenting growth compared, for example to the growth path along OA, because of relatively limited expansion of NK employment. Admittedly, technology OB may indeed be more productive, especially if economies of scale are assumed to exist, yielding a higher value-added per unit of cost: but such technology is also more biased and rewarding to owners of K since it utilizes more capital-intensive technology. Morevoer, to the extent that OB is imported technology, owned by non-residents, then the share of value-added retained locally is correspondingly reduced.

Thus, the capitalization bias in economic development can occur in two distinct, but reinforcing ways: first, by substitution as a result of pro-capital relative factor pricing policy, and second, by means of corporate investment decisions that favour capital-intensive technology. Neither of these biases are results obtained on a 'level playing field': they are induced by deliberate policies or production choices reflecting the view that growth is capital accumulation. The dynamic shift in income shares in favour of K is deliberate, not accidental, resulting from constantly augmenting the capital stock through converting NK into new stock of K.

A more pro-labour growth strategy in a labour-abundant economy is the promotion of appropriate technology shown by a technique OC relative to OA. In this case, optimal production point would be the tangency at c (followed by d *ceteris paribus*) with an expanding labour share of output resulting in higher standard of living for the community.

In the postwar period, capitalization in developing countries has occurred thanks to collusive behaviour on the part of rent-seeking domestic elites eager to import technology from the West and to collaborate with Western capitalist interests. The so-called 'Asian miracle' in Southeast Asian tigers (see pp. 113–120) is an excellent case in point. During this period of 'miracle growth', ruling elites in countries like Indonesia and Malaysia allowed, indeed encourged, underpricing of environmental (e.g. the rainforest) and labour resources (in particular, women and children in sweatshops and on industrial estates and cheap migrant labour in plantation sectors) as part of government policy deliberately aimed at manufacturing comparative advantage in order to capitalize these resources with excessive inflows of foreign capital. While capital asset values sky-rocketed, generating windfall gains for foreign speculators and investors, alongside rents for domestic ruling elites, workers were exploited and the environment degraded. Ultimately, the bubble burst with the currency collapse of 1997–8, a topic discussed on pp. 117–120 below.

Monopolistic underpricing

Figure A1.2 illustrates the mechanics of monopolistic underpricing of Third World prices. Under competitive market conditions, equilibrium occurs at point *e* at the intersection of marginal cost,

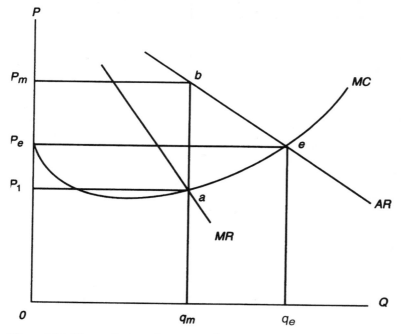

Figure A1.2 Monopolistic underpricing of Third World resources

MC and average revenue, AR. Here the market clears establishing a price, p_e, and quantity bought, q_e, with producers earnings only 'normal profits'.

If and when production occurs under monopolistic conditions, (the standard state in the Third World) then the typical producer enjoying market power would maximize profits at point a where marginal revenue, MR, equals MC. The selling price would rise to p_m, quantity bought would decline to q_m, and the producer would realize 'supernormal profits' of 'a–b' per unit of output. These 'supernormal profits' are rents, i.e. unearned bonus, which enrich monopoly interests. It is these huge rents which allow rent-seeking behaviour (i.e. corruption through influence-peddling, a subject discussed in Chapter 6). In standard economic theory, these profits are monopolistic profits representing the fact that whereas the economic cost of resources used up in production is represented by the area under MC, value-added is the significantly higher area of the rectangle under point b on the demand curve. This is surplus value extracted out of Third World resources by monopolistic (Eurocentric) interests for transfer to the North. Mainstream economists ignore this transfer simply because they continue to assume that pricing occurs under competitive conditions, i.e. that Third World markets clear as at point e, which is a myth.

2

CLASSICAL (PRE-1914) ECONOMIC DEVELOPMENT THEORIES

Economic development was a central concern of Western classical economists from the eighteenth century onwards, but this concern was 'with the capitalist development of their own Western world' (Arndt 1987: 30). This is quite understandable since Western countries were then in the early stages of economic development via industrialization. The challenge of economic development for classical theorists was 'opulence', or how nations prosper. Adam Smith's classic treatise was entitled *The Wealth of Nations* (Smith 1776). Smith, who was a professor of moral philosophy, is acknowledged as the founder of mainstream economics as a positive, value-free science.

The classical economists equated economic development with growth (Meade 1962; Hahn and Matthews 1964; Eltis 1987), although in post-1945 literature, the two terms became increasingly separated and even conflicting (Herrick and Kindleberger 1988: chap. 2; Clower *et al.* 1966). The objective of classical theorists was 'opulence', that is, national wealth. The way to greater opulence was through growth of output, the value of which was the exchange value determined in the market. Higher output was made possible by higher productivity of a given stock of factors of production (due to technical change), or as a result of net increase of the factors, particularly of labour and capital, since land (i.e. European land) was assumed to be fixed as a constant. Trade extended the size of the market, promoted specialization and acted as the engine of growth, leading to greater opulence.

The classical model of economic development is not the work of any one person; rather it represents the cumulative contribution of Western economic thinkers, British, French and German, 'the worldly philosophers' (Heilbroner 1961), most notably Adam Smith

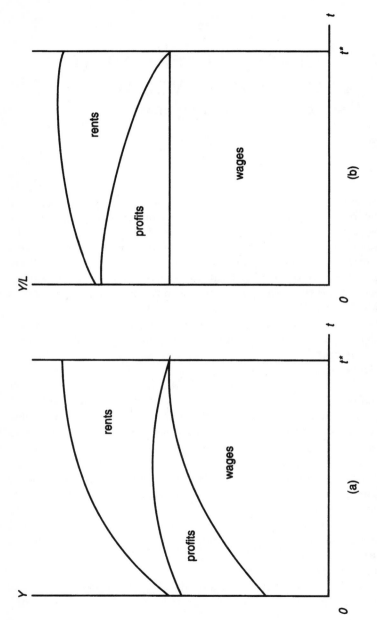

Figure 2.1 The Ricardian theory of rising rents and falling profits: (a) national income; (b) per capita income

(1723–90), Robert Malthus (1766–1834), David Ricardo (1772–1823) and John Stuart Mill (1806–73).

THE RICARDIAN GROWTH MODEL

We start with the Ricardian growth model, first in a 'closed' (i.e. domestic) economy context (i.e. England), and subsequently in an 'open' context with free trade. This approach has the merit of demonstrating clearly the classical view of 'trade as the engine of growth' as opposed to an autarkic, 'closed' economy which reaches maturity and exhausts all profitable opportunities, ultimately sinking into stagnation.

Figure 2.1 summarizes the Ricardian economic growth and decline in dynamic terms. Panel (a) refers to the growth of national income over time driven by profit-oriented investment. With no trade and technological progress, fixed land and expanding population, investment becomes increasingly unprofitable, and the limit of growth is reached at some future year, t^*, when profits fall to 0, precisely when rents and wage costs are at their maximum. In panel (b), where incomes are measured in per capita terms, it is noteworthy that wages are constant throughout at subsistence, whereas rents increase at the expense of profits. Overall, the theory predicts the ultimate decline of capitalism as a 'closed' economy as profits melt down towards 0 in a stagnating, stationary economy.

Vanishing profitability was a consequence of the classical concept of the 'stationary state', a concept equivalent to stagnation in a 'closed' island economy like England. It was a pessimistic model. Ricardo and Mill, as well as Malthus, were prophets of doom, fearful of the ultimate demise of capitalism due (to put it in Schumpeterian terms) to exanding capital stock against the backdrop of vanishing investment opportunities. For Ricardo, as for Mill, stagnation resulted from the natural tendency of profits to fall and 'the consequent chocking off of capital accumulation' (Higgins 1968: 66), i.e. overcrowding in capital markets. Mill, who believed that stagnation was just round the corner for England unless it adopted free trade, put the matter explicitly:

> When a country has long possessed a large production, and a large net income to make savings from, and when, therefore, the means have long existed of making a great annual addition to capital; (the country not having, like America

[1848], a large reserve of fertile land still unused) it is one of the characteristics of such a country, that the rate of profit is habitually within, as it were, a hands' breath of the minimum, and the country therefore on the very verge of the stationary state.

(Mill 1917: 731)

How could such a gloomy prospect be avoided? Mill's solution was English capital exports in search of global profits. Ricardo took the argument further and stated it in terms of free trade so that England could exchange cheap food for industrial products. Food imports kept wages at subsistence level, while export earnings from industrial products increased profits, generating new savings and further growth, enhancing the national wealth in the process. An inverse relationship between profits and wages, which he repeatedly restated in his *Principles of Political Economy and Taxation* (1911: chaps v and vi) was the essence of Ricardo's Comparative Advantage Theory (1911: chap. 7). A few examples of Ricardo's reasoning can be cited: 'The whole value of (production) is divided into two portions only: one constitutes the profits . . . the other the wages of labour' (Ricardo 1911: 64). 'If, therefore, by the extension of foreign trade, or by improvements in machinery, the food and necessaries of the labourer can be brought to the market, at a reduced price, profits will rise' (Ricardo 1911: 80).

In brief, the Ricardian trade was capitalist growth, good for profits. It was an escape route for the otherwise gloomy industrial prospects in a 'closed economy' for an overcrowded England. Ricardo's theory of rent and income distribution, institutionally and historically, matched the transition from agriculture to industry, while showing how growth affected income shares accruing to owners of land, labour and capital. It demonstrated the changing sectoral composition of national income. His rent theory was the original model of a rent-seeking society: Given fixed supply, Ricardo predicted that land (British land) would become increasingly scarce, its return (i.e. rent) would continuously rise, and, expressed in per capita terms, the share of rents in national income would increase. On the other hand, Ricardo believed that the share of wages would remain constant at subsistence, and that the profit share of industrialists would vanish in accordance with the declining productivity of capital and labour inputs per unit of output.

Growth for Ricardo, like all classical economists, meant national income resulting from 'accumulation'; that is, from capital accumulation determined, not by government, but by profit-seeking capitalists. Capital accumulation was private investment, financed by private savings. At any point in time, with given capital stock, profitability, as a return on capital, depended on the price of food, which determined the cost of labour, or, in Ricardo's own words: 'The natural price of labour which is necessary to enable labourers, one with another, to subsist and to perpetuate their race, without either increase or diminution' (quoted in Eltis 1987: 188).

Thus, in David Ricardo's growth model the king-pin is the real wage of industrial workers, which is the supply price of labour shown in eq. (1.8) above. If wages could be held in check through cheap food imports, then any profit, as net revenue, shown in eq. (1.2), would ensure sustained growth of capitalism. The 'gains of trade', derived from exchanging industrial exports for food imports, was the essence of Ricardian analytical prescription to guide policy makers in charge of British industrial strategy.

Were the Ricardian analysis and prescription 'value-free' and universal? No. Ricardo was a product of his social context and his premises were nationalist. He was also a politician and a lobbyist. 'Essentially a conservative economist' (Abbot ed. 1946: 275), he championed the cause of the repeal of the Corn Laws on behalf of the business lobby. His theorizing coincided with the fact that England was emerging as the first industrial nation, and, as such, it possessed a manufacturing base quite different from agricultural production, the dominant mode in other countries. Industrial revolution had made England unique. Ricardo's unstated value-premise was the uniqueness of the British national interest, giving Britain a strategic head start as the first industrial nation. Ricardo's 'gains of trade' were similar to Schumpeter's 'pioneer profits'. When seen in its relative social reality context, the Ricardian theory is as nationalistic, as is pointed out, for example, by the German economist Frederich List (see below pp. 51–53), as the postwar 'Japan Inc.' model.

Ricardo's analytical originality lay in the fact that his theory redefined factors of production and economic relations in the light of this new commanding social reality. His theory supported and promoted the new captains of industry in Manchester and other industrial centres since they were rapidly displacing the landowning aristocracy as the controlling interests. The crucial role of the cost of food in Ricardo's theory coincided exactly with the interest of the industrial and capitalist classes who, in turn, determined England's comparative advantage. The Ricardian theory was, in a real sense, a

'Britain Inc.' or Pax Britannica model based on the premise that, with the domestic price of corn rising, the industrialization of England was doomed unless access to cheap food for the working classes could be obtained. Free trade, based on exchanging industrial goods for cheap food imports, was the prescription to realize the gains of trade and expand the profit horizon of British capitalism.

In the global context, Ricardian theory was Eurocentric, even though at first sight his theory appears objective and universalistic. Free trade provided markets for the new 'captains of industry' and made England the 'workshop of the world'. As a doctrine it rationalized exchanging British industrial goods for cheap agricultural products, and, in the process, it de-industrialized British India and other colonies (Stavrianos 1981), for the cause of arresting and reversing the otherwise inevitable decline of the 'closed' British economy. The colonial policy-makers who built empires on capitalist foundations were schooled on, and believed they were practising, free trade doctrines. In fact, the results were the plantation economies in British West Indies (Beckford 1972), Malaya (Emerson 1964; Bauer 1948), in Dutch Indonesia (Higgins 1968; Himawan 1980) and in Africa built and managed on mercantilist criteria, financed largely with capital from the London money market, thereby returning huge annual dividends and surpluses from colonies to the treasury of the mother country (Drake 1961; Pauuw and Fei 1973). The welfare or socio-economic development of local populations in colonies did not matter: it was an idea totally alien in classical economics or in the education of colonial administrators (Arndt 1989). Moreover, these administrators were schooled on the notion that there is an inherent conflict between growth and population, between wages and profits, and, hence they possessed a stereotyped anti-labour worldview.

THE MALTHUSIAN POPULATION THEORY

In his *Essay on the Principle of Population* (1798), Robert Malthus advanced a deterministic theory of economic development in which the state of nature, as constructed by Rousseau and other egalitarian and radical *philosophes*, such as Condorcet, was turned on its head, ideologically speaking, and given a conservative and anti-revolutionary character; analytically it was equated with Adam Smith's supply–demand theory of market forces. These, in turn, were judged as morally valid according to a Christian divine scheme of the universe caught in a perpetual oscillation between scarcity of food and man's natural tendencies for indolence and other vices.

Malthus's theory of economic development was a pessimistic theory founded on the 'impossibility' (Winch 1992: xix) of remedying poverty through social policy intervention. Not surprisingly, it earned economics, in the words of his contemporary Thomas Carlyle, the label of the 'dismal science'.

According to Malthus, population–food dynamics are determined by three 'propositions' governing human progress (See Box 5):

> 1. Population is necessarily limited by the means of subsistence. 2. Population invariably increases, where the means of subsistence increase, unless prevented by some very powerful and obvious checks. 3. These checks, and the checks which repress the superior power of population, and keep its effects on a level with the means of subsistence, are all resolvable into moral restraint, vice, and misery.
>
> (Bk I, chap. ii)

Malthus classified two types of checks to population growth: positive checks that contribute to shortening human life such as 'extreme poverty, bad nursing of children, great towns, excesses of all kinds, the whole train of common diseases and epidemics, wars, pestilence, plague and famine' and preventive checks by which he meant 'moral restraint' in gender relations and delayed marriages: 'Promiscuous intercourse, unnatural passions, violations of the marriage bed, and improper arts to conceal the consequences of irregular connexions, clearly come under the head of vice' (Winch 1992: 23–4).

Behind this moralistic high ground lay the British economic interest. At the time when Malthus was theorizing, large parts of the earth, such as Canada and Australia, were unpopulated and his prescriptions were directed at British emigration policy. This was explicitly stated in the 1817 edition (Bk III, chap. iv) of his *Essay* (Winch 1992: 88) in order to promote colonial emigration as a cause 'worthy of . . . humanity and policy'. In spite of this, he believed that emigration provided no more than a temporary outlet that could in no way overcome the superior power of population growth to outstrip the power of the means of production (Winch 1992: 370).

The Malthusian population theory was, in reality, culture-specific and moralistic in the extreme, even though it was presented in universalistic terms: 'taking the whole earth, instead of this island,

---

Box 5

Malthus: on population–food dynamics

The Rev. Malthus was a highly moral man whose views on development were shaped by his religious convictions. His population–food theory was a mixture of his own Christian ethics and economic realism.

Malthusian theory was anti-labour and pro-capital. Thrift was a virtue of the capitalist classes who alone would save in order to make investment a reality. Working classes merely consumed what they earned, and, moreover, unless their 'vices' were checked, they would over-populate and over-consume, becoming a drag on economic growth. These anti-labour views shaped later theories of neo-classical economics, while also influencing generations of colonial administrators in charge of settlement and development.

---

emigration would of course be excluded; and, supposing the present population equalled to a thousand million, the human specie would increase as the numbers, 1, 2 , 4 , 8, 16, 32, 64, 128, 256, and subsistence as 1, 2, 3, 4, 5, 6, 7, 8, 9' (Bk I, chap. 1).

Here were have the 'law' of population – in actual fact a market solution to population policy – most often associated with Malthus, namely, the geometric growth of population compared with the arithmetic growth of the means of subsistence. This supply–demand theory predicts a long-term tendency for population to stabilize at the subsistence level of real wages, a culturally defined minimum income necessary for physical survival. If, in the short run, rising wages raise income per capita, then better health and nutrition will tend to reduce death rates. In due course, the population will increase, but the food supply will not be able to keep pace due to the limited availability of land and natural resources. The excess population will force wages below subsistence and inadequate income per capita will cause starvation, epidemics and war. As a result, the market will clear: food–population balance will thus be restored, and wages and income per capita will be restored at subsistence level. Malthus, the reverend moral philosopher, had little confidence in anti-poverty programmes, opposed the English Poor Laws, and would have rejected the idea of a Welfare State built on social safety net; most telling, unlike neo-Malthusians, he would have condemned national birth control policy as 'contrary to God's beneficent design' (Winch 1992: xiv).

The Malthusian population theory had a decisive influence in subsequent colonial emigration and resettlement policies. Malthus himself was, from 1805, a professor at East India College at Haileybury, an institution designed to train civil servants prior to duty in British India. However, it must be pointed out that Malthus himself was first and foremost a moralist, who emphasized the moral responsibility of the individual and who trivialized emigration and colonial interests which other contemporaries such as Wakefield promoted with great force. Nevertheless, his population theory advanced the cause of colonialism, a systematic exploitation of global resources in the interest of the mother country. It complemented Ricardo's theory in that colonization opened new possibilities for extensive farming in Canada, Australia and elsewhere, thereby solving one of the critical constraints identified in Ricardo's 'closed economy' growth model, namely, fixed supply of British land.

In theory, the Malthusian population–food dynamics represented a pioneering example of supply-side economics; more specifically, a demographically driven labour market theory which subsequently rationalized a cheap labour policy to safeguard capitalist profits at home and in the colonies. This was the essence of the Iron Law of Wages centred on the constancy of long-run real wages at subsistence level, an anti-working class bias. This is illustrated in Figure 2.2.

In Figure 2.2, real wages (RW) settle along the long-run labour supply curve, LR_s where subsistence level of income, S_w equals RW_0. The employed portion of the labour force, shown on the horizontal axis, is determined by population growth. The optimal population size, however, is determined by the labour market equilibrium E_0 and is exactly equal to L_0. This is 'optimal' because the workers' earnings, shown by the area of the rectangle under E_0, is exactly equal to the subsistence cost of sustaining them. In other words, these workers consume what they earn, i.e. their level of savings is zero. In Malthusian (or classical) terms, the workers' contribution to accumulation (i.e. growth) is nil!

Now, suppose that in the short run, labour supply is reduced (say, as a result of emigration). Short-run labour supply shifts from S_0S_0 to S_1S_1. The new equilibrium is at E_1. The employment level falls to L_1

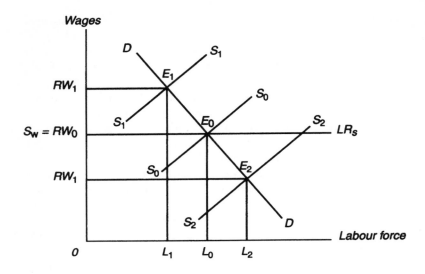

Figure 2.2 The Iron Law of Wages

but relative labour scarcity pushes real wages to RW_1 which implies rising income per capita. Since workers consume but do not save, higher incomes result in more marriages, possibly at earlier ages, accelerating multiplication of population. In due course, population growth expands labour supply and may reach $S_2 S_2$ with a labour market equilibrium at E_2. Employment at this equilibrium is L_2 and the real wages, RW_2, are markedly below subsistence level of income. Such an excessive population is untenable, and substandard consumption and nutrition levels will either lead to starvation, pestilence or plagues (Malthus might have added AIDS), or massive emigration. In the end, wages and living standards will revert to, and stabilize at, the subsistence level along LR_s at the constant real wages RW_0.

In the above model, two behavioural assumptions are particularly notable. First, unlike Smith's trade model, the Malthusian model is entirely supply driven. Demand for labour is totally passive: it does not shift throughout the entire analysis; this is quite unrealistic and, historically, quite incorrect. Labour productivity has increased dramatically as a result of better education and technical know-how. Second, workers are merely inputs in the production system: they have value merely as tradables, consuming what they earn entirely, making no contribution to growth. Thrift, for Malthus, was a virtue limited to capitalists because savings for investment, the essential engine of capitalist growth, was all their contribution. This classical assumption of labour–capital conflict predates Marx.

The anti-labour bias of Malthusian theory guided not only the emigration policies of colonial administrators in resettling excess Europeans in the New World; they also rationalized the cheap labour policies in the building of plantations and mining enterprises in the colonies. The perennial problem of the colonial capitalists carving plantations out of the jungle or opening mines was the shortage of indigenous labour (Parmer 1960; Jackson 1968).

The labour shortage problem arose because the local inhabitants generally refused to work on European terms, in particular, for low wages. In the typical case, the opportunity cost of such labour was higher than wages offered and colonial administrators in many cases resorted to land titles and taxes, payable in cash, effectively coercing indigeneous people into wage-employment. Peasant rebellions followed such colonial policies (Scott 1976, 1985). Wage-employment was miserable work, unhealthy and often away from the family; supply response was, therefore, erratic. Any unanticipated earnings might mean an opportunity to return to the family, even at the risk of absenteeism. The classic colonial explanation, however, was in terms of the Backward-sloping Supply Curve Hypothesis (Bauer and Yamey 1957; Berg 1961), stressing perverse or irrational supply response on the part of local people. Therefore, immigrant labour from other colonies had to be imported to supply labour to capitalists operating mines and plantations at subsistence wages as in the Iron Law of Wages. The real motive, of course, was the pursuit of profits on a global scale. It was this global search for profits which drove colonial interests, entrepreneurs and policy-makers into teamwork, creating the population mixtures of many countries today, presuming that these people were incapable of national or cultural sentiments. Thus, the Chinese and Tamils were shipped into Malaya for tin mines and rubber plantations; African tribes, near and far, were mobilized into South Africa to provide labour pools for the gold mines; Indian coolies were taken to build railways in East Africa; African slaves, and later Indians too, were imported to supply cheap labour to sugar plantations in the West Indies; and so on. They were all justified and rationalized by economic development theorizing in the mother country. None, however, was more powerful than the free trade theory.

TRADE AS THE ENGINE OF GROWTH

The 'us and them' dichotomy has always lain at the root of trade, from Marco Polo to mercantilists, and persists down to the present, mirroring a zero-sum view of the potential benefits of trade. The greatest minds of Western orthodox economics have sought to construct a win–win trade theory, but no theorist put theory above national interest.

Adam Smith, David Ricardo and their disciples viewed trade as the path to expanding the wealth of England. Without trade, the English economy would remain 'closed' and, as a small, overcrowded island, it could only experience declining living standards since a lack of investment opportunities would ultimately force the profit rate to decline towards zero. Opening free trade and settling the New World pushed the limits of nineteenth-century capitalism to new heights of prosperity. As Adam Smith put it, trade extended the size of the market, promoted specialization and generated prosperity through its gains.

SMITH'S VENT-FOR-SURPLUS THEORY

The pioneering concept of 'trade as the engine of growth' is Adam Smith's vent-for-surplus theory (Myint 1958, 1971), a simple or 'crude' theory, lacking rigour. Nevertheless, Myint considered it 'more suitable' (1958: 327) for developing countries than the more modern Hecksher-Ohlin factor-endownment theory (see below p. 54) because: (1) it promoted a more efficient 'balanced growth' relationship between domestic and foreign trade, and (2) it emphasized agricultural development first in economic development instead of protecting of manufacturing (Myint 1977).

The central logic behind the vent-for-surplus theory is that trade brings national prosperity through gains of trade. Exporting surpluses to foreign markets increases national income with exchange earnings thereby extending the size or the productive capacity of the domestic market. Thus, foreign markets act as 'vents' attracting the surplus output of the exporting country. Output that is extra to domestic consumption earns foreign exchange with which to finance imports. This represents the first of the 'two distinct benefits' of Smith's trade-cum-development approach (Myint 1977), namely, gains of trade. The other, higher allocative efficiency, in the domestic economy is realized when trade promotes full employment through higher productivity, since otherwise idle or underemployed labour, land and other resources are more productively employed. As a result, economic welfare, or consumers' 'enjoyments', rise. To cite a famous passage in Adam Smith's words, foreign trade

> carries out that surplus part of the produce of their land and labour for which there is no demand among them, and brings back in return for it something else for which there is demand. It gives a value to their superfluities, by exchanging them for something else, which may satisfy a part of their wants, and increase their enjoyments. By means of it, the narrowness of the home market does not hinder the division of labour in any particular branch of art or manufacture from being carried to the highest perfection. By opening a more extensive market for whatever part of the produce of their labour that may exceed the home consumption, it encourages them to improve its productive powers, and to augment its annual produce to the utmost and thereby to increase the real revenue and wealth of the society.
>
> (Smith 1776: vol. I: 413)

Smith's vent-for-surplus theory is illustrated in Figure 2.3. Suppose a hypothetical country's maximum potential output in the state of autarky is Q_0. At this output, the labour endowment of the country, shown by the vertical supply schedule SS is fully employed. The level of domestic demand, shown by DD, results in market equilibrium at E_0 determining a unit price of P_0. This price level, however, is below the 'natural' price (determined subjectively by custom or convention) equivalent to P_1. In other words, at the prevailing price level, P_0, there is surplus output (over and above the natural or normal consumption level Q_n) equal to Q_nQ_0.

Now suppose that this surplus were to be exported to foreign markets. As a result, price and consumption would revert to normal levels and market equilibrium would be established at E_n. While domestic price level would rise from P_0 to P_n, this would merely eliminate abnormally depressed prevailing prices. On the positive side, the surplus output exported would earn foreign exchange and thus enable the attainment of a higher standard of living demonstrated by higher average income per capita.

What holds true for one specific country, holds in general for other trading countries. In other words, all trading countries can realize

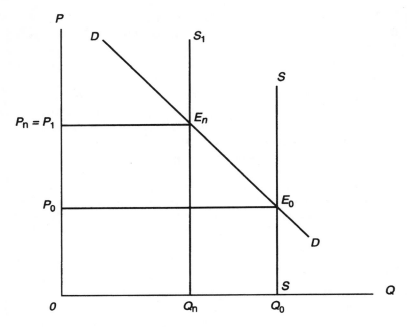

Figure 2.3 Trade as vent-for-surplus

gains of trade through specialization and exchange through free trade. In short, trade would operate as an engine of economic development enhancing global prosperity in a world without trade barriers, if and when resources are allocated according to the principles of division of labour and free trade.

Adam Smith's trade theory was simple and lacked the formal rigour of Ricardo's comparative cost theory. Accordingly, mainstream theorists have generally judged that 'Smith was not a great trade theorist' (Bloomfield quoted by Myint 1977: 231), a view which the Burmese economist Myint has, as discussed above, challenged. Myint's defence notwithstanding, it remains unexplained as to why an underdeveloped country would produce a surplus over and above its consumption in order to trade, unless it was first guaranteed market access. Also, Smith's theory was based on the principle of absolute advantage, i.e. the assumption that each country participating in free trade enjoys a cost advantage, a highly dubious assumption (See Box 6).

To see this, let's take a hypothetical two-country and two-good (2 × 2) model, with each country specializing in the production of

---

Box 6

Absolute and comparative advantage

Generally, it is regarded that Adam Smith, the father of modern economics, was a poor trade theorist. His trade theory was based on *absolute advantage*, i.e. that each trading country in free trade enjoys a cost advantage in a given product so that gainful exchange through trade is always possible. This 'naive' theory ignored the obvious question of what happens when no absolute advantage exists.

Ricardo's *comparative advantage* theory provided the missing explanation. With the aid of the wine-for-cloth example in the case of Portugal and England, Ricardo demonstrated that, even when England enjoyed absolute advantage in both goods, specialization and exchange under free trade was better for both countries, so long as England enjoyed greater cost advantage in one product (i.e. cloth) over Portugal.

The major weakness in Ricardo's theory, however, is that it is not a dynamic theory of trade; it is only a static theory. Unfortunately, this weakness has not prevented the spread of Ricardian theory as the Western gospel of free trade, and as universally valid under all situations.

---

the good which it can produce cheaper than the other, and exchange these in free trade to the mutual gain of both countries. But what if one possessed both the advantages, while the other had none: was gainful trade still possible? This was the question which Adam Smith ignored. The puzzle had to await David Ricardo whose theory will be analysed presently, following a fuller exposition of the absolute advantage principle, an essential step to the analysis.

The absolute advantage principle can be illustrated by a table comparing productivities in the standard 2×2 model. Consistent with the classical view that the value of a commodity is the opportunity cost of labour required in its production, Table 2.1 measures productivity in terms of output per unit of labour.

In this example, England is depicted as having absolute advantage in cloth production and an absolute disadvantage in wine, whereas Portugal has an absolute advantage in wine production and an absolute disadvantage in cloth. Gains of trade would accrue to both if

Table 2.1 Output of one man-year's labour

Commodity	England	Portugal
Cloth (yds)	12	10
Wine (gals)	4	5

the two countries specialized in the production of commodities in which they enjoyed absolute advantage and engaged in free trade.

RICARDIAN COMPARATIVE ADVANTAGE THEORY

But what if a given country enjoyed absolute advantage in both commodities? Would free trade still be justified in the sense that there would be gains of trade for both countries? Adam Smith did not deal with this question. David Ricardo provided the missing answer.

Ricardo, in the famous chapter vii on foreign trade of his *Principles of Political Economy and Taxation* (1911: 77–93), demonstrated, using a simplified version of the 2 × 2 example, that free trade would still be gainful 'with the universal good of the whole' (1911: 81), even when English labour was more productive than its Portuguese counterpart in the production of both commodities, provided only that English labour was comparatively more productive in one commodity. In other words, comparative advantage stemmed from inter-industry productivity differences. Ricardo chose cloth (i.e., the industrial product) for England and left Portugal wine (i.e., the agricultural product). Ricardo's numerical example assumed that, in a state of autarky, England could be self-sufficient in the production of cloth and wine, but the former would need 100 men for one year for 120 in the case of the latter. Ricardo argued:

> To produce the wine in Portugal might require only the labour of 80 men for one year, and to produce the cloth in the same might require the labour of 90 men for the same time. It would therefore be advantageous for her to export wine in exchange for cloth. This exchange might even take place notwithstanding that the commodity imported by Portugal could be produced there with less labour than in England. Though she could make the cloth with the labour of 90 men, she would import it from a country

where it required the labour of 100 men to produce it, because it would be advantageous to her rather to employ her capital in the production of wine, for which she would obtain more cloth from England, than she could produce by diverting a portion of her capital from the cultivation of vines to the manufacture of cloth.

(Ricardo 1911: 82)

Here, in a nutshell, was Ricardo's comparative cost theory centred on the principle of opportunity cost applied to illustrate inter-industry productivity differences.

The choice of this particular product mix, cloth and wine, the former industrial and the latter agricultural, is of fundamental importance, for therein lies a vital, though unstated, pro-capital value-judgement: namely, that, by Ricardo's time, England was uniquely industrialized and hence, as the base of capital-intensive manufacturing, would always derive the lion's share of any gains of trade. If we recast this value-problem within a two-country world (i.e. England and ROW – Rest of the World), a zero-sum Euro-centric worldview clearly emerges! For, as has been pointed out by Myint (1977), Ricardian trade theory has nothing to say about the domestic impact of trade in ROW, beyond the fact that it should so reallocate its resources as to subordinate itself entirely to the requirements of its trading partner. Under such conditions, how could the gains of trade be shared equitably to fulfil Ricardo's promise of 'the universal good of the whole'? It seems impossible. We shall return to this question shortly.

First, however, it is necessary to examine further the general view amongst mainstream theorists regarding the superiority of the Ricardian doctrine of comparative advantage over Smith's absolute advantage, while keeping in mind that Portugal may be thought of as a ROW or the future Third World.

In Table 2.2, it is assumed that England should indeed specialize in the production of cloth entirely, leaving wine production to Portugal, notwithstanding the English absolute advantage in both products. This stems from the fact that the marginal productivity of English labour is higher in cloth production than wine; in fact, it is twice as productive. Therefore, it would be more profitable if England were to specialize in cloth production. But how can the Portuguese specialization in wine be justified? Ricardo's reply would be on the basis of opportunity cost, i.e. the amount of cloth production which would be sacrificed in order to produce a gallon

Table 2.2 Output of one man-year's labour

Commodity	England	Portugal
Cloth (yds)	12	6
Wine (gals)	4	3

of wine. In Portugal, where the productivity of one man-year's labour is either 6 yards of cloth or 3 gallons of wine, the marginal opportunity cost of wine is 2 yards of Portuguese cloth; however, measured in terms of forgone English cloth, 1 gallon of Portuguese wine is worth 4 yards of cloth. Consequently, if England were to specialize in cloth and Portugal in wine production and exchange the two commodities in free trade, both would derive gains of trade. Portugal, for example, would receive twice the quantity of English cloth per gallon of wine compared to what it would cost her to manufacture cloth at home; likewise, England would be able to import a gallon of Portuguese wine at the cost of 2 yards of cloth, whereas it would cost her 3 yards if she were to produce wine in England.

But Ricardo's numerical calculations contain several crucial flaws. The analysis is strictly 'static' based on constant costs and no productivity gains due to technical progress or 'learning by doing'; there is free mobility of labour domestically, but not internationally; while capital is free to move freely anywhere, seeking highest profits. This means that England, designated as the industrial country, will always enjoy comparative advantage in manufacturing. Thus, Portugal (or Japan and others) would never industrialize, but remain an agricultural country, a wine producer forever. If English tastes were to change so that wine consumption dropped drastically, Portugal would be in a serious economic crisis owing to its external dependence or vulnerability. Read 'primary producers' for Portugal, and we can see the precarious permanent dependency position of primary producing economies on externally driven exports, fluctuating around a boom–bust cycle generating instability of foreign earnings. Also, there is a psychological weakness amongst the exporting circles, as an 'inhibiting export mentality' (Watkins 1963: 150), perpetuating a division of labour as hewers of wood and drawers of water; in short, there is no incentive to move up the industrialization ladder. The static Ricardian model is solidly constructed on an unequal trading relationship in the short and long term.

In the above 2 × 2 model production functions are homogeneous in the first degree, i.e., there are no economies or diseconomies of scale in production. Therefore, each country must specialize completely, as well as permanently, in commodity production to be exchanged for imports of industrial products (but not parts or components), and on terms of trade determined exogenously, beyond its control. Effectively, therefore, trading partners are 'trapped' in existing productivity differences reflecting initial differences in technologies and know-how with no prospect of shifts in comparative advantage as a result of growth dynamics. In the Ricardian worldview, England would always remain the pre-eminent industrial country.

Do these assumptions make Ricardo's free trade a value-free, objective theory, independent of British national interest? Some would argue in the affirmative. Others would concur with Joan Robinson, who clearly acknowledged the nationalistic roots of Ricardo and other classical economists, when she put it succinctly: 'The classical economists were in favour of Free Trade because it was good for Great Britain, not because it was good for the world' (Robinson 1962: 117). Ricardo, like Adam Smith, supported navigation laws to protect and maintain English maritime supremacy, considered essential not only for defence but for trading. On colonial trade he was uncharacteristically vague and waffling, generally siding with English monopolistic interests arguing that export duties in colonies were 'a measure of internal policy, and could not easily be imposed by the mother country' (Ricardo 1911: 228). Moreover, he shared the standard Victorian biases of his time and readily attributed the poverty and underdevelopment of poor countries to 'the ignorance, indolence, and barbarism of the inhabitants' (Ricardo 1911: 56).

In Europe, at least one of Ricardo's contemporaries was unpersuaded by free trade arguments. Frederich List dismissed Ricardo and Adam Smith, 'the cosmopolitan theorists' as he labelled them, in favour of a protectionist (i.e. infant industry) strategy and argued that Ricardo was wrong because he had ignored existing inequalities and differences in economic development levels between different countries. Therefore, List believed that

> under the existing conditions of the world, the result of general free trade would not be a universal republic, but, on the contrary a universal subjection of the less advanced nations to the supremacy of the predominant manufacturing, commercial, and naval power [i.e. Britain] . . . A universal republic . . . i.e. a union of the nations of the

earth . . . can only be realised if a large number of nation-
alities attain to as nearly the same degree as possible of
industry and civilisation, political cultivation, and power.

(List 1885: 126–7)

In other words, even if universal free trade is regarded as an ideal,
under the existing status quo characterized by economic disparities
amongst nations, the first question has to be how to get from here
(i.e. the status quo) to there (i.e. the ideal). Otherwise, List would
argue, a free trade regime would merely transform the more advanced
countries into 'predatory victors' (Darity 1985: 494).

List had a great influence on Bismarck, the architect of German
unification. In particular, he inspired the formation of Zollverein,
the German customs union, and economic policy after 1870 was
more along the lines of state capitalism, commencing with state
monopolies and direct state intervention in the economy. Today, it
is difficult to argue that German economic development since
List's time has been any less impressive than England's since
Ricardo's time. 'Protectionism versus free trade' have remained as
the two opposite strategies of national commercial policy.

What, in brief, were the essentials of List's economic development
theory?

In Chapter 10 on the 'teachings of history', deduced from ancient
and modern times, List summarizes his own theory of economic
development for national wealth and power on the basis of three
stages: 'in the first stage', it is necessary for the emerging nations
to adopt 'free trade with more advanced nations as a means of raising
themselves from a state of barbarism, and of making advances in
agriculture; in the second stage', protectionist policies are required
for 'promoting the growth of manufactures, fisheries, navigation,
and foreign trade by means of commercial restrictions; and in the
last stage, after reaching the highest degree of wealth and power,
by gradually reverting to the principle of free trade and of unrest-
ricted competition in the home as well as in foreign markets, that
so their agriculturalists, manufacturers, and merchants may be pre-
served from indolence, and stimulated to retain the supremacy
which they have acquired' (List 1885: 115). Evidently, List was no
doctrinaire protectionist; he merely saw it as a necessary condition
for the launching of infant industries under state guidance. Once
the third stage, the commercial stage, is reached by trading partners,
only then can free trade, gainful to all partners, start; but not
before.

List, the economic nationalist, also rejected the *laissez-faire* individualism of classical economists from Adam Smith on, supporting instead the interests of a collectivity such as the state or nation. He denounced as 'sophism' the doctrine of individual rationality, guided by self-interest alone , as the sufficient condition of national prosperity. It is not true, List argued, '*that the wealth of the nation is merely the aggregate of the wealth of all individuals in it, and that the private interest of every individual is better able than all State regulations to incite to production and accumulation of wealth*' (List 1885: 170, italics in original). For List, the state has a duty to promote and guide economic development for the good of the nation as a whole which had an identity of its own in the international community:

> Between each individual and entire humanity . . . stands
> THE NATION, with its special language and literature,
> with its own peculiar origin and history, with its special
> manners and customs, laws and institutions, with the
> claims of all these for existence, independence, perfection
> and continuance for the future, and with its separate terri-
> tory . . . It is the task of national economy to accomplish
> *the economical development of the nation*, and to prepare it for
> admission into the universal society of the future.
> (List 1885: 174–5, italics and capitals in original)

No wonder List, more than Ricardo, found favourable response in post-Meiji Japan (Fallows 1994).

Both the British and German approaches to economic development, though utilizing radically different theories, were nevertheless conditioned by the same commanding objective: national interest. For both, investment was the engine of growth to achieve national wealth. The two differed in their interpretation of the role of investment: public investment for List, private investment for Ricardo, was the trigger for economic development to make their nation rich. This, in the final analysis, is what places economic nationalists like List and free traders like Ricardo in the same Eurocentric framework. List's Eurocentricity was explicitly stated when he ruled out any prospect for non-Europeans, such as the 'Asiatic people', of achieving autonomous civilization or progress.

> Hence the entire dissolution of the Asiatic nationalities
> appears to be inevitable, and a regeneration of Asia only pos-
> sible by means of an infusion of European vital power, by the

general introduction of Christian religion and of European moral laws and order, by European immigration, and the introduction of European systems of government.

(List 1885: 419)

Of the two, of course, David Ricardo's work has had the greatest theoretical impact. In the early twentieth century, it spawned Hecksher–Ohlin's multi-factor endowment theorem (Hecksher 1919; Ohlin 1929) which replaced the classical labour theory of value on which Smith and Ricardo had built their theories. But these were abstract, 'pure' theories, constructed in the ideal perfect competition framework with no empirical basis.

'PURE' TRADE THEORY: TEXTBOOK ANALYSIS AND EMPIRICAL REALITY

Standard textbook analysis (Heller 1968; Kindleberger and Lindert 1982) of Ricardian and Hecksher–Ohlin theories are more exercises in abstract logic than policy-relevant theory. They use Edgeworth–Bowley box diagrams, production possibility frontiers and social indifference curves, all non-empirically constructed, reflecting a set of assumptions from Euclidian geometry and Aristotelian logic. However, this logic bears little resemblance to the real world of trade increasingly dominated by oligopolistic corporations, of mixed nationality, handling a growing volume of parts and components sourced from varied, and often undefinable, origins and regulatory jurisdictions.

The aim of such abstract theorizing was originally twofold: to demonstrate theoretically (1) that free trade based on exchange and specialization enhances world economic welfare in potential terms, and (2) that the gains of trade, again potentially, could improve national economic welfare within trading countries. This theoretical result required that the international terms of trade (i.e. the ratio of import and export prices) should settle somewhere in the 'wedge' or band bounded by pre-trade domestic price relatives. But what if they did not? In the case of a small trading country, too small to have any influence on terms of trade, trading may occur on the dominant country's terms that were actually determined by the power of influential interest groups and middlemen therein.

The inherent flaws of the heuristic theorizing of the 'pure' trade school became especially apparent subsequently (see below) when tested empirically. But, this kind of empirical work did not begin until after the World War II, and the results shocked mainstream theorists. What the empirical findings demonstrated was the simplistic and unrealistic nature of these theories. This was the main conclusion of the Leontieff Paradox (1953) which showed, contrary to expectations, that the USA was exporting labour-intensive products and importing capital-intensive ones, a result which was verified in several subsequent applications by Leontieff's students. Similarly, empirical work on the terms of trade between industrial and primary producing countries (Singer 1950; ECLA 1950; Prebisch 1959) reinforced doubts about the validity of the 'pure' trade theory. What these studies demonstrated was a long-term steady impoverishment of primary producers since the mid-nineteenth century for the greater benefit of European trading powers. We shall return to this below (see pp. 79–80).

MARKETS AND ETHICS

Having briefly surveyed the classical theories of economic development, what main conclusions emerge?

Undoubtedly, the classical economists formulated their theories with great sophistication, displaying fine analytical skills in Aristotelian logic and Euclidian geometry to present their theories as cosmopolitan or universalistic. However, neither the logic of Ancient Greece, nor the classical theories of mainstream economists can be universal. Behind the logic and theories, there are subjective value-loaded premises. In this context, the following themes, as summary to this section, are noteworthy.

First and foremost, the classical theorists believed that the path to economic development lay in the *laissez-faire* market-exchange mechanism. What exactly is this mechanism? An abstraction of buying and selling in the domestic as well as in the world marketplace without government; an unrealistic worldview reducing such heuristic theorizing into 'empty boxes'. Realistic theorizing needs to take the state into account, and to ask the question: Why are some states better at economic and social development than others? (Onis 1991; Wade 1988, 1990). We shall return to this question later in the context of the East Asian NICs which succeeded in economic development primarily because they charted their own independent course, though with much learning and adapting from the West – more from List than Ricardo.

Second, the economic development theories before and after Adam Smith made national prosperity the ultimate end. Efficiency and productivity were de-linked from ethical values and equilibrium, as in the Walrasian ideal, was equated with optimality. By removing ethics from efficiency and productivity in abstract models that had no objective empirical content from non-European worlds, the classical economists provided Cecil Rhodes and Raffles and other empire builders from the West with the theoretical rationalization needed to pursue profits aggressively, and if necessary by force and oppression. The surplus value generated by the enterprises of such men, nevertheless facilitated the greater enrichment of the colonial powers.

VALUES, INSTITUTIONS AND EUROCENTRICITY

Although classical economic thinkers believed that they were constructing value-free models of markets that were objective in determining prices for valuing production, in fact, their reasoning was shaped by their own historical and social conditioning. It is no surprise that their theorizing coincided with the Industrial Revolution and the rise of European nationalism.

Classical economic development theorizing coincided with the rise of nation-states. When the city-state gave way to the nation-state at the end the medieval era, new political and economic institutions emerged to replace old ones. In politics, parliament replaced the divine right of kings in law-making; in economics, guilds disappeared in favour of markets. The *raison d'être* of Western market enterprise became profit-driven capitalism, increasingly international in outlook, but nationalistic in its premises. Thus, Adam Smith's treatise was dedicated to the hope that 'the progress of England towardss opulence and improvement [would continue] in all future times' (quoted in Arndt 1989: 13). Whenever the English national interest collided with economic principle in *The Wealth of Nations*, nationalism won. Thus, at the end of Book III Smith declared England was 'well fitted by nature . . . to be the seat of foreign commerce' (Smith 1776 vol. I: 391), and in the second part of Book IV, when Smith discusses the notion that the economy of England depended on the number of its sailors and shipping, he judged that the 'act of navigation . . . *very properly* endeavours to give the sailors and shipping of Great Britain *the monopoly of the trade* of their own country, in some cases, by absolute prohibitions, and in others by heavy burdens upon the shipping of foreign countries' (Smith 1776 vol. I: 427, italics added).

Nationalism is the ideology of the nation-state, and it is a purely European innovation (Kedourie 1966; Hobsbawm 1992). Classical economic theories were constructed to promote the common good of the nation-state. These theories, in turn, enabled formulation of public policy instruments in which economics, as much as defence, played the key role. Behind theory and policy instruments was another new European innovation: *interest*, national and personal. Until the eighteenth century, honour was the overwhelming virtue in human affairs (Hirschman 1977). Subsequently, interest replaced honour as the driving ethic of Western behaviour, meaning, of course, Western honour as in gentlemanly conduct limited to Westerners. The Industrial Revolution affected moral values no less than the techniques of production (Mumford 1934). The British and continental theorizers attuned their theories to the respective national interest. Collectively, these Europeans had shared values, strictly bound by Europeanness or being Western, the Protestant Ethic, in which 'earthly advancement' (Mumford 1934: 43) as demonstrated by 'earthly goods' and personal wealth, however acquired from others (non-Westerners), was seen as the necessary condition for ultimate divine grace. Rational behaviour, guiding 'earthly' pursuits masked self-centred utilitarianism and the new 'science' of positive economics made it all look objective, rational and value-free! But, deep in their hearts, European theorists, Smith and Ricardo not excluded, were nationalistic with little understanding, and less tolerance, of non-Western peoples.

Eurocentricity lay at the very heart of a self-righteous ethic which justified a zero-sum game worldview, legitimizing for the enrichment of self—us at the cost of the impoverishment of others. In the age of European colonialism, economic development theorizing was for 'us', i.e. for Europeans exclusively, and catchy phrases like 'gains of trade' and 'colonial development' in reality meant enrichment of the colonial powers. While in theory, the existence of the 'other' was acknowledged, often in exotic terms as in Wallace, this was akin to 'barbarians' in Ancient Rome and Greece. From the Renaissance on, as the Western capitalist system evolved, so also emerged with it an integral mythology constructed around the 'irrationality', i.e. inferiority of the 'other'. Accordingly, the 'other' was hedonistic, beyond reason, incapable of culture or national existence. 'The whole of Eurocentricity lies in this mythic construction' (Amin 1989: 11).

3

POSTWAR NEO-CLASSICAL
THEORIES, 1945–1973

World War I destroyed the old colonial trading system, but it did not end flawed economic development theorizing from the West. In fact, idealization of the West accelerated, under a new American vision mirroring the shift of the economic centre of gravity from the eastern to western Atlantic: in the process, the US dollar gradually replaced the pound as the lynchpin of the international financial system and Americanization became increasingly synonymous with Westernization of the former colonies. The pre-1914 narrow conception of Eurocentricity was henceforth broadened into US–Eurocentricity. Westernization of the former colonies took on a new meaning and mission led by mainstream economists.

Between the two world wars, the industrialized countries were transition economies preoccupied with the domestic problems of postwar reconstruction and then the Great Depression. Theoretically this reconstruction was justified by the new macroeconomics of John Maynard Keynes (1936), stressing fiscalism via government deficit spending; this was implemented first in the USA, then Europe, and finally introduced to the Third World under a new agenda, complete with a new terminology, but still solidly resting on Western premises which left no room for any alternative worldview. In particular, the Western multinationals emerged as the key agents of the Westernization of the Third World.

NEW AGENDA, NEW TERMINOLOGY: THE
TWO-AXES WORLDVIEW

The post-1945 order was re-invented by US–Eurocentric mainstream rationalists with a new agenda and terminology centred on three brand new themes: (1) the Cold War bipolarity, (2) modernization, or better yet Westernization of former colonies, and (3) modelling of economic development as a linear, homogenized process.

This new agenda involved the stereotyping of development economics in textbooks on the basis of stylized characteristics of 'the typical underdeveloped country' (Hirschman 1986: 3), as if such a country really existed! Moreover, the new 'pioneers in development' (Meier and Seers eds 1984) became spokespersons of the orthodoxy that development was capital accumulation; a technocratic task of grand designs, simultaneous equations, balanced growth, plannable with mathematical precison. They were optimists, convinced that 'the natural progress of opulence' (in Adam Smith's words) – what we would call today 'development economics' (Lewis in Meier and Seers eds 1984: 121) – would emancipate primitive societies from backwardness and modernize them. In theory, based on ideal markets, prosperity via tricklism would cure all problems of underdevelopment. In practice, however, Eurocentric interests took advantage of market imperfections and failures.

The bipolar worldview: redefining 'us' and 'them'

The label 'Third World' itself was a postwar invention that was originally coined by Alfred Sauvy and was modelled on the Third Estate in the French Revolution (Harris 1987: 18). It was a product of the US–Eurocentric mindset, shaped by the passing of the old Victorian colonial order at the end of World War II, and the onset of decolonization and the Cold War. The Third World leaders, revolutionary, charismatic and utopian, the 'Bandung generation' (Harris 1987: 171), which included Nehru, Tito, Nkrumah, Nasser and the host Sukarno, were unintentional partners in this venture; for while they sought to construct a separate ideological world interspaced between the First and Second, they were often secret admirers of the 'mystique of the West', actively promoting Western tools and techniques of development planning.

The Eurocentric worldview post-1945 was constructed mirroring the American hegemony of the West, in a two-axis, bipolar world. In this worldview, the Third World was ranked last, behind the First and Second: and it was stereotyped, as in Victorian times, in the us–them dichotomy. To develop the latter (as a transitive verb) emerged as the mission of the new field of development economics. Variously described as backward, undeveloped, underdeveloped, developing (and sometimes worse), the Third World became the new frontier for Western economists who went out on missions to win hearts and minds, and to modernize and Westernize the peoples of Asia, Africa and Latin America. This was part of the big power rivalry, the politics of 'containment' as articulated by George Kenan, the mysterious author 'X' of the celebrated article in July 1947 of *Foreign Affairs*, the voice of American diplomacy.

The big power politics were played on two axes: An East–West security axis that focused on the ideological confrontation between the First (capitalist) and Second (communist) Worlds; and a North (rich)–South (poor) development axis. The Third World, emerging out of colonialism, was suddenly discovered as lacking autonomous capacity for development. Mainstream economic development theorists, without inquiring into the history of this underdevelopment, rushed forward with new sets of US–Eurocentric prescriptions and paradigms to reconstruct the Third World. These were all dependent upon aid and technology flows from the First World caught in an ideological competition with the Second.

The inner logic of this new US–Eurocentric worldview was the 'containment' of communism worldwide as articulated by George Kenan: militarily along the East–West axis, and developmentally along the North–South axis. Thus, Third World countries, newly independent politically ('flag independence' – as aptly described) but economically backward, undeveloped, underdeveloped and developing, were targeted as objects of foreign aid flows from the North to become modern and be converted to Western capitalism.

The new agenda of economic developmentalism for Third World development was thus set. It was an entirely Northern agenda mapping the course of economic development in the Third World from outside, defining goals, and selecting policy instruments for state-sponsored capitalist development within, all ultimately justified with reference to rational behaviour. Domestic constraints and institutional capacity inside the Third World seemed not to matter all. It was as if developing countries were all empty, ready for a brand new start. What about the post-independence generation of Third World leadership? It played a surprisingly marginal role.

Modernization and national leadership

In political terms, the Western agenda for the Third World was drawn up to fit the new 'rising expectations' of post-colonial independence. It set the stage for political development (Higgot 1983) paralleling economic development. As befits an era of optimism,

Western theorists came up with the modernization theory made in Europe or the USA. It was based on the view that development was modernity, defined as 'the passing of traditional society' (Lerner 1958) or 'becoming modern' (Inkeles and Smith 1974); it embraced the Western political institutions and norms as 'universal reference' (Eisenstadt 1987).

During the first quarter century after World War II, post-independence leadership elites in the South played a generally submissive or accommodating role in economic development, facilitating the transfer of Western planning techniques. Rhetorically much emphasis was placed on social and economic development as part of decolonization. In spite of this, national leaders, especially the 'Bandung generation' (Harris 1987: 171), including those who had fought for liberation, were unashamedly conditioned by the 'mystique' of Western rationalism, mistaking pseudo-scientific planning as virtuous. A couple of examples may be sufficient. Thus, Eric Williams, the Prime Minister of Trinidad and Tobago from 1956 to 1981, in a conference on planning at Sussex University in 1969, declared that 'planning is like discussing virtue. It is a good thing . . . [intended] to impart discipline and enthusiasm to the pursuit of development effort by both the public and private sectors of the economy' (Williams 1972: 39). India's Nehru, who succeeded Gandhi, went even further in his admiration of Western techniques while rejecting Gandhian egalitarian economics focused on villages and rural people (Myrdal 1968: 753–6). Nehru favoured capital-intensive technocratic central planning transferred from the West. Naively he declared:

> Planning and development have become a sort of mathematical problem which may be worked out scientifically . . . Planning for industrial development is generally accepted as a matter of mathematical formula . . . Men of science, planners, experts, who approach our problems from purely a scientific point of view rather than an ideological one . . . agree, broadly, that given certain pre-conditions of development, industrialization and all that, certain exact conclusions follow almost as a matter of course.
>
> (Nehru quoted in Lindblom 1977: 318)

This pseudo-scientific approach ultimately ended in a dramatic failure. It pushed India into a severe balance of payment crisis and forced a new planning strategy based on agriculture (Frankel 1969). The Indian planning failure was subsequently repeated in Africa and elsewhere causing food deficits and rural underdevelopment. Having won national liberation, it became fashionable for Third World leaders to rely on Western advisory teams (such as UCLA or Harvard mafias), supplied under foreign aid programmes of doubtful effectiveness (Griffin and Enos 1970). It was astonishing how often these Western technocrats seemed to be encountering severe failure and 'culture shock' (Seers 1962; Byrne 1966; Edgell 1973/4)!

Of course, the newly independent countries of the Third World faced daunting challenges of nation-building. They were short of such critical resources as human capital (Harbison and Myers 1973) as well as domestic savings and investment, and possessed a weak administrative capacity, especially at the sub-national level (Esman 1978; Uphoff et al. 1979; Rondinelli 1983). Typically Western educated, the post-colonial leadership continued in the footsteps of their colonial masters, rejecting rural development and opting for urban-biased strategies. They banked on the mystique of Western scientific techniques and aid, hoping for a repetition of the Marshall Plan. In this approach, the new gospel was Keynesian macroeconomics, particularly with its interventionist fiscalism.

The new macroeconomics

The architect of the new macroeconomic doctrine was John Maynard Keynes whose *General Theory of Employment, Interest and Money* (1936) was formulated, as with other Western theories, for solving Western problems. Keynes favoured active state intervention through deficit financing and the magic of 'the multiplier' (Keynes 1936: 115; Harrod 1963: 441–2) to cure deficiency of aggregate demand in pump-priming a depressed economy operating below its full productive capacity and manifesting severe involuntary unemployment made up of workers 'unemployed [yet] who would be willing to work at less than the existing real wage' (Keynes 1936: 228). This was a situation typical of developing countries, but Keynes's policy prescription was meant for Western economies then in deep depression. The Keynesian solution, via deficit financing, found an especially receptive response initially in the USA, and led to a full employment policy which paved the way to what subsequently emerged as the 'Welfare Sate' initiated under the New Deal era of public make-work and other social infrastructural projects.

Where did Third World economic development fit into the new macroeconomics of Keynes? Despite the relevance of involuntary unemployment, it did not fit anywhere because the Third World was still in the future: it had to await the age of decolonization. Thus, in its origins, Keynesian macroeconomics was no less Eurocentric than microeconomics! Starting in the 1940s, even before the Third World was invented, seriously flawed versions of Keynesian macroeconomic theorizing began to be extended and applied to developing countries. A case in point was the pro-capital orthodoxy known as the Harrod–Domar model (Harrod 1948; Domar 1946; Sen ed. 1970) which was transferred to the Third World by disciples (Nurske 1953; Agarwala and Singh eds 1963). It emerged as the key theory to popularize capitalization of Third World development. To this end it mobilized state intervention in the economy with state enterprises and central planning (Tinbergen 1964; Bettleheim 1959; Vernon 1966), often on shaky facts and figures (Stolper 1967; Myrdal 1968: Appendix 3) using 'sophisticated tricks invented (but seldom tested) in the most advanced countries of the world' (Watson and Dirlam 1965: 305).

THE GOLDEN AGE OF MODELLING

The 20-year period from 1950 to 1970 can be labelled as the golden age of Eurocentric modelling to shape Third World economic development (Morawetz 1977; Tolbert and Baum 1985). During this period, Keynesian disciples pioneered the extension and application of macromodelling to the Third World, which ultimately evolved into the national accounting system adopted by the World Bank and the United Nations. Notable among these theorists were Harrod (1948), Domar (1946), Nurske (1953), Tinbergen (1964, 1967) and Kuznets (1959, 1966). Some of their theories will be further examined in the pages below. However, as one example at this stage, and in view of its subsequent importance, reference can be made to Joan Robinson's concept of 'disguised unemployment' (Robinson 1936). This concept was formulated on the basis of massive and widespread under-employment in industrial economies during the Depression years. Subsequently, it was utilized most effectively by Arthur Lewis (1954) in his Nobel-winning contribution, namely, the two-sector theory of capitalist economic development with unlimited supplies of labour (see below pp. 74–79).

VICIOUS CIRCLES OF POVERTY AND THE
POPULATION TRAP

The logical origin of Western efforts to modernize the Third World through economic development was the premise of circular under-development, crystallized as the vicious circles of poverty (Todaro 1977: 74; Myrdal 1968: Appendix 4). In standard textbooks on economic development, undeveloped (or underdeveloped) countries (as they were labelled at the time) were generally considered poor because they were peopled by 'traditional societies' which resisted change (Zuvekas 1979: chap. 3). Local histories and cultures were dismissed as 'barriers' to economic growth by leading economists (Lewis 1955; Kindleberger 1958) and other modernization theorists. Peasants who resisted high-risk, capital-intensive technologies were regarded as 'irrational', recalling the earlier 'backward sloping supply' theories (Bauer and Yamey 1957). In fact, this unjustified, paternalistic view of peasant conservatism did not begin to change until the early 1970s after the 'optimizing peasant' paradigm (Lipton 1968) found its way into mainstream theorizing and more sympathetic analysis of peasantry gained respectability (Scott 1976, 1985). By this time, Eurocentric theorizing had acquired a strong anti-rural bias, in effect condemning peasant communities to stag-nation in a low-equilibrium trap, while Western donors supplied cheap food aid and concentrated on building urban industries and infrastructure.

Thus began the Western inflow of food and technical assistance programmes intended to modernize and transform the Third World and narrow the gap between the rich and poor countries (Shonfield 1961; Myrdal 1968; Ranis ed. 1972). Boserup has observed (1981: 189–90) that, whereas in the nineteenth century England and other Western countries had imported food in exchange for exports of manufactures in their trade with low-income countries, in the post-1945 period, industrial, high-technology countries have achieved a 'reversal of trade in food' exporting surplus food as well as capital-intensive manufactures to low-technology, high-density Third World countries. This virtually ensured that the West mono-polized all productivity gains as well as the gains of trade, thereby invalidating, simultaneously, the theories of both Malthus and Ricardo.

As abstract theory, however, the vicious circles of poverty argu-ment was heuristic. Figure 3.1(a) illustrates the population trap at a low level of income per capita shown by point A. Aggregate

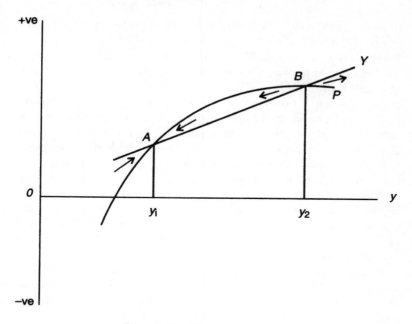

Figure 3.1(a) The population trap

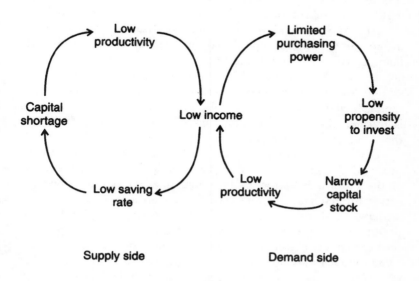

Figure 3.1(b) The vicious circles of poverty

income (denoted by Y) and population (denoted by P) are both positively related to income per capita, y, and the growth rate, g. Point A is a stable equilibrium because any deviation around it will generate automatic forces of corrective change in the dynamics of P and Y to restore equilibrium at point A. Thus, to the left and below A, when Y exceeds P, higher incomes per capita will induce higher savings and investment generating further growth towards point A. To the right and above point A, however, P will exceed Y, and as a result, the standard of living will be checked à la Malthus.

Figure 3.1(b) illustrates the permanent stagnation in which the low-income economy is trapped. On the supply side, low income generates a low saving rate, capital shortage and low productivity; on the demand side, low income is responsible for limited purchasing power, a low propensity to invest, a narrow capital stock and low productivity. Thus, persistent poverty was causally linked to capitalization.

Adherents to the vicious circles of poverty prescribed two remedies for escaping the trap. One was population policy, with emphasis on birth control. This was met with resistance in some developing countries as well as from the Catholic Church. The other and more determined prescription was the Big Push theory of industrialization (see below), which aspired to dramatically convert a low-income country into a high-income country. Thus, if point B in Figure 3.1(a) at the substantially higher income per capita of y_2 could be achieved as a result of Big Push industrialization, then sustained income growth would indeed become a reality because, unlike A, point B was an unstable equilibrium implying that to the right and above it, Y would exceed P; as such, it would generate additional savings leading to sustained income growth and higher income per capita. In short, once the threshold level of income per capita of y_2 is reached, there is no looking back. The trick was reaching this threshold level of per capita income.

Despite its elegance, the vicious circles theory was no more than a distorted projection of non-European 'irrationality', the reverse side of the rational behaviour assumption: in neo-classical orthodoxy, extra children are 'inferior' goods! Such orthodoxy was counter-factual because it was a non-institutional conception of Third World poverty. It ignored the colonial roots of this poverty, and exaggerated the capacity of central authorities to impose population and birth-control policies (as, for example, Indira Gandhi found out to her regret) in a top-down, authoritarian manner (Mamdani 1972: esp. chap. 6 on the family, and chap. 7 on how the villagers see birth control). 'Soft' and 'hard' states (Myrdal 1968) were equally assumed to be capable of implementing drastic population policies and of intervening and managing economic development on a grand scale. Thus, the theory formed an essential ingredient of favouring large-scale industrialization with strong pro-capital and urban-biased assumptions. It legitimized a technocratic conceptualization of economic development as a more or less mechanical or engineering task of construction; it was divorced from peoples and cultures.

THE BIG PUSH THEORY OF INDUSTRIALIZATION

State intervention in economic reconstruction began first in and for a Europe devastated by World War II. Even before World War II ended, economists were busy at the drawing board with master-plans and blue-prints for postwar reconstruction of Europe. Paul Rosenstein-Rodan (1943), the father of the Big Push theory of economic development, argued emphatically that industrialisation 'is *the* way of achieving a more equal distribution of income between different areas of the world by raising incomes in depressed areas at a higher rate than in rich areas' (Rosenstein-Rodan 1943: 203, italics in the original). Industrialization was defined as the increased use of capital per unit of output, especially in the manufacturing sectors where all 'growth poles' were thought to exist. These were then linked to capital-intensive technology imports from the West with complete disregard to factor endownments in labour-abundant developing countries.

After the war, the Marshall Plan, and the European miracle which it financed, seemed to confirm the Big Push theory based on massive infusion of American aid. So, in this optimistic climate, the European success story was set to be replicated in the newly emerging Third World under American leadership.

What were the premises of the Big Push theory? They were pro-capital and pro-big: large-scale manufacturing and mega-projects were favoured over small-scale works in the belief that the highest returns and productivity gains were to be found in the capitalist 'growth poles' of secondary industry. 'Bigness' in industrialization was justified on two sets of criteria: economies of scale and modern technology. The argument in favour of modern technology was of recent origin: it favoured capitalist industrialization via higher productivity (Kaldor 1967: 13–14), based on an empirical and positive correlation, known as the Verdoorn Law, between output growth and productivity. The economies of scale argument was older and more complex. It classified the benefits of large-scale industrialization as internal economies (e.g. more efficient division of labour within a firm) and external (e.g. cross-fertilization amongst firms in an industry), both helping to generate dynamic benefits such as learning by doing. These, especially the high quality of human capital embodied in highly dynamic and motivated Europeans, had been responsible for the miracle of Europe.

Originally formulated by Allyn Young (1928), the theory of increasing returns to scale postulated that the rate of economic development could be accelerated if large, capital-intensive manufacturing industries were built instead of many small ones. (Significantly, it may be noted in passing, this is *not* what happened in Taiwan where small firms were promoted, see pp. 114-117). In the Big Push mindset, small firms were risky and unprofitable because their unit costs would be relatively high since their production runs would be correspondingly limited. On the other hand, large firms, able to mass-produce, could utilize the latest capital-intensive techniques of production, achieve the minimum efficient scale of operation and, by minimizing unit costs, maximize the rate of return. In addition to these 'internal' economies, an agglomeration of large, industrial firms in a given (previously depressed) region would be in a more advantageous position of realizing external economies of scale. For example, vertically or horizontally complementary service industries (trucking and warehousing) or engineering firms could be established providing specialized activities, promoting further specialization and extension of the market size.

A version of the Big Push theory of industrialization is presented in Figure 3.2 where the horizontal axis represents the quantity of production, Q, and the vertical axis refers to unit price and/or cost. Suppose that initially, in an underdeveloped region, a particular manufacturing industry is characterized by ten firms, each typically small and facing demand conditions represented by dd. The cost per unit of production, shown by the average cost curve, ATC, lies uniformly above the individual demand curves dd. Accordingly the typical firm makes an economic loss. This industrial organization is non-viable and in the long run, the firms will have to shut down.

The Big Push theory implied a 'minimum efficient scale' by replacing the ten uneconomic firms into by single firm large enough to meet the total market demand, shown by DD. The one

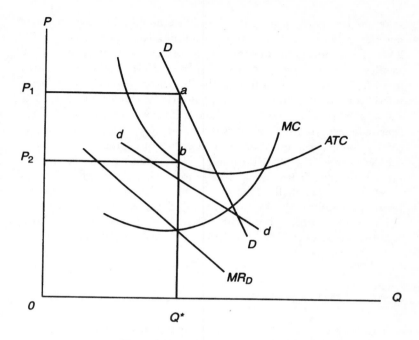

Figure 3.2 Big Push industrialization

large firm would overcome lumpiness of capital and use the most modern (i.e. capital-intensive) technology and thereby minimize unit costs. The optimal level of production would then be OQ^* determined by the point of intersection between the marginal cost, MC, and the marginal revenue, MR_D. At this level of production, the large firm would be economic, realizing total profits of P_1abP_2.

A profitable industry developed according to the Big Push theory would act as a leading sector in the depressed region, creating productive jobs and generating an income multiplier process. In turn, this would stimulate, through backward and forward linkages, the development of several other related and complementary industries. Thus, strategically selected Big Push manufacturing industries could promote general economic development.

The Big Push theory failed to replicate the European success story in the Third World. Why? Early critics (Agarwala and Singh eds 1963) argued in terms of economic doctrine. Ellis (1958) objected to its strongly interventionist assumptions. Streeten (1963) argued that while it was sound to argue in favour of an investment package as in the Big Push approach, it should be noted that 'investment is not the only component' (in Johnson and Kamerschen eds 1972: 236) of the development strategy. Streeten also cautioned against 'careless use of Western concepts' (ibid.: 233). Rosenstein-Rodan himself, in a look back, admitted that his theory had been 'over-optimistic' due to its '"rationalist" assumptions' (Meier and Seers eds 1984: 215–16). In other words, the Big Push was admittedly a Eurocentric conceptualization: it was exceedingly pro-capital, and it totally ignored the questions of ownership of capital imports from the West and the distribution of value-added generated in the growth process. It had worked in Europe where it was first formulated for the Marshall Plan, largely for cultural and institutional reasons, including the high quality of European human resources. Additionally, behind both the Marshall Plan and Third World reconstruction were ulterior political and ideological motives.

THE ROSTOWIAN STAGES THEORY

The Cold War ideology spawned two major modernization theories, both based on the Eurocentric premise of Third World development as Westernization: one was political development and reconstruction of the Third World (Higgot 1983); the other was stages-of-growth theorizing. Both were conceived as part of the American-led global strategy for the containment of communism.

The stages-of-growth theory was Rostow's brain-child (1956, 1963), which explicitly regarded Third World economic development as an extension of US foreign and military policy. Rostow, the economic historian, was, like Marx, his ideological nemesis, Eurocentric; their theories were linear, deterministic and guided by Western history perceived as the universal law of development. Just as Marx regarded (European) feudalism, capitalism and socialism as necessary stages in his materialistic determinism, so Rostow, whose book was subtitled *A Non-Communist Manifesto*, believed that the hearts and minds of the people of the Third World could be won over for American capitalism through a Marshall Plan type of foreign aid. His optimism was derived from his Eurocentric worldview which led him to the conclusion that 'the lesson [of economic history, i.e. Western experience] . . . is that the tricks of growth are not that difficult' (Rostow 1960: 166). Rostow saw capitalist development as historically inevitable; European and American

experiences were confirmations of a long-term uni-directional transformation that could be subdivided into:

> (1) distinct time segments, characterized by different sources
> and patterns of economic changes, (2) a specific succession of
> these segments, so that *b* cannot occur before *a*, or *c* before *b*,
> and (3) a common matrix, in that the successive segments
> are stages in one broad process – usually one of development
> and growth rather than of devolution and shrinkage.
>
> (Kuznets summary quoted in Meier 1989: 69)

Each one of these stages was interlinked through a dynamic theory of
production where transition from one to the next was characterized
by certain changes in the composition of investment. 'Turning
points' and 'leading sectors' were the essential elements of the
Rostowian stages theory.

Rostow's 'distinct time segments' along an inevitable path of uni-
directional growth consisted of five stages: (1) the traditional society,
(2) the preconditions for take-off, (3) the take-off, (4) the drive to
maturity and (5) the age of mass consumption. The developing countries of the Third World were in the first three stages, whereas countries of the First World were in the last two.

As an economic growth theory, the most important Rostowian
stage was the 'take-off.' It was the launching pad of accelerated capitalist growth. It is here that Rostow saw the trigger or the magic
wand of economic growth; or, more precisely, how its rate could
be *deliberately* accelerated. The take-off was defined 'as requiring all
three of the following related conditions' (Rostow 1963: 36-40):

1 a rise in the rate of productive investment from say, 5 per cent or
  less to over 10 per cent of national income (or net national
  income);
2 the development of one or more substantial manufacturing
  sectors, with a high rate of growth; and
3 the existence of quick emergence of a political, social, and institutional framework that exploits the impulses to expansion in
  the modern sector and the potential external economy effects of
  the take-off and gives to growth the ongoing character.

Thus, given appropriate institutional framework, the two core
elements of the Rostowian theory were: (1) the manufacturing as
the 'leading sector' and (2) the investment ratio. The trigger of

economic growth was change in investment activity concentrated in manufacturing sectors designated as 'the modern sector'. By implication rural and agriculture sectors were relegated to traditional stagnant sectors, hence giving rise to 'urban bias' (Lipton 1977).

Rostow's *Non-Communist Manifesto* was not *laissez-faire* capitalism with reliance on the invisible hand of the market. In fact Rostowian prescription favoured state capitalism. By strategic decisions affecting resource allocation designed to stimulate investment in leading sectors, a society (i.e. government) could engineer economic growth and accelerate the growth rate. Thus, quite paradoxically, Rostow, the prophet of capitalism, far from advocating reliance on market forces, ended up legitimizing state intervention in Third World development, based on planning and foreign aid – a contradiction which did not escape the attention of another prophet of capitalism, Milton Friedman (1958).

BALANCED VERSUS UNBALANCED GROWTH

The next paradigm debate amongst Eurocentric theorists following the Big Push theory was the Balanced verus Unbalanced Growth theory debate. The former was, in essense, an annex to the Big Push theory, favouring as it did a simultaneous or 'synchronized application of capital to a wide range of different industries' (Nurske 1952 in Agarwala and Singh eds 1963: 256). Nurske's argument was based on the principle of complementarity, in turn derived from the increasing returns argument: 'Most industries catering for mass consumption are complementary in the sense that they provide a market for, and thus support, each other. This basic complementarity stems, of course, from the diversity of human wants. The case for "balanced growth" rests ultimately on the need for a "balanced diet"' (ibid.: 257). But, such an approach was too extravagant in terms of required investment outlays for the typical developing country. Choices had to be made and priorities ranked.

The chief critic of the Balanced Growth theory was Albert Hirschman. In his *The Strategy of Economic Development* (1958), Hirschman argued that economic 'development depends not so much on finding optimal combinations for given resources and factors of production as on calling forth and enlisting for development purposes resources and abilities that are hidden, scattered, or badly utilized' (1958: 5). In contrast to balanced growth, Hirschman envisaged development as a chain of disequilibria:

> Therefore, the sequence that 'leads away from equilibrium' is precisely an ideal pattern of development from our point of view: for each move in the sequence is induced by a previous disequilibrium and in turn creates a new disequilibrium that requires a further move . . . At each step, an industry takes advantage of external economies created by previous expansion, and at the same time creates new external economies to be exploited by other operators.
>
> (Hirschman 1958.: 66–7)

Thus, Hirschman emphasized linkages, backward and forward, to generate and sustain the growth dynamic. His preference was for industrial growth and infrastructural investment to create a modern leading sector. Hirschman's strategy was aimed at deliberately creating imbalances and shortages, to operate as incentives and generate external economies which would strengthen growth. Coinciding with the prevailing Western preoccupation with infrastructural mega-projects, Hirschman's strategy favoured inflationary finance, on the rationale that the creation of imbalances and shortages (e.g. in electricity or highways) would stimulate appropriate investments to be undertaken to expand aggregate supply before inflationary pressures could get out of hand.

Simultaneously, the expectation was that backward and forward linkages in inter-industry demand would stimulate aggregate demand, leading to specialization and sustained growth. What was overlooked in this prescription was the capital-intensive character of these mega-projects, delays and bottlenecks in project implementation, food shortages, and the implied dependence and uncertainty on capital imports from the North, always subject to political considerations. Subsequently, and in view of chronic inflation, balance of payment crises and internal inequalities in several Latin American countries, Hirschman changed his views, adopting a less inflationary, more pro-agricultural position, as well as becoming more interdisciplinary (Hirschman 1981, 1984, 1986).

These industrialization strategies shared some important common flaws: They were pro-capital, and favoured heavy industry over food production and rural development. They were ambitious grand designs with little appreciation of implementation or logistical problems. A highly influential example of such a 'grand design' theory in action was the Indian Mahalanobis model (Bettleheim, 1959). Its theoretical roots were derived from balanced growth and, as with former Soviet planning, it had great mathematical consistency as in general equilibrium analysis. As masterfully analysed in Gunnar Myrdal's *Asian Drama* (1968: Part III), grand planning designs proved disappointing in practice. While some of the reasons were clearly domestic (as for example, lack of appropriate statistical information), in many cases the causes of failure stemmed from unrealistic models constructed as if general equilibrium prevailed everywhere, with total disregard for actual Third World realities; these models assumed that unlimited capital imports from foreign donors would be forthcoming. But more significant than Western aid was the entry of Western multinational corporations (MNCs) originally as part of the ISI strategy (see pp. 79–84 below).

ECONOMIC DUALISM: THE LEWIS TWO-SECTOR MODEL

Dualistic theories became very fashionable in the 1950s and 1960s. Dualism was by no means a new concept. One of the most Eurocentric of these was the 'social dualism' of Boeke (1953), the nineteenth-century Dutch economist of colonial Indonesia, which built upon and extended such earlier abstractions as the Marxist idea of the Asiatic mode of production or Kipling's poem about 'East is East, and West is West, and never the twain shall meet'. Boeke's 'Eastern economy' which clashed with 'high capitalism' imported from the West, was soundly criticized by Higgins (1956) as factually false. In the postwar era, the idea of dualism was reformulated, typically on neo-classical foundations but with numerous variants, emphasizing different aspects, as briefly noted below.

One variant was 'technological dualism' (Eckaus 1955) which was based on the notion that 'the American way' of production was the only modern way, even though capital lumpiness created a 'factor proportions' problem. Hla Myint coined 'financial dualism' (Myint 1971: 324–31) and, more recently, 'organizational dualism' (Myint 1985). All these variants shared one fundamental assumption: the coexistence of 'traditional' (i.e., indigenous = primitive) and 'modern' (i.e. Western = productive) techniques of production. Modern techniques were American or European, capital-intensive, fit for the capitalist sector, labelled 'the modern sector', in constrast to backward agriculture or rural sectors. Economic development, as modernization, focused on the capitalist growth in the former and Western MNCs emerged as agents of capitalization to expand the capital base in the modern sectors.

The single most influential postwar dualistic theory of economic development was the neo-classical two-sector model formulated by Arthur Lewis, originally from St Lucia, in his celebrated article 'Economic Development with Unlimited Supplies of Labour' (1954). It was a typical example of abstract, *a priori* pro-capital and anti-rural theorizing in the best tradition of Eurocentric mainstream economists, demonstrating that not all Eurocentric minds are necessarily European-born. Lewis's article had a huge intellectual impact, which was generally negative in terms of living standards for the masses in developing countries. In mainstream development literature, it led to a vast volume of theoretical contributions (Fei and Ranis 1964; Meier 1989: Part III), and it ultimately won Lewis the Nobel Prize for Economics. It also had a great impact on the planning, policy and practice of economic development (See Box 7).

Lewis's point of departure was the plausible fact that developing countries are labour-surplus economies, especially in the large agricultural sectors dominated by low-productivity traditional farming which relied on unpaid family labour for subsistence production. On the other hand, there was the small, urban-centred capitalist/modern sector. In this dualistic framework, Lewis identified the

---

Box 7

The Lewis two-sector model

Originated by Arthur Lewis, the two-sector (dual) growth model was arguably the most influential postwar abstract theorizing to guide Third World development.

It was Eurocentric as it was designed in the West on purely abstract, neo-classical foundations, for imposition on a developing world, then in the process of decolonization.

The UN and other Western donors eagerly became implementing agencies for this urban-biased development strategy which, subsequently, caused, as a result of unplanned urbanization and rural–urban exodus, so much dislocation and destruction in the Third World.

---

modern, capitalist sector as the engine of economic growth, justifying this selection on the basis of higher productivity due to modern (imported) capital-intensive technology. In short, the traditional (rural/agricultural) sector was identified as the source of underdevelopment. As a result, Lewis rejected *in situ* pro-rural development via investment in rural communities. This anti-rural bias was a well considered position since Lewis was fully aware of the classic conflict of interest between wages and capital, and between capitalists and peasants/workers. In his *Manchester School* article in a Marxian passage he stated that 'the level of wages in the capitalist sector depends upon the earnings in the subsistence sector' and that therefore 'the capitalists have a direct interest in holding down the productivity of the subsistence workers' in a manner matching the imperialists' exploitation of colonial workers by keeping wages low for greater profits (Agarwala and Singh eds 1963: 409–10).

Lewis's aim was capitalist accumulation through pro-urban industrialization dependent on capital imports from the West. The key element of this strategy was to transform the presumed surplus labour in the traditional sector into wage-labour for additional national income in the capitalist/modern sector. In short, Lewis recommended large-scale inter-sectoral labour transfers. He believed that such transfers would not reduce agricultural production, since 'the marginal productivity of labour is negligible, zero or negative' (Agarwala and Singh eds 1963: 402). Therefore, additional income in the modern sector would be net growth, hence accelerating the rate of economic development. He also dismissed the possibility that even skilled labour might be more than a transitory limiting constraint on growth: 'it is only a very temporary bottleneck, in the sense that if capital is available for development, the capitalists or their government will soon provide the facilities for training more skilled people' (Agarwala and Singh eds 1963: 406). Seeing capital as the 'real bottleneck', Lewis ended by recommending capital imports from the West for capitalist growth.

Figure 3.3 illustrates the Lewis two-sector model focusing in particular on wage determination, the principal mechanism for labour transfers. In panel (a), there is a graphical illustration of the neo-classical production function where $Q = F(K, L)$. The capital stock, measured on the vertical axis is given, and together with L_1, it determines full-employment level of output, Q_a on the production-possibility curve, F_1F_1. In this neo-classical model economic development is driven by capital accumulation with the significant twist of capitalizing L which is availabale in unlimited quantities. Theoretically the Lewis model implies an outward shift of the production-possibility curve to F_2F_2. Since K is fixed, in the Lewis model growth of national income (denoted by Q_b) implies a larger volume of employment measured by increase of labour from OL_1 to OL_2.

The core of the Lewis model is illustrated in panel (b). The initial labour force in the developing economy is N_0N_3, of which ON_0 is in the traditional sector, and the smaller proportion, ON_3 is in the modern sector. In the traditional sector, (i.e. the subsistence agriculture), labour demand is D_0D_0 so that N_0N_1 portion of the agricultural labour force represents disguised unemployment, with labour having a marginal product which is zero or negative. In addition, a second portion, i.e. N_1N_2, has a marginal product that is positive but less than the subsistence level of wages SW. Therefore, the total amount of labour surplus is N_0N_2. Lewis believed that this surplus could be transferred out of the traditional sector *without any loss of agricultural output*, and that it could be put to productive employment in the modern sector for income growth.

The modern sector is a relatively high-productivity sector because it utilizes capital-intensive technology. The labour demand in this sector initially is defined by D_1D_1. Given the initial labour force in the modern sector (i.e. ON_3), the prevailing wage-rate is W_m. Therefore, if the modern sector is designated as the 'leading' sector or the 'growth' pole, then net national income can be realized by transferring surplus labour out of the traditional sector and expanding employment in the modern sector. National income growth can be achieved without having to raise W_m; moreover, such growth can be realized indefinitely as long as there were unlimited (and transferable) supplies of surplus labour.

The Lewis model aspired to lead labour-surplus, capital-short economies of the Third World out of the poverty trap. However, it was based on anti-rural and other questionable premises chiefly resulting from a presumed 'irrationality' in the traditional sector. Thus, the assumption of zero or negative marginal productivity of agricultural labour was refuted (Schultz 1964) along with costless migration (Todaro 1969). Although subsequently it was demonstrated that the negative marginal productivity assumption was not essential (Uppal 1969), in practice the Lewis model has not been very successful. Significantly, the newly industrializing countries of the Far East, such as South Korea and Taiwan, industrialized precisely because they started first with agricultural modernization,

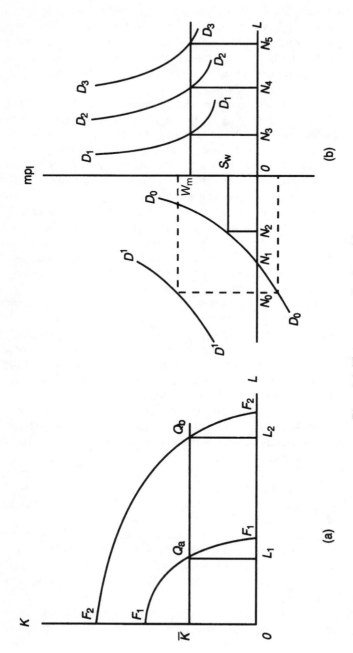

Figure 3.3 The two-sector Lewis model

which included land reform and investment in rural human resources to enhance labour productivity; hence, these countries delayed labour transfers to non-agricultural sectors until after the successful completion of agrarian development and the expansion of non-farm income and employment opportunities. Thus, the NIC success is 'at variance' (Tan 1992: 39) with what Lewis would have recommended.

In more general terms, as a review article of agriculture has shown, 'few countries have achieved sustained economic growth without first, or simultaneously, developing their agricultural sector' (Birkhaeuser and Feder 1991: 607). This is also consistent with the priorities of classical economists in particular Adam Smith (Myint 1977).

On this basis, therefore, the Lewis model was a mis-specified neo-classical model with a distinctive anti-rural bias of 'treating the traditional sector as a "black box" which exists merely to provide "unlimited supplies of labour" to the modern sector' (Myint in Meier ed. 1989: 139). In the context of Figure 3.3, a pro-rural development strategy à la Taiwan and Korea, for example, would be capable of increasing labour demand in the left quadrant to D^1D^1, possibly even higher than the urban wage W_m. In retrospect, the anti-rural bias of the Lewis model was both the cause and the effect of the then prevailing Eurocentric mindset of equating economic development with a 'modern' sector dependent on imported Western technology and capital.

IMPORT SUBSTITUTION INDUSTRIALIZATION (ISI), EXPORT PROMOTION AND THE INFANT INDUSTRY ARGUMENT

Lewis's Eurocentricity reflected the then dominant Western intellectualism. As such it facilitated the flawed, protectionist industrialization theory: the ISI. Paradoxically, when it came to the design of Third World industrial strategy, Western neo-classical theorists did not seek to transplant the free enterprise theories of classical economists; and they only reverted to export-promotion following the successful emergence of the Far Eastern NICs (Lee ed. 1981).

How this paradox came about is quite revealing. It was as if postwar designers of Third World industries had opted for the ideas of List (pp. 51–54 above) rather than those of Adam Smith and Ricardo. The case for protectionism was argued in dynamic terms, partly in order to expand domestic demand, but mainly for reasons of external trade in primary products for which foreign demand is relatively inelastic; therefore a socially optimal tariff would improve its trade balance (Meier in Agarwala and Singh 1963: 73).

The central ISI argument was the so-called infant industry argument, namely, that developing countries of the Third World should nurture new industries, subsidizing and protecting them with tariffs and other incentives on grounds of increasing economies (Allyn Young 1928; Agarwala and Sing eds 1963: Part 4). This protection was necessary until the new (i.e. infant) industries could achieve dynamic efficiency from 'learning by doing' and other external benefits to face competition from imports in the long run. In other words, ISI strategy necessitated state protection for the immediate and foreseeable duration in return for long-term economic social benefits. Significantly, this same argument was utilized in the case of export-led strategies; whereas Japan, Taiwan and South Korea implemented industrial strategies in a manner which did not discriminate against domestic firms, ISI generally empowered Western MNCs and their branch plants. Indeed, these emerged as the principal beneficiaries of immediate protectionism in developing countries in exchange for dubious long-term benefits.

Surprisingly, in retrospect, the ISI industrialization received its initial theoretical boost from the early revisionist trade theorists. Pioneers in this movement were Raul Prebisch (ECLA 1950, 1957) and Hans Singer (1950). Writing at about the same time and utilizing the same data sources, Prebisch and Singer launched a powerful, empirical attack on the classical view that trade operates as an engine of growth. Their results showed that the terms of trade seemed to be biased against primary producers and that these terms had been deteriorating for these producers almost since the beginning of relevant statistical series: nearly a hundred years. Accordingly, far from working as an engine of growth, diffusing gains of trade to all countries that were specialized and traded according to Ricardian theory, trade had actually impoverished primary producers. This is the central argument of the dependency, as distinct from Marxist, theorists (Weaver and Berger in Wilbur ed. 1984), who argue that no autonomous economic development can occur in the South as long as the latter is not delinked from its traditional dependence on capital, technology and markets of the North. Later, especially during his ECLA years, Prebisch (in Wilber ed. 1984) moved closer to the dependency school, espousing socialism. In the final years of his life, Prebisch shifted his position once again, adopting a mid-way stance, hoping to reconcile socialism (which he regarded as necessary for the 'social use' of surplus) and economic liberalism (Meier and Seers ed. 1984: 191). Singer, for his part, remained a strong voice for the 'trade, not aid' school (ibid.: 296).

Mainstream neo-classical theorists, also, began to reach conclusions which stood the Ricardian free trade theory on its head. Thus, at about the same time that the Prebisch–Singer hypothesis was being put forward, Leontieff (1953) came up with new empirical evidence casting serious doubts on the empirical validity of the Ricardian theory. Prebisch (1959) further demonstrated, using productivity ratios and income elasticities, that economic development in the countries of the periphery was bound to lag behind the growth rates of industrialized countries of the metropole as long as the structure of international commercial relations was maintained. At the same time, Bhagwati (1958), using neo-classical analysis, was able to show that primary producing countries could actually promote immiserizing growth as a result of excessive specialization.

The Prebisch–Singer results on the terms of trade question, as well as the findings of Leontieff and Bhagwati, were of fundamental importance and should have alerted Third World neo-classists of the inherent weaknesses of 'pure' trade theorizing based on equilibrium economics. Monopolies, oligopolies and other forms of market imperfections in Western market economies should have dampened the general mainstream idealization of rational behaviour modelling of trade and equating industrialization with modernization. Neither theoretical nor empirical findings seemed to deter neo-classical modellers and rationalists of Third World development from their anti-rural, pro-capital obsessions.

Thus, the ISI emerged as the new gospel for Third World industrialization. The creation of enclave manufacturing sectors by active government intervention became virtually synonymous with industrialization. To encourage ISI industries a wide range of incentives were utilized such as tax holidays, duty-free imports of producer goods, subsidized utility rates and infrastructural facilities, cheap labour and capital, and, of course, tariff protection against competing imports. In a relatively short period of time, the 'enclave sectors' (usually on industrial estates specially built by host governments at public expense) became dominated by branch plants of Western multinational corporations (MNCs), sometimes labelled transnational corporations or enterprises, producing brand new consumer products, (e.g. textiles, plastics and cigarettes) as well as more durable goods (e.g. assembled automobiles, kitchen appliances and electronics), all originally developed in the West. The Third World was thus captured as part of the 'global supermarket' in the global reach of the MNCs, superimposing Western tastes and marketing techniques on local cultures (Barnet and Muller 1974).

Increasingly, the MNCs became the centre of a new multi-sided controversy. Hymer (1970) utilized the tools of positive economics to demonstrate the monopolistic market power of MNCs as a causal determinant of uneven development. Others argued that national sovereignty was being eroded (Vernon 1971) or cultures were being invaded (Sunkel 1972) as a result of the power of MNCs. Others pointed to transfer pricing and other monopolistic practices of the MNCs indirectly, sometimes illegally, shifting value added out of host countries (Vaitsos 1978). For example, Western pharmaceuticals have been accused of 'gene piracy', a dubious practice of searching and exploiting rare disease-resistant genes found in certain indigenous people in the tropics, for highly profitable new drugs.

The most controversial debate concerning MNCs concerned capital-intensive technology transfer to labour-abundant countries (Lall 1978). While some argued in terms of constraints in the absorptive capacity of host countries (Dahlman *et al*. 1987), the dominant view was Eurocentric and pro-capital. It justified imports of direct foreign investment (DFI), embodying new Western technologies, transferred by MNCs; thus DFI promoted foreign ownership and control. There were notable exceptions, however, in particular the Far Eastern NICs (Enos 1989). The case of Korea is particularly instructive: 'Korea has not relied upon direct foreign investment as a source of foreign technologies. Korea has hired technology but has not hired production; Korea has welcomed foreign techniques but has not encouraged foreign ownership. Together with the modern capital goods that Korea has imported in such large quantities has come the know-how to operate them; but in the main Korea has purchased both the capital goods and the know-how rather than let foreign firms possess them' (Enos and Park 1988: 39).

In the much of the Third World, foreign ownership and control of DFI minimized the benefits of industrialization. These issues highlighted a growing debate on the subject of inappropriate technology transfer. The debate was, of course, not new. Eckaus, in an early paper (1955), attributed inappropriate technology transfer to fixed capital–labour ratios which resulted in 'indivisibilities' or lumpiness of capital, implying wasteful and excessive capitalization. Leibenstein (1978), on the other hand, argued that inefficiency in industrialization in developing countries resulted from qualitative human and management factors, euphemistically termed the 'X-efficiency' factor in development.

In retrospect, it is clear that the ISI industrialization failed to work as expected by the rational, trickle-down theorists because Western DFI, aid and technology transfers were part and parcel of inherently flawed (i.e. Eurocentric) prescriptions which tended to minimize, rather than maximize, developmental benefits for host countries. Capitalization increased foreign ownership and control, while capital-intensive techniques biased productivity gains in favour of Western interests. At the same time, job creation was limited and retained income share of value-added minimized. The ISI strategy was also anti-rural, discouraging food production while concentrating modern/capitalist sectors in urban centres, thereby causing an ever-increasing rural exodus. In its political assumptions, ISI was statist, enhancing, rather than reducing, state intervention to

---

Box 8

The ISI strategy

Pioneered by revisionist theorists like Prebisch, Import Substitution Industrialization (ISI) was intended to promote domestic industry in developing countries under state protection and subsidy, in much the same manner as List's ideas had shaped German development in the ninteenth century.

In fact, however, ISI became a captive strategy of MNCs, a process willingly encouraged by post-independence leadership, eager to attract Western capital and technology with all sorts of capital-biased incentives such as tax holidays, duty-free imports of capital goods and subsidized interest rates.

This leadership mistakenly came to equate 'development' with 'industrialization' and accepted blueprints such as the two-sector models, as failsafe recipes for rapid economic growth.

ISI lead to massive infusion of direct foreign investment (DFI) in LDCs, along with inappropriate (i.e. capital-intensive) technology transfers, rising foreign control and indebtedness, which ultimately led to the structural problems in the 1980s ushering in WB–IMF 'structural adjustment' programmes.

---

generate comparative disadvantages in labour-abundant economies (See Box 8).

In short, the ISI strategy was a powerful force promoting capitalization via foreign equity ownership, especially when account is taken of transfer pricing opportunities from intra-firm transactions designed to spread the tax obligations of MNCs across different jurisdictions (Dunning 1992: chap. 18.3). It is no surprise that within a relatively short period of time ISI led to host-country–MNC conflicts while also contributing to subsequent chronic balance of payments crises and foreign indebtedness (see pp. 125–133 below).

NEO-CLASSICAL GROWTH AND DISTRIBUTION THEORIES

The roots of these negative consequences lie in the neo-classical growth theory which guided the design of postwar economic development in developing countries. This 'capital-is-everything' theory, exemplified in the famous Harrod–Domar models (see pp. 99–102 below), sacrificed basic human needs and people-focused development for capital accumulation. The origins of this pro-capital bias are to be found in the Western conception of development as growth. As we saw in the previous chapter, the origins of this concept extends back to the classical economists to whom neo-classical theorists of the postwar period turned for guidance (Meade 1962; Hahn and Matthews 1964).

What was this standard growth theory? Its essential characteristics can be illustrated with the aid of Figure 3.4. The vertical axis refers to y, output per capita, where $y = Y/N$. The horizontal axis represents k/n, the incremental capital-labour ratio, where $k = dK/K$ and $n = dN/N$. The ray from the origin, OI, is the net investment requirement or capital accumulation, representing net addition to capital stock. On the other hand, aggregate output is the production function Oy; it is a positive function of capital accumulation but a negative function of population growth. In turn, capital accumulation is a function of the saving rate net of depreciation, d, and population growth, n. In other words, population and depreciation are both drags on growth, a basic tenet of classical and neo-classical worldview.

The steady-state growth is where savings, sy, are just sufficient to maintain the investment requirement, namely, $(d + n)k$. This happens at points such as a and c when the capital–labour ratio

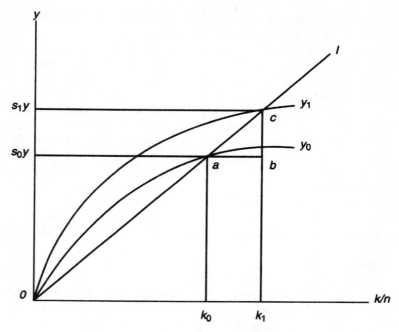

Figure 3.4 The neo-classical growth theory

exactly matches savings. At a higher capital–labour ratio, such as k_1 relative to k_0, savings corresponding to y_0 falls short of required investment. Either a higher savings must be generated such as s_1y to achieve state–state growth at point c, or a lower capital–labour ratio must be realized through greater capital efficiency.

Figure 3.4 is no more than a bird's-eye view of a large volume of literature (Sen ed. 1970). This literature is complex and often confusing, reflecting different questions of theory such as the savings function, the nature of technology, the adjustment and stability of growth and moving equilibrium in a capitalist economy. Yet, the various paradigms have one crucial common feature: they were constructed on common (i.e. Western) assumptions of rational, reductionist and optimising behaviour.

Paradigm debate over growth modelling often appeared as a sterile Byzantine argument far removed from the realities and requirements of developing countries. In these exercises the Cambridge UK versus Cambridge USA schools held centre-stage. The former was led by Joan Robinson, and the latter by Robert Solow; both focused on a real model, with no fiscal or monetary policy, and hence no policy levers linked to economic development. Robinson (1956 and 1962 in Sen ed. 1970) and her colleagues concentrated on such issues as the problem of defining and measuring capital, and the properties of equilibrium growth on the basis of comparisons of alternative steady growth, 'golden age' and Harrod's 'warranted' rate of growth, which were further differentiated from natural and actual growth (see pp. 99–102 below). On the other hand, Solow (1956) and his followers concentratred on the properties of the adjustment mechanism as movements from one equilibrium to another. In these, as well as in subsequent two-sector and other extensions of the neo-classical growth model, the usual perfect competition assumptions were made such as inter-factor substitutability, perfect foresight and complete price flexibility in labour and money markets, in a manner which ignored not only actual reality, but also such important theoretical contributions as Keynes's wage stickiness and liquidity trap.

The same type of unrealism and abstraction prevailed in the case of production functions work, starting with Cobb–Douglas assuming constant returns along with perfect competition in factor and product markets (Yutopoulos and Nugent 1976: chap. 6) that hardly matched the actual realities of developing countries. In effect, neoclassical growth modelling was distorted by the illusion that there could be no surplus value in the growth process since income growth would be fully and entirely returned to factors of production in accordance with the marginal productivity theory in which factor shares match, and are determined by, productivity. The entire question of the political economy of pure surplus, originally raised by Marx, was dismissed, despite impressive contemporary contributions (Sraffa 1960; Dobbs 1960). Likewise, although much attention was devoted to savings and thrift, investment and entrepreneurial behaviour was ignored, as were the all-important questions of ownership and control of capital, and international capital mobility to finance growth (Mehmet 1983).

About the same time as the Cambridge vs. Cambridge debate was raging in the pages of Western economic journals, the 'residual growth' paradigm emerged. The problem here was the fact that neo-classical growth theorizing left a significant unexplained component of income growth. This failure was not recognized until the pioneering work of Denison (1962) which followed Schultz's classic re-invention of the human capital theory (1961). (It was well known to Adam Smith and Marshall to name but a couple authorities.) Denison, using USA data, showed that up to 40 per cent of long-term growth derived from investments in education in a manner which neo-classical growth theory was unable to explain.

Denison's findings initiated the 'residual' growth paradigm (OECD 1964), which was later transformed into total factor productivity, and most recently endogenous technological change (Lucas 1988; Romer 1990). It reflected growth-enhancing investment in education, training, entrepreneurship and new technology. In the meantime, growth along these lines was further reconfirmed by the experience of Japan and the Far Eastern NICs (Mehmet 1988, Enos 1989). However, during the ISI period, investment in human resource development (Harbison and Myers 1973) was virtually ignored in growth modelling by mainstream Western theorists in much of the Third World; indeed, manpower development was scorned as unworthy of serious economic theorizing (Arndt 1989).

Prior to the 1970s, at the height of tricklism, neo-classical growth theorists treated income distribution as a secondary objective which should best be postponed until after the 'cake', i.e. GNP, was sufficiently enlarged. In the meantime, the distribution literature reflected Western capitalist bias justifying income inequality on the ground that savings were determined by profits. Kaldor (1957) formalized a neo-classical growth model in which, following Malthus, workers made no contribution to aggregate savings. This was a false assumption which was partially corrected by Pasinetti (1961–2) who extended the Kaldor model to incorporate income distribution.

The most influential work on income distribution in economic growth was Kuznet's inverted U-shaped hypothesis (1955, 1966). It was a theory based largely on Western historical experience, which tended to provide empirical support for the neo-classical scenario of economic development. Kuznet's inverse relationship between income inequality and income per capita during the take-off stages quickly became a cornerstone of economic development orthodoxy. Western neo-classical economists applied this finding, without questioning its relevance on theoretical or cultural grounds, to developing countries.

THE 'TRICKLE-DOWN' THEORY AND WESTERN CAPITALISM

In the mainstream Western theorizing of Third World development, economic and social equity were sacrificed for capitalist growth through industrialization dependent on Western technology and equipment. Kuznet's empirical findings legitimized what Todaro has aptly called the trickle-down theory (see p. 13 above) while Arthur Lewis, in a major textbook, *The Theory of Economic Growth*, boldly declared: 'Our subject matter is growth, not distribution' (Lewis 1955: 9).

The trickle-down orthodoxy was that making the wealthy richer in the take-off stage was justified because in due course, and without any special intervention (i.e. automatically), accelerated economic growth would filter down and spread across, bringing the benefits of capitalist growth to the poorer segments of developing societies. While not all would agree that trickle-down bias was a deliberate intention on the part of postwar theorists (Arndt, 1983), the consequences of the tricklism orthodoxy are undeniable: it relegated poverty alleviation to the bottom of the development agenda and with total disregard of the inherent factor-endowments of LDCs; it also encouraged labour-saving technologies, often by creating foreign indebtedness to pay for Western capital and technology imports.

The trickle-down theory was, of course, a Western derivation from rationalism. Third World ends and means were redefined by these outsiders in rather arrogant, paternalistic terms recalling the worst days of missionaries bent on saving the souls of natives, even if it meant using violence in the process! In standard technocratic terms, Western experts and middlemen with 'know-how' determined targets and priorities for, as well as amounts of capital inflows into, the Third World countries, and merely 'assumed' that these decisions and inflows would have no adverse impact on recipient societies, cultures and institutions.

Western resource inflows were initially justified on the plausible enough ground of inadequate domestic savings and modern technology in developing countries. Very quickly, however, foreign resources distorted not only income and asset distribution, but also the geographic distribution of population because of the 'urban bias' (Lipton 1977) of Western prescriptions. Even then, the aim was seldom the development of competitive capitalism; typically Western theorists worked as handmaidens of monopolies and uncompetitive industries, justified by protectionist ISI strategies which institutionalized rent-seeking behaviour (Krueger 1974).

Western MNCs entered the Third World and were initially welcomed as agents of economic prosperity for all. At the height of ISI, they were actively promoted by development-minded, modernizing elites with generous and numerous incentives (Higgins

1968). Indeed, until the mid-1960s the prospects of Third World development, designed according to Western blueprints, were generally viewed with optimism. Gustav Papanek's *Robber Barons* (1967), a promising account of Western-style capitalism initiated by US aid in Pakistan, is a good example of misguided Western efforts to promote capitalism top-down in a Third World cultural environment inconsistent with the Protestant Ethic.

DISENCHANTMENT WITH THE 'TRICKLE-DOWN' THEORY

Beginning in the second half of the 1960s empirical evidence from developing countries increasingly demonstrated that Western economic development theory was not working as expected. Not only was the gap widening between the First and Third Worlds; domestic inequality between the rich and poor within developing countries was getting worse. The title of a book on Liberia captured the new theme: *Growth without Development* (Clower *et al.* 1966).

Four major signs of concern, in particular, emerged about the Western 'trickle-down' capitalism: (1) rural exodus and the emergence of 'informal sectors' (Hart 1973; ILO 1972; Weeks 1975) mushroomed around overcrowded, subhuman settlements in shanty-towns and slums; (2) worsening unemployment problem (Turnham and Jaeger 1971) in the wake of capital-intensive ISI industrialization, manifesting an increasingly acute conflict between the income and employment objectives of economic development (Streeten and Stewart 1971); (3) increasing poverty and social injustice (Adelman and Morris 1973; Chenery *et al.* 1974; Mehmet 1978) and (4) feminist theorists began to document the gender-bias of Western mainstream theories of development (Boserup 1970).

MIGRATION MODELLING

Urbanization brought migration into the mainstream of economic development studies. Its scale was largely unexpected and unplanned, catching Western designers of postwar industrialization by surprise. Large-scale labour migration in colonial times, as in South Africa, Southeast Asia or the Caribbean, were largely organized affairs regulated by colonial interests to supply cheap labour to plantations and mines (Murray 1980; Parmer 1960; Beckford 1972).

But the postwar urbanization and rural exodus, occasioned by urban-biased ISI, was unprecedented in its scale, rate and impact. As always, mainstream economists rushed, *ex post facto*, to offer new paradigms.

One of the most important migration theories, which is solidly based on neo-classical assumptions of rational behaviour, is the Todaro model (Harris and Todaro 1970) formulated to explain the postwar phenomonenon of rural exodus. In this model the migration decision, as rational act, is quantified and evaluated as a benefit–cost exercise on the basis of comparisons of expected additional income at destination with the earnings forgone at the original place of residence net of the cost of migration. Thus, both pull (i.e. urban wage employment) and push (i.e. farm mechanization) factors influence migration behaviour, but only in a narrow economic sense.

The Todaro model generated a great deal of theoretical discussion (Meier 1989: 142–7) which was generally focused on the urban bias of industrialization. While new urban-based industries in the modern sector received all the attention of economic planning and policy, they generated too few jobs. Explosive Third World urbanization forced Western theorists back to the drawing board to come up with new explanations of the labour market process (Williamson in Chenery and Srinivasan eds 1988).

One alternative theory was that of the dual labour market based on the coexistence of formal and informal sectors (Mazumdar 1976). Initially, the informal sector was viewed in negative terms as a reservoir of cheap labour waiting in a long queue for the limited opportunity of some wage employment in the formal sector. But, as we have observed above, this sector was dominated by MNC branch plants which tended to utilize capital-intensive imported technology; this reduced the labour absorptive capacity of the economy, thereby pushing new comers into the informal sectors (Sethuraman 1976; Rodgers ed. 1989; Lubbel 1991). Subsequently, the negative opinion gave way to a more 'benign' (Tokman 1978) view that the informal sector could become a key to small-scale, indigenous economic development. However, the informal sector remains an elusive concept, and however defined, activities in it are high risk (Evers and Mehmet 1994) and subject to a complex and costly set of licensing regulations (de Soto 1989). By contrast, macroeconomic policy, in particular formal banking and credit institutions, continue to favour large-scale, foreign-owned industries.

During the 1980s urban labour market conditions in developing countries have generally worsened, not only because of rising internal migration flows, but also because of policy-induced factors. Thus, the transition to export-oriented industrialization under structural adjustment and stabilization policies (see pp. 125–133) often necessitated labour market de-regulation which meant declining real wages and weakening labour standards (ILO 1994: 43–4) in order to generate export earnings to repay foreign debts (Dornbusch 1985: 533).

GENDER BIAS OF DEVELOPMENT

Another major source of bias in neo-classical theorizing was the issue of gender in economic development. The question of whether economic development helped or hindered the status of women was originally raised by Esther Boserup (1970). Boserup's approach was primarily in the tradition of liberal, orthodox economic theory which has come under attack both at the macro- (Corner 1992) and the micro-theory level (Hart 1992; Woolley 1993). Gradually, Western feminists split into different camps: the women-in-development (WID); and a more radical, neo-Marxist gender-and-development (GAD) paradigm (Tinker ed. 1990; Rhode *et al.* 1990; Moffat *et al.* 1991). A popular theme was a critique of the subordination of female workers, typically unprotected by labour codes, in 'sweatshops', cottage industries or on the assembly lines operated by MNCs which promoted a new international division of labour (Nash and Fernandez-Kelley eds 1983). Some theorists also challenged traditional gender roles from the perspective of domestication in production, as well as household and patriarchal relations. Neo-Marxist class categories and terminology were also utilized (Mies 1986; Agarwal ed. 1988; Vickers 1990) to attack the Western, male-biased capitalist growth as the product of the 'rule of fathers' (Mies 1986: 37) and to call for a complete redefinition of 'the fundamental questions, concepts and approaches of our societies' (Bunch in Tinker ed. 1990: 72).

The dual labour market theory was also utilized to analyse gender issues in development. Thus, the labour market was separated along gender lines into a primary market for professional, well-paid jobs typically reserved for males; and a secondary market dominated by lowly paid, casual jobs, overcrowded by female workers, reflecting gender discrimination and increased vulnerability under structural adjustment (Lele 1986; Gladwin ed. 1991). Most recently, however, Third World women have articulated their own views and visions

(Sen and Grown 1987; Shiva 1989), implicitly or explicitly equating Western (i.e. Eurocentric) 'sisterhood' with paternalistic motives.

Feminist theorizing of development has expanded in several important directions, especially in post-modernist, deconstructionist directions (Marchand and Papart eds 1995). As a result, gender has now moved centre-stage in development studies. Broadly speaking, there are two major groupings in this feminist literature. One is the largely negative group of writings that present women as 'victims' or 'casualties' not only of structural adjustment and stabilization programmes, but also of environmental degradation (Cutter 1995) and unsafe health and epidemics like HIV/AIDS (O'Leary and Lemmott eds 1995). From a more positivist, policy-oriented perspective, gender is seen by donors and governments as occupying the crucial link leading to 'desirable outcomes' such as better standard of living for sustainable development or social capital (See Box 13, p. 140).

THE BASIC NEEDS APPROACH

After the mid-1960s, the conflicting nature of the income and employment objectives of economic development had become a leading issue. Compelling empirical evidence began to show that ISI was too capital intensive (Baer and Herve 1966; Streeten and Stewart 1971; Turnham and Jaeger 1971) to generate adequate job opportunities for the exploding numbers of job-seekers. This was partly due to the rapid growth of the labour force, but more significantly, also to rapid internal migration.

The International Labor Organization (ILO), which has been committed to social justice since its inception in 1919, took the initiative in popularizing the Basic Needs a'pproach (BNA). It was first implemented in the Kenya employment mission led by Singer (ILO 1972), and subsequently in other official reports (ILO 1976; Jolly 1976). Food, clothing, shelter, education and jobs emerged as the focus of BNA, and Western theorists went to work to provide answers and solutions for the most appropriate ways and means of fulfilling basic needs (Streeten 1979).

New schools of thought emerged, and many Western NGOs mushroomed, all sharing a common Eurocentric premise of outsiders targeting poverty, especially amongst rural communities which had finally been 'rediscovered'. Western 'bottom-up' theories aspired to replace earlier 'top-down' ones, emphasizing grassroots institution-building and empowerment (Esman 1978; Uphoff *et al.* 1979; Rondinelli 1983). Neo-classical theorists constructed rational behaviour models for peasant farmers in a new attempt at redesigning pricing and other intervention policies (Lipton 1968; Southward and Johnston eds 1967; Bateman ed. 1988; Timmer 1988). However, little heed was paid to voices like Schumacher's (1973) for more attention to Third World cultures studied endogeneously from within that could produce such successful grassroots institutions as the Grameen Bank (Yunis 1988).

The BNA initially seemed to win friends and allies in unexpected places. The World Bank, under McNamara, surprisingly endorsed it, commissioning the highly acclaimed growth with equity paradigm (Chenery *et al.* 1974). In due course, the BNA won some powerful advocates such as Paul Streeten and Mahbub ul Haq and their associates, (Streeten 1979; Streeten *et al.* 1981) who hoped to orient development policy towards 'people first' and poverty redressal as the primary indicator of economic development. As such, BNA aimed first at satisfying food, shelter, clothing, education and health ahead of infrastructural and mega-projects, implying a trade-off between social equity and maximization of GNP. This trade-off, however, led to a heated debate between the new paradigm and neo-classical economists (Srinavasan 1977), with the latter arguing that any diversion of scarce development resources from 'productive' investment to basic needs would harm the development prospects of LDCs.

As long as McNamara presided over the World Bank the BNA retained a commanding position. It changed its lending priorities away from infrastructural projects and started to bank on the poor, with increasing importance now being given to education, health and social sectors. There was, of course, good supporting evidence on standard rationalist criteria for this shift in the Bank's lending. Empirical studies of investment in human capital formation (Schultz 1961; Psacharopoulos 1973) promised impressively high rates of return on such investment. Also, the experience of the Far Eastern NICs such as South Korea and Taiwan, seemed to validate growth with equity, (GwE), as measured by declining Gini coefficient during a period of rapid income growth based on labour-intensive, export-oriented industrialization (Ranis 1978; Westphal 1978; Lee ed. 1981; Chen 1979; Balassa *et al.* 1982). Some, however, expressed doubts about export-led growth on grounds of export pessimism (Cline 1982).

Box 9

The BNA

This was the first egalitarian strategy for Third World development in the 1970s. Although originated by the ILO, it became 'legitimized' once it was suddenly and unexpectedly embraced by the then World Bank Chairman, Robert McNamara.

Intellectual architects who made major contributions to the popularization of the BNA included Mahbub ul Haq (who subsequently fathered the UNDP's *Human Development Reports*), and Paul Streeten. Despite its early endorsement by Western donor agencies, it was never seriously adopted by the developing countries themselves; futhermore, after the commencement of 'structural adjustment' policies in the 1980s, it was gradually relegated to the backburner.

Once McNamara stepped down at the World Bank, the BNA and GwE theorizing were quickly dethroned (See Box 9). The World Bank abandoned banking on the poor in favour of structural adjustment lending along standard neo-classical orthodoxy, at least until the late 1980s when Mahbub ul Haq and others sought to revive donor interest in human development, especially in the context of global equity and sustainable development (UNDP 1992, 1993; Cornia *et al*. 1986; Singer 1989).

4

MODEL-BUILDING AND
MACRO-PLANNING

The failure of Western development tricklism to provide productive jobs or meet basic human needs in the Third World was not accidental. It stemmed from the pro-capital bias of Eurocentric theories. Prescriptions based on these theories were top-down and technocratic, i.e. ahistorical, abstract and macro, all based on the universality of Western rational behaviour. As such, the Western theories were anti-labour and inherently in conflict with the realities and resource endowments in developing countries.

In this period, the Western hegemon, the USA, basking in the success of the Marshall Plan (Mehmet 1978: chap. 1) became the principal source of technology and skill transfer to introduce 'the American way' (Eckaus 1955). Economic planning techniques (Chenery and Clark 1959; Tinbergen 1967) and model-building by Western experts donors quickly emerged as the new magic wand to guide Third World economic development. Foreign aid through multilateral and bilateral channels became an elaborate system (OECD 1990). Thus was the 'mystique of planning' born, ignoring the possibilities of what economic planning could really achieve given the shortcomings of these theories as well as the limited administrative capacities of host countries themselves (Killick 1976; Watson and Dirlam 1965).

NEO-CLASSICAL STRUCTURALISM

Technocratic modelling was first initiated by neo-classical structuralism based on certain predictable transformations in the structure of outputs and employment as part of the process of economic development. Neo-classical structuralism shared similarities and weaknesses with the Rostowian stages-of-growth theories. As an empirically testable observation, it was originally formulated by Colin Clark (1940), almost entirely derived from Western economic history. It divided an economy into three sectors, namely, P, S and T sectors referring to the primary, secondary and tertiary sectors. It hypothesized that the P sector (agriculture) would experience secular decline, both in terms of shares of output as well as labour force, while the S sector (i.e. manufacturing) would expand, followed subsequently by the relative growth of the T (i.e. service) sector. Kuznets (1965) subsequently verified the Colin Clark hypothesis, using Western and some developing country experience. Chenery *et al.* (1975) further developed the neo-classical structuralism which, of course, differed fundamentally from neo-Marxist or dependency structuralism of Frank, Amin, Dos Santos and Wallerstein, to name a few (Wilber ed. 1984; Meier ed. 1984: 133–42).

THE MYSTIQUE OF PLANNING

At the height of the Western obsession with the planning mystique, abstract designs, analytical techniques and economic model-building emerged as the standard tools for the economic development of 'underdeveloped' countries. How 'underdeveloped' countries could manage such an ambitious task was ignored. The economists simply 'assumed' that the required administrative capacity existed! Hence, institution-building was brushed aside; instead, the Western experts concentrated on technocratic modelling based on a 'how-to-do' cookbook mentality. Economic development came to be viewed as a process of planning by targets and instruments. Five-year plans, though originally created in the Soviet Union, were borrowed in India (Bettleheim 1959) and elsewhere. This approach was promoted by Western donors, who had their own programming needs in the cause of capitalist development (Lewis 1966; Vernon 1966; Manne 1974; Taylor 1979), and popularized by such multilateral bodies as the UN agencies (UN ECAFE 1960). For the latter, development planing became a new mission, a *raison d'être*.

The planning process was conducted in an environment of state-led, top-down developmentalism (Mehmet 1990: 41–2). But it lacked social and historical fit with prevailing institutional and economic realities; seldom were the needs of target groups or the efficiency of decision-makers in developing societies considered. In fact, little or no attention was paid to domestic aspects of development. Thus, institutional efficiency, indigenous history and cultures were ignored and such critical issues as land reform was dismissed as 'unplannable'. In newly created planning agencies controlled by Western experts, blueprints of investment projects, derived from equilibrium economics, were relied upon to generate plans and strategies in abstract. When these failed, Western technical experts suffered culture shock (Seers 1962; Byrne 1966).

Initial failure was attributed to the 'other'. Therefore, rural and agricultural development failure was explained in terms of 'urban bias' (Lipton 1977), 'extension bias' (Johnston *et al.* 1972) and a 'backward-sloping supply curve' (Yutopoulos and Nugent 1976: 131–7), regardless of the appropriateness of Western technology in question. In the industrial sector, failure was attributed first to engineering 'factor proportions' problems (Eckaus 1955), subsequently to managerial 'X-efficiency', (Leibenstein 1978) and later, by the neo-conservative public choice school, to 'government failure' (see pp. 122–125 below).

In fact, technocratic development theorizing was mostly pseudo-planning; initially a case of 'planning without facts' (Stolper 1967; Faber and Seers eds 1972), it was an exercise aimed at servicing the programming interests of Western donors. Focused on project aid and performed by Western advisers for Western consumption, effectiveness was judged on the basis of Western criteria and targets (e.g. 0.7 per cent of GNP earmarked for official development assistance) rather than the developmental impact on the actual living standards of populations in developing countries.

Abstract models, elaborate input–output tables, general equilibrium and linear programming models were typically formulated as if perfect competition and rational behaviour prevailed everywhere in developing countries. Prices in these models were surrogate (i.e. artificial), obtained from the dual solution from a hypothetical Walrasian competitive economy (Blitzer *et al.* 1975). Rather than concentrate on eliminating price distortions through market reforms, investment decisions and project selection were based on highly complex and ambitious 'shadow pricing' and 'social benefit–cost' techniques (Little and Mirrlees 1974; Meier ed. 1989: 480–90) which proved of little practical help.

Abstraction in model building masked pro-capital investment advice given to developing countries, still heavily agrarian in production and structure. In agriculture, premature capital-intensive mechanization was introduced from the West as part of the 'green revolution' technologies movement without significant land reform, in effect leaving intact feudalistic land tenures (Warriner 1969).

While MNCs such as Massey-Ferguson marketed large numbers of tractors, millions in rural communities in labour-abundant countries lost their livelihoods and joined the rural exodus to urban centres in vain hopes of finding jobs. As a result of tractorization, land distribution was made more unequal, benefiting large landowners and impoverishing the smallholders (Griffin 1976). In some cases, impressive gains in physical agricultural output were achieved by commercialized agriculture, as in the case of the Sudan, while local consumption declined as land was shifted from food to cash crops and the output was earmarked for export markets to earn foreign exchange (Griffin and Ghose 1979). In cases of food deficit, dumping of food aid from Western donors was relied upon. Large imports of food under US PL 480 often distorted local agriculture and food markets. While such aid benefited Western interests, as for example 'grain merchants' (Morgan 1980) and subsidized farmers in USA or Europe (Lofchie and Cummins 1981), food aid worked as a disincentive to farmers in recipient countries (Singer 1988). Much moral blame adheres to Western donors for the drastic decline in food production in Africa after 1970 and for the desertification and mass hunger generated as a result of this (Griffin ed. 1987). While food aid remains an urgent need in cases of humanitarian and relief situations, there is little justification for its continuation, especially in countries once self-sufficiency in food production is achieved or when the beneficiaries are civilian or military elites. The only successful agricultural development occurred in Taiwan and South Korea, thanks to modernizing elites who, to their credit, rejected both the Lewis model and the 'green revolution' presciptions, in favour of egalitarian land reform (Lee 1979) as a precondition for export-led development (see pp. 114–117 below).

MACRO-MODELLING

Now, we shall briefly, but critically, survey five of the most influential cases of macro-modelling utilized in the postwar design of economic development by Westerners:

1 the Harrod–Domar model,
2 the two-gap theory,
3 the Keynesian macro-model,
4 input–output analysis,
5 computable general equilibrium models.

These models were Western constructions, originally developed from experience and realities in the West, to solve Western problems. Subsequently, they were transferred and applied in developing countries, but without the necessary institutional and theoretical adaptation or test of fitness. None was constructed inductively.

The Harrod–Domar model

The Harrod–Domar (H–D) model was the ultimate expression of Eurocentric, pro-capital modelling, popularizing and legitimizing the view that capital constraint is the only important rein on economic development. It became a tool of capitalization by assigning top priority in economic development on expanding the capital base in the developing country by all means and at all costs.

Although Harrod (1939, 1948) and Domar (1947, 1946) worked independently, in England and United States respectively, they were interested in the same central question: What is the rate of income growth necessary for smooth economic development? Their models (Sen ed. 1970) were essentialy the same, with the usual strong assumptions of perfect competition, and such unrealistic assumptions as the existence of initial full employment equilibrium, closed economy, *laissez-faire* capitalism and only one product.

The conclusion of Domar's model is that the full employment growth rate, g, is the rate of net investment, dI, which must equal the product of the marginal propensity to save, α, and the marginal productivity of capital, σ:

$$g = dI = \alpha\sigma \tag{4.1}$$

In the original Harrod version the warranted rate of growth, Gw [subsequently corrected to G, the actual rate of growth – see footnote 1 in Sen ed. 1970: 43], is a positive function of the saving rate, s, and a negative function of the incremental capital-output ratio, C:

$$Gw = s/C \tag{4.1a}$$

Effectively, the right-hand side of eq. (4.1) and (4.1a) were identical with Domar's α being equivalent to Harrod's s, and similarly with σ and C.

Thus, as a result of the Harrod–Domar modelling, economic development emerged as a single-issue concern reduced to investment decision-making to increase the capital stock of developing countries. All other determinants of economic development, such as administrative, managerial or institutional, were ignored. While Western neo-classical economists initiated an ever-growing paradigm debate over growth models, splitting hairs over the nature of technical change (whether it was embodied or biased), they entirely ignored the relevance of perfect competition assumptions to the developing countries.

The UN, specifically its arm charged with promoting economic development in the Third World, took the initiative to popularize H–D modelling based on the crucial incremental capital–output ratio (ICOR). Economic planning manuals were drafted, as if ICOR and savings represented the 'magic wand' of macro-planning. Thus, in a standard reference manual on planning methodology, ECAFE (the Economic Commission for Asia and the Far East) declared:

> The rate of economic growth may be analytically considered as being the function of two factors: (a) the rate of capital formation, and (b) the capital/output ratio. Accordingly, economic development policies may be described as aiming at increasing the former, reduce the latter, or both.
>
> (UN ECAFE 1955: 25–6)

As late as 1960, another group of UN experts confidently declared:

> After estimating the current rate of savings, the crucial question will be what amount of net national output can be expected from investment to be made on the basis of the estimated savings.
>
> (UN ECAFE 1960: 10–11)

While the H–D modelling was being widely introduced in the Third World, however, it came under increasing criticism in the West. What exactly is capital and how can it be measured? The paradigm debate centring on these questions, known as Cambridge vs. Cambridge, between differing American and British schools of thought, (Solow 1956; Robinson 1962; and others such as Kaldor, Swan, Tobin *et al.* collected in Sen ed. 1970), were largely remote from actual Third World realities or requirements. It was conducted in Western terms – highly abstract, with vintage models of capital stock, variable factor prices, embodied and disembodied technical change, Hicks and Harrod neutralities and other stylized facts of little practical relevance to the developing countries, which were then in the midst of the protectionist ISI strategy utilizing capital-intensive technology transfers managed by Western multinational corporations. During this period, Japan and soon the Four Dragons were applying pragmatic, 'made-at home' versions of endogenous economic development (see pp. 114-117 below) on the road to what became their miracle developments.

This is how Third World development planning was set on the wrong track under Western intellectual leadership and the transfer of inappropriate techniques. With the H–D model as the new gospel, all the complex theoretical assumptions were dropped in actual planning and policy exercises; instead, the gospel was applied uncritically as a mechanistic, simplistic tool, to justify and spread the new Western prescription of: (1) 'capital is everything' and (2) economic development is planning by a government dependent upon Western technical advice and resource transfers.

These Eurocentric premises were strongly endorsed and legitimized by the mainstream opinion of the leading neo-classical economists. For example, Arthur Lewis bluntly stated that the task of economic development was 'growth and not distribution' (Lewis 1955: 9). He explicitly argued that:

> The central problem in the theory of economic growth is to understand the process by which a community is converted from being a 5 percent to a 12 percent saver – with all the changes in attitudes, in institutions and in techniques which accompany this conversion.
>
> (Lewis 1955: 225–6)

Lewis's view became an essential core of the neo-classical orthodoxy. It encouraged further intellectual theorizing in the tradition of Harrod–Domar whereby the sole constraint in economic development was seen as capital. Thus, capital accumulation was identified with capital-intensive techniques, symbolizing modernization (i.e. Americanization or Westernization) and economic development, which was expected to generate higher income via productivity. While in theory a correct link was established between capital-intensive techniques and higher productivity through savings, the vital issue of ownership of the capital accumulated was overlooked; hence retained income from producitivity gains was ignored. In fact, many of the gains accrued to Western interests. Herein lies a fundamental Eurocentric bias in the 'capital-is-everything' mentality. The bias arose because of the neo-classical assumption that, given the inadequacy of domestic savings in the newly decolonized Third World, growth was a function of foreign aid and capital transfers from the West. This was a presumption enthusiastically accepted by the post-independence leaders and followers alike. Tricklism and Western intellectualism were powerful forces.

The two-gap theory

This is a somewhat more sophisticated model, pioneered by Chenery and his associates (Chenery and Bruno 1962; Chenery and Strout 1966), in that it adapts the H–D model to the open economy and allows domestic savings and investment to interact with trade policy and foreign aid. The central logic of the model is the basic macroeconomic identity: aggregate income = aggregate expenditure. Algebraically,

$$Y = C + I + (X - M) \tag{4.2}$$

where C and I are total (public and private) consumption and investment expenditures, and X and M are expenditures on exports and imports.

Rearranging the identity such that sources of resources used in the economy equal uses of resources in the economy:

$$Y + M = C + I + X \tag{4.3}$$

Furthermore, Y can be defined as savings, S, plus C. Finally, deleting C from both sides in eq. (4.3) and transposing:

$$M - X = S - I \tag{4.4}$$

where the left-hand side of eq. (4.4) represents the foreign exchange gap, while the right-hand side represents the domestic savings gap. One of these gaps will dominate and will serve as the binding constraint. While in the early stages of economic development domestic savings may limit growth, at a later stage of industrialization this may be overcome by the inflow of foreign aid. Hence, projecting foreign aid requirements, under various assumptions of 'aid productivity', export earnings and growth rates in recipient countries, emerged as important activities of Western economists working in aid agencies or planning agencies in recipient countries.

As a planning technique, the two-gap theory was utilized by planners to analyse the independent desires of consumers/savers, investors, importers and exporters and to attempt to influence these desires in the light of domestic economic realities in conjunction with external economic circumstances. In particular, export and import levels could be influenced by pricing policies such as foreign exchange rates, savings could be augmented by foreign inflows, and investment levels could be influenced by tax incentives and by interest rate policies. In short, the two-gap theory seemed to offer planners and economic policy-makers room to manipulate each one of the four variables specified in eq. (4.4), in order to forecast prospective targets and balances and to keep regularly monitoring actual values of these variables against planned target levels.

However, as with the H–D model, the two-gap theory was an unrealistic prescription designed to promote Western foreign aid in the shorter term and Western corporate interests in the longer. The growth rate in LDCs was thus tied to inflows of development aid on the expectation that there was a positive correlation between aid and development. This expectation was later questioned empirically, in particular because foreign aid seemed to displace domestic savings and encourage conspicuous or superfluous consumption (Griffin and Enos 1970). No less importantly, the two-gap theory missed crucial questions of distribution and social policy objectives of development in accordance with tricklism. In the meantime, Western foreign aid facilitated equity ownership and control in modern/capitalist sectors dominated by MNCs. The net result was that much of the productivity gain in these sectors accrued to Western interests at the expense of domestic-retained income.

The Keynesian macro-model

Of all the Western models, the Keynesian macro-model seemed the most appropriate for Third World development. Conceived as an aggregate disequilibrium model, it fitted well the circumstances of the developing countries as did the concept of 'disguised unemployment'. Moreover, Keynesian macroeconomics promised decision-makers potentially powerful policy instruments, in particular fiscal policy levers derived from the income-multiplier analysis.

For this reason, it is instructive to sketch out the Keynesian macro-model in some detail in order to highlight the role of fiscalism in development. This will be done with the aid of a simple macro-model featuring an open economy and fiscal policy. We start with the key identity between aggregate income and expenditure:

$$Y = C + I + G + (X - M) \qquad (4.5)$$

where all notations, except one, are as defined before. G, government spending, is the new variable which introduces fiscal policy featuring income tax and government spending including transfer payments, TR. Consumption, C, is a function of disposable income, Y, and the marginal propensity to consume, b, which is greater than zero, but less than one. Disposable income is net of income tax plus transfer payments. The rate of tax, t, is a determined by fiscal policy.

$$C = bY_d \qquad 0 < b < 1$$
$$= b[(1 - t)Y + TR] \qquad\qquad (4.6)$$

Investment, government spending, transfer payments and export earnings are all assumed, for simplicity, to be autonomous. But, imports, are a function of aggregate income, Y and the marginal propensity to import, m:

$$M = mY \qquad\qquad (4.7)$$

After incorporating these definitions into the basic Keynesian identity in eq. (4.5) and performing the standard operations, we derive the income determination:

$$Y = A/[1 - b(1 - t) + m] \qquad\qquad (4.8)$$

where A is the sum of all autonomous variables. The coefficients inside the [ ] are, respectively, the marginal propensity to consume, marginal tax rate and the marginal propensity to import. The reciprocal of [ ] is the income multiplier, so that the larger the value of the [ ], the smaller the multiplier. While the marginal propensity to consume stimulates income, the tax rate and import propensity have negative impacts; accordingly, the larger the values of t and m, the smaller will be the multiplier.

Now for the deficiencies of the Keynesian macro-model in Third World planning. For one thing, Keynesian modelling could only be applied in countries where highly detailed and reliable information was available for empirical consumption functions, savings, investment and numerous other variables and where monetary and fiscal policies and institutions existed to a sophisticated degree. In addition, many developing countries suffered from 'financial dualism' (see p. 74 above), 'monetary repression' (Fry 1982) and capital market imperfections (Meier ed. 1989: 205–12). In these environments it was foolhardy to base development policy on elaborate Keynesian models (Blitzer *et al.* 1975; Taylor 1979, 1990); it could be even more misleading for policy-makers to rely on computable general equilibrium models (Robinson in Chenery and Srinivasan eds 1988). We shall return to this topic presently (see pp. 108–110 below).

In developed countries, the Keynesian macro-economics encountered increasing criticism from monetarists led by Milton Friedman and others and lost ground after the 1970s. Empirical problems also emerged in developing countries. The stability of empirical consumption (and saving) functions became a key problem (Yutopolous and Nugent 1976: 172–6). Also, unemployment in developing countries was soon realized to be more complex than the Keynesian open unemployment variety (Uppal 1973; Krishna 1973; Edwards 1974). These countries had large informal sectors and labour markets which were subject to causal or seasonal employment and income patterns (Hart 1973; Weeks 1975). Consequently, the path to full employment in the Third World could not simply be prescribed by means of conventional aggregate demand management via deficit financing.

The shortcoming of consumption and saving functions reduce the effectiveness and policy relevance of the income multiplier formula. This is the chief Keynesian policy lever intended to provide the fiscal policy-maker with a powerful instrument of employment policy. The basic income multiplier relationship is quite simple:

$$dY = k^* dA \qquad (4.9)$$

where k, the income multiplier, is the reciprocal of the denominator in eq. (4.8); dA is the required amount of additional autonomous injection to achieve a given amount of income growth.

But the realities of Third World economies make eq. (4.9) an extremely hazardous tool of fiscal policy to promote full employment. Four limitations, in particular, can be cited here, in addition to the unemployment problem already discussed above. First, transitory or casual income variations, which are frequent due to seasonality of agriculture or informality of employment, reduce the multiplier to mere guesswork. This is especially true in the case of regional multipliers which are subject to inter-regional expenditure leakages, as for example when construction expenditures in a low-income province revert to urban centres or the capital city from where most sourcing originates.

Second, the Keynesian concept of disequilibrium as a temporary state, which can be overcome by pump-priming public spending also fails to apply, in view of the permanence of underemployment disequilibrium in developing countries thanks to remittances and the support systems within extended family networks (Mehmet 1971b; Pack 1974). Third, as demonstrated by the heated debate on monetarism and structuralism (Meier ed. 1989: 193–216), the Keynesian model also suffers from several institutional weaknesses. Tax efficiency is extremely low, with extensive tax avoidance and evasion (Toye ed. 1979; Goode 1984: chap. 4). There is financial repression (Fry 1982) and a lack of financial deepening, especially in the rural areas of developing countries where money lending and other forms of informal credit prevail (Wharton 1962). Reform and liberalization of monetary and fiscal policies in developing countries are of very recent origin, and, as we shall see presently (pp. 126–127 below), they are influenced to a great extent externally, in particular by the World Bank and International Monetary Fund 'conditionalities'.

Input–output analysis

In economic planning, the single most extensive tool in Third World development has been the linear input–output (I–O) analysis (Todaro 1971, 1981: chap. 15). Though costly and time-consuming in construction, the I–O analysis is a simple technique which logically lends itself to public sector budgeting and such medium-term planning as the standard five-year plan.

Logically, the I–O matrix is an inter-industry model derived from the fact that the various sectors of an economy are interdependent. This interdependence is reflected in inter-industry transactions whereby products of various sectors are used up in producing the output of any given sector. Each sector is assumed to specialize exclusively in just one product, produced in fixed factor proportions, thus reflecting constant unit costs, no technical change or productivity gains. Clearly, in Third World economies with rapid structural change, these mechanical production/transaction relations do not prevail. Therefore, the reliability of IOA is considerably reduced, if not entirely negated.

Furthermore, the I–O model is a general equilibrium model, presuming the existence of perfect competition throughout the economy. This is essential for 'closing' the I–O model, i.e. to ensure that total output of any sector equals total demand. Total output (TO) is the sum of intermediate demand (ID) and final demand (FD); total purchases of inputs (TP) is the sum of intermediate purchases (IP) and value added by primary resources (VA):

$$TO = FD + ID \tag{4.10}$$

$$TP = IP + VA \tag{4.11}$$

Mathematically, the I–O matrix is a square, each sector appearing twice, once in rows, as a producer of a given output, and once in columns, as a purchaser of inputs. This ensures internal consistency of the matrix, demonstrated by the equality of total output and total purchases. In the matrix, the last row and column add up exactly to the value of the last cell of the matrix.

The I–O matrix is partitioned into four quadrants:

1 the final demand quadrant, based on the macro-identity: $FD = C + I + G + X - M$;
2 the intermediate demand quadrant, reflecting inter-industry transactions of the productive sectors of the economy;
3 the value-added quadrant, reflecting the contribution of primary inputs such as labour, capital, land as well government services and imports and
4 own use quadrant relating to the use of primary inputs by components of final demand.

The basic I–O equation, for a matrix with n sectors, and hence n equations, is:

$$\Sigma\, x_{ij} + Y_i = X_i$$

where $i = 1, \ldots, n$

$$j = 1, \ldots, n \tag{4.12}$$

What eq. (4.12) states is that in all sectors, total production (X_i) exactly equals deliveries to other industries ($\Sigma\, x_{ij}$) plus deliveries to final demand (Y_i). Inter-sectoral deliveries, known as intermediate demand, (x_{ij}), are a fixed proportion of total production, reflected by constant input–output coefficients, a_{ij}:

$$x_{ij} = a_{ij}X_j$$

where $i = 1, \ldots, n$

$$j = 1, \ldots, n. \tag{4.13}$$

By substitution, final demand can be derived as the difference between total production and intermediate demand:

$$Y_i = X_i - \Sigma\, a_{ij}X_j. \tag{4.14}$$

In the standard I–O matrix elegance and mathematical consistency prevail over Third World realities. Elegance and consistency are achieved by strong assumptions. For instance, the assumption of general equilibrium contrasts sharply with the actual imperfections in markets dominated by monopolies, oligopolies and 'administered prices'. Similarly, the requirement that each sector produces only one product can only be accomplished by using artificial classification or grouping of products and industries. The constant returns to scale condition denies the possibility of technical or structural change. Since economic development, by definition, entails technical and structural change occurring under conditions of market imperfections, the restrictive assumptions underlying the I–O analysis render the technique unreliable and costly as a basis for policy and planning.

Computable general equilibrium (CGE) modelling

If the I–O analysis is the product of Western economist's obssession with ideal world of perfect competition, the CGE modelling must be regarded as his ultimate masterpiece! With the advent of the computer age, Western modelling for Third World economic development has become ambitious and sophisticated. Large-scale I–O matrices, 100×100 or even larger varities, are now technically feasible, as well as linear and non-linear optimization models known as CGEs. Only a brief comment on CGEs needs to be made since their formal elegance far exceeds their utility or policy relevance in the cause of development.

In theory, the relative merit of these CGEs is the endogeneity of such key economic variables as prices and incomes along with their capacity to vary levels of production and consumption under conditions of perfect substitution. But this endogeneity is achieved at the cost of realism. It is realized by the assumption of perfect competition so that consumers and producers act as rational optimisers and the markets for factors and products entirely and fully clear. This is the standard love affair of the Western economic mind with the abstract ideal known as the Walrasian economy manifesting automatic and instantaneous market equilibrium. Since, however, the actual conditions in developing countries do not even come close to the Walrasian economy, prices and costs in CGEs are derived indirectly from dual solutions in linear programming (LP) models as imputed values on the basis of more or less arbitrary guesswork. This practice has been defended by a leading practitioner with the argument that: 'If we had a better theory of prices and market power than the Walrasian one, model builders would clearly use it . . . If competition is basically the only game in town, you might as well play it with elegance' (Taylor in Blitzer *et al.* 1975: 100).

Some CGE applications have gone further and constructed social accounting matrices (SAM) as a guide for agricultural or social policy evaluations (de Melo 1988; Pyatt 1988), while Taylor (1979, 1983) and others have attempted to blend 'macro-structuralist' with Walrasian CGEs. As stated by Stern (1989: 648), 'the very special structures assumed for the sectoral markets in these models' are so limiting that they generate little, if any, useful information for decision-makers in contrast to professional benefits realized by the analysts themselves. In short, there is little advantage in creating 'incomprehensible black boxes constructed from narrowly stereotyped or weak components and *casually invented parameters*' which make such modelling 'worse than useless' {Stern, ibid., italics added).

All in all, this survey of main techniques of planning leads us to a pessimistic conclusion. Although introduced from the West with great optimism and with high expectations, the record of macro-modelling and planning has been disappointing. Western mainstream economists, unable or unwilling to divorce themselves from ideal markets, have put abstraction before reality. Where facts did not exists they have simply manufactured facts by presumption. In contrast to this theoretical abstraction, the actual markets have been dominated by Western corporate interests such as the MNCs actively promoting capitalization of Third World resources. These corporations did not lose sight of bottom lines: they exploited monopolistic powers to derive monopoly profits (Hymer 1970), retarding rather than promoting economic development in the Third World.

This disappointing Western record contrasts sharply with the pragmatic, problem-solving approach of the Far Eastern NICs, where modelling and techniques were indeed used in planning and development policy, but only after appropriate adaptation to fit the environment and to serve local requirements. The result has been inductive, pragmatic, policy-relevant modelling and techniques in the service of economic development with social justice. On the other hand, and against rising disenchantment with modelling and planning in much of the Third World, in the early 1970s the North–South agenda experienced yet another dramatic swing of the development pendulum ushering in another paradigm debate. This time it was the onset of the new international economic order debate (Bhagwati ed. 1970).

5

THE NEW ECONOMIC ORDER:
FALSE START 1973

In October 1973 the OPEC oil crisis hit the world economy when oil-producing countries unilaterally decided to triple, and then further increase, the price of oil sold to consuming countries. This act represented the first time that a group of primary-producing countries had acted in concert, as a cartel, to determine the terms-of-trade of a strategic commodity worldwide. The act had two immediate effects. First, in consuming countries it created a supply shock, shortages and long queues at filling stations, exposing the vulnerability of rich, industrialized countries of the North to the actions of primary-producing countries of the South, generating fears of more 'producer cartels' (Bergsten and Krause eds 1975; Bergsten 1976). Second, in the South, it led to calls for the new economic international order (NEIO), suddenly empowering the G7 countries in the United Nations Conference on Trade and Aid (UNCTAD). UNCTAD, originally created in 1964 in the spirit of 'trade, not aid', was expected to counter GATT, the General Agreement on Tariffs and Trade, which was generally perceived as a rich man's club (Walters 1973).

What was NEIO all about? And why did it fail as quickly as it rose?

NEIO was, essentially, a demand from the South for global equity; to restructure the old unequal 'colonial' trading system which kept generating uneven development (Hymer 1970), thus making the rich Northern countries richer while impoverishing the primary pro-ducers in the South (Helleiner ed. 1976). It was the product of the Algiers Conference of 1973 which led to the Sixth Special Session of the UN General Assembly which adopted a Declaration and Program of Action on the Establishment of a New International Eco-nomic Order. This was proclaimed in Resolutions 3201 and 3202 followed by the Charter of Economic Rights adopted as Resolution

3362 of the Seventh Special Session of the General Assembly (Meier ed. 1984: 758–62).

NEIO failed within a few years for a multiplicity of reasons. For one thing, the G7 countries of the South were disunited and overly ambitious and/or unrealistic in their expectations, often vague and conflicting. For example, UNCTAD's Integrated Commodity Fund, intended to stabilize the export earnings of core commodities, failed to get off the ground: it did not even get the necessary endorsement of primary producers' themselves, let alone winning any support from rich, industrialized countries which regarded UNCTAD no more than the 'poor relation', at best, of GATT (Helleiner ed. 1976).

The October 1973 OPEC crisis had several immediate and long-term consequences. In the short term, the crisis contributed greatly to credit expansion in the Eurocurrency market, originally stimulated by Nixon's cheap monetary policies coupled with high German interest rates (Kindleberger 1989: 225). Oil-surplus countries such as Saudi Arabia and Kuwait, highly dependent on Western advice, decided to keep their windfall profits, as petrodollars, in Western banks which ensured the stability of the Western financial and banking system. But these burgeoning petrodollar accounts led to sudden credit expansion in Western banks which then began lending recklessly to Third World borrowers on such a massive scale that Kindleberger subsequently, and very aptly, spoke of 'speculative manias' (1989: 28).

Here is the fundamental cause of what later became the Third World debt problem. In fact, 'the problem' was a Western creation due to reckless credit expansion which Darity and Horn have appropriately termed 'the phenomenon of loan pushing'. The practice, reminiscent of the South Sea Buble of the nineteenth century, worked within a flawed credit allocation system featuring the following critical elements:

> There was the promotional-cum-persuasion aspect, where the initiative to borrow comes from the lenders. Borrowers received more credit than they themselves conceived as feasible or necessary at the outset . . . The foreign lending wave involved nepotistic connections and corruption in the arrangement of loans . . . [They] performed a market-making function for numerous US-producers . . . When concrete evidence of softness in the ability of the borrowers to meet their obligations became visible, the lenders initially tried to resolve the situation by continuing to

lend . . . Eventually, the lenders withdrew altogether from
providing funds ('revulsion' took hold).
(Darity and Horn 1988: 3–4)

In short, it is in the Western financial system that we must look for
the basic origins of the debt crisis of the 1980s. It was during this
time that 'the chickens [came] home to roost' (Kindleberger 1989:
26), i.e. borrowing countries began to default on payments and ask
for debt rescheduling and/or structural adjustment lending from
the World Bank and IMF. In turn, this led to new 'conditionalities',
i.e. Western terms with little account of social and domestic policy
constraints in borrowing countries. Ethnic conflict in Sri Lanka
and several African countries followed in the wake of such new
'conditionalities'.

In the meantime, the dramatic hikes in OPEC prices after October
1973 generated 'supply shocks' in oil-dependent developing countries, exposing, in dramatic fashion, the inappropriateness of capital-
and oil-intensive industrialization strategies of the previous quarter
century. However, easy lending available from Western banks and
temporarily high commodity prices cloaked the basic structural
imbalances of these countries, though not for too long!

The OPEC cartel's initial success in reversing terms of trade did
have a long-lasting unintended impact on world trading links. It
provided a new stimulus for South–South cooperation, it encouraged
regional integration movements in several areas of the Third World
(UNCTAD 1976), which were influenced in part by the success of
the European Common Market. Seldom, however, have these movements fulfilled the initial expectations (Vaitsos 1978), in a large
measure owing to the power of MNCs, but also due to the inherent
weaknesses of the primary producers' themselves in delinking, or
at least diversifying, their trading along a North–South axis. It
seemed that prospects for 'autonomous' development in the South,
as argued by radical theorists from Baran (1957) to Samir Amin
(1976) might, after all, be premature (Meier ed. 1984: 133–43).

THE FOUR DRAGONS

Autonomous, or rather endogenous, economic development in the
Third World did occur in the case of the Four Dragons or Tigers of
the Far East, namely, the authoritarian regimes of South Korea and
Taiwan, and the city-states of Singapore and Hong Kong. How did

they do it? And what did their experience really mean for Western economic development theorizing? It presented, until its sudden demise in 1997 (see pp. 117–120 below), a new challenge, no less significant than Japan's earlier economic ascent.

THE NIC CHALLENGE: THE RISE AND FALL OF THE ASIAN DRAGONS

From the mid-1960s, the NIC challenge thrusted export-led, labour-intensive industrialization to the top of economic development theorizing. Their success brought into the development debate the 'look East' model of the 'Four Little Dragons' (Vogel 1992; World Bank 1993). Taiwan, South Korea, Hong Kong and Singapore emerged as the pioneering set of countries graduating out of the class of developing countries and into the coveted group of newly industrialized countries (NICs). Graduation of the Dragons came right on the heels of the Japanese miracle and it caught Western development theorists by surprise. These theorists were still preaching ISI strategy for the Third World when the Dragons had already discovered export-led growth! For example, the earliest comprehensive study of the new export-led strategy did not appear until 1970 (Little *et al.* 1970), by which time outward-oriented 'growth with equity' in the Far East was largely an established fact.

Policy pragmatism, shaped by endogenous cultural values, rather than Western economic theory, was a major factor behind the rise of export-led growth in the case of the Far Eastern Dragons. Governments in the city-states of Singapore and Hong Kong, and in the former Japanese colonies of Taiwan and Korea, recognized developmental intervention as a necessity (Wade 1988, 1990); in reality they had no choice but to rely on exporting and services to promote development (Tan 1992). Singapore, recently thrown out of the Malaysian Federation, had no other choice but to opt for exporting. In the early 1950s South Korea and Taiwan were 'basket-cases', war-torn and military-ruled, and they started industrialization with agricultural modernization (in direct opposition to the Lewis model, it should be noted). They utilized assistance from the USA (Jacoby 1966; Mason *et al.* 1980) effectively to promote egalitarian development. Exports were encouraged for efficiency and equity reasons. Thus, redistributive policies were interlinked to growth-stimulating policies right from the outset. It was a strategy first implemented through massive egalitarian land reforms, as in

Taiwan and South Korea, in order to expand food production for the domestic market. Subsequently, the same egalitarian strategy was repeated through active labour market policies to maximize employment creation. The positive correlation between exports and employment was realized simply by following an industrial strategy which aimed at maximizing value-added of domestic factor endowments. This, in turn, ensured growth with equity. The importance of redistribution, as a complement of growth, stemmed from endogenous cultural values which assigned high social weight to the family and other group values in sharp contrast to Western individualism. Overall, the Far Eastern model was an example of organic growth (Mehmet 1990: 220–1).

The NIC experience of export-led development was in sharp contrast to the poor economic performance of other Third World countries which, following Western advice, ignored distribution in favour of growth by relying on protectionist ISI theories. By 1990 the Japanese miracle (Johnson 1982; OECD 1982) was replicated not only in the Four Dragons, but also in Southeast Asia (Tan 1993). The obvious question examined by several observers became: Can the Asian model be generalized for 'lessons' transferable to the Third World (Ranis 1978; Cline 1982; Hamilton 1987; Berger and Hsiao eds 1988)? Apart from the speed of its achievement, the Asian NICs' success was remarkable in promoting growth with equitable income distribution (Papanek and Kyn O 1986; Islam and Kirkpatrick 1986). It verified empirically the wisdom of investment in education, human resource development and land reform (Ahluwalia 1976; Jacoby 1966; Fei, Ranis and Kuo 1979), strategies sadly ignored in the rest of the developing world.

Until the Asian currency collapse of 1997, the Asia-Pacific region was the envy of the world as the most dynamic area in the global economy (Bergsten and Noland ed. 1993). By contrast, Western economies remained bogged down in recession, especially in Europe where high levels of unemployment presented new problems of 'social exclusion'. With the opening of China, the twenty-first century may see, for the first time since Marco Polo, the economic centre of gravity in world trade shifting from the West back to the Orient. Several observers have begun labelling the twenty-first century *the Pacific century* (Elegant 1991; Inoguchi 1994; Kristof 1993). The basic issue behind the NIC challenge became: How did these high-performing economies generate rapid growth? This question led to a heated debate which has continued to grow (Wade 1990; Islam 1992; Tan 1992; World Bank 1993).

In this debate, the neo-classical theorists took the high road, arguing in terms of market ideology emphasizing private sector and export-oriented industrialization (Westphal 1978, 1990; Little in Lee ed. 1981; Balassa and Associates 1982; Tsuru 1976; Riedel 1988; Hicks 1989). These theorists, associated with the World Bank, initially stressed the importance of 'getting prices right' and more recently 'getting the fundamentals right' (World Bank 1993: 347). Deepak Lal was perhaps the most assertive; in his book *The Poverty of Development Economics* (1985) he attacked the 'dirigiste' dogma of early postwar theorists, such as Myrdal and Hirschman, for sacrificing market forces for various forms of government intervention in the economy. Lal's criticism, symbolic of neo-classical *laissez-faire* doctrine, was that state intervention has caused 'policy-induced' distortions worsening, rather than helping, economic development:

> The empirical assumptions on which this *dirigisme* was based have been belied by the experience of numerous countries in the postwar period. The most serious current directions in many developing countries are not those flowing from inevitable imperfections of a market economy but the policy-induced, and thus far from inevitable, distortions created by irrational *dirigisme*.
>
> (Lal 1985: 103)

This kind of neo-classical position has not gone unchallenged. For example, many (Lim 1983; Wade 1990) have rejected 'the myth of the free market', as have neo-Marxists (Hamilton 1983), based on *laissez-faire* doctrines, and have argued that the "Little Dragons" transition to an export-promotion strategy was government-led capitalist industrialization dependent on the USA. Feminists (Corner 1992; Tinker 1990; Vickers 1990) criticized the subordination of low-wage female and child labour in the sweatshops of the new international division of labour. Others argued in terms of 'export pessimism' (Balassa *et al.* 1980; Cline 1982; Bhagwati 1984), pointing out that rising levels of protectionism in the North, coupled with an increasing number of NICs in the South, would result in untenable export penetration. Others emphasized cultural factors such as the Japanese culture and work ethics (Nakane 1970), overseas Chinese capitalism (Redding 1993), government–business partnership (Johnson 1982), labour–management relations (Gordon 1982) and 'learning by doing' through innovative education and human resource development (Mehmet 1988; Selvaratnam 1994).

In this inter-paradigm debate no single Western theory has managed to provide a full explanation for the NIC challenge. Even though it reflects strong capitalist tendencies, there are enough cultural and organic characteristics to support a 'new Asian capitalism' (Papanek and Kyn O in Berger and Hsaio eds 1988). In particular, it is an Asian variety that rejects individualism in favour of solidarity of the group or family, managed top-down by an authoritarian state. This non-Western variety has also contributed to the emergence of new prospective graduates in Southeast Asia under significantly differing (e.g. Muslim and plural) cultural circumstances (Islam 1992; Tan 1993).

Analytically, this fact validates the endogenous sources of economic development of Third World countries based on 'home-made' prescriptions. In these 'home-made' prescriptions, there is undoubtedly much borrowing from Western development theories; however, the vital element is deliberate blending by indigenous modernizers of what is borrowed with local requirements. Blind imitation of Western theories is finally becoming a thing of the past. But Eurocentricity in theorizing, and its major product, namely, global inequity, are by no means at an end.

THE ASIAN CURRENCY COLLAPSE, 1997

The floating of the Thai bhat in August 1997 marked the onset of the currency crisis which abruptly ended the 'Asian Miracle' (World Bank 1993). The crisis was private-sector generated in financial markets that were prematurely and excessively liberalized without the necessary supervision of banks (Culpeper 1998). Under these circumstances, private short-term borrowing reached unprecedented levels, resulting in excessive debt–equity ratios, as a result of greedy investors and speculators seeking quick returns in high-income real estate and luxury-goods markets. The crisis quickly transformed itself into a political challenge to several authoritarian regimes who were themselves vulnerable, not only on account of corruption but for maintaining overvalued currencies and for inadequate supervision of banks and financial institutions. Almost overnight the crisis wiped out the economic gains of the preceding quarter century, so painfully achieved with so much sacrifice on the part of the ordinary citizens. Popular revolt, in the wake of currency devaluation and austerity measures recommended by the IMF, led to unexpected regime change in South Korea and, even more surprisingly, in Indonesia.

In reviewing the Asian collapse, three issues come to mind: the explanation for the crisis, the recovery of these economies, and finally, the theoretical significance of the experience. Let's briefly examine them.

First, what led to the collapse of these Asian economies? Clearly, the root causes of the crises are a set of of domestic and external reasons. Chief among the internal causes of the collapse must be the premature liberalization of capital and financial markets in an environment with an extensive system of *crony capitalism*. In this climate, authoritiarian development states manipulated fiscal and economic policies to channel high savings into high debt–equity obligations while financing dubious pet prestige projects (e.g. 'the national car' project of Tommy Suharto in a joint venture with Kia Motors of Korea) (Lim 1998). Overall, the system was managed for corruption and rent-seeking behaviour which has been extensively documented elsewhere (Mehmet 1986, 1994, 1997).

Equally significant, internal causes of the Asian meltdown include deliberate under-pricing of environmental and labour resources in order to generate comparative advantage and make the Tiger economies attractive to foreign investors. The under-valuation of environment and labour inputs basically exaggerated the rate of return on capital, creating excessive inflow of foreign funds looking for quick windfall gains. The nominal GNP growth rates of 8 per cent or over were artificial because they relfected over-valued asset pricing. On a net accounting basis, a nominal GNP growth rate of 8 per cent was more like 3–4 per cent or less, after allowance is made for the social costs of environmental damage and labour exploitation.

Externally, the Tigers relied excessively on foreign borrowing, especially short-term private loans, with little or no controls within a macroeconomic policy framework committed to trade and financial liberalization. These were the pillars of the IMF orthodoxy on which Asian macroeconomics were founded. As late as November 1996, the IMF confidently declared that the Southeast Asia region 'is poised to extend its success into the twenty-first century and that governments still have a major role in driving this process . . . [This confident projection] . . . was rooted in the region's strong macroeconomic fundamentals' (IMF, quoted in Kapur 1998: 114).

Box 10

The Asian currency collapse of 1997

This was not a purely 'Asian' crisis, but, rather, a crisis of globalized Western capitalism. Like its predecessor, the Mexican peso crisis of 1994, it was the byproduct of the inherent instability of the system. As explained in Chapter 1 (the basic mainstream model, pp. 16–19), the capitalist system requires swings in the market process in order to generate profits that drive the system. For, under equilibrium, there can be no profits.

The Asian crisis had several domestic and external causal factors and there are important lessons for domestic leaders in these countries as well as for global management of the world economy. The chief lessons to be learnt are that 'authoritarian states', however committed to development and 'Asian values', cannot exploit their workers and degrade the environment to manufacture comparative advantage. Exploitation can only attract excessive foreign funds looking for short-term windfall gains and they can exit as suddenly as they enter, causing a meltdown in their wake.

A few short months later the Asian financial meltdown took place; so much for the IMF's judgement on 'fundamentals'! (See Box 10.)

Are these Asian economies likely to recover? In due course, they will, but it is virtually certain that these economies will be quite different: more self-reliant and less hospitable to Western financial inflows. The Asian financial collapse was a failure of capital markets. It was not a failure of Asian creativity or enterprise. Paul Krugman (1994) overstates his case when he argues that the Asian miracle was a 'myth', since it was based on exploitation of resources, which is subject to the law of diminishing returns. While this is true so far as it goes, Krugman's knowledge of the region is scanty (Haggard and Kim 1997). Asia-Pacific Tigers have great reserves of human creativity and enterprise. In due course, the spirit of Asian dynamism will be revived on the basis of a more sustainable development, founded on a more realistic pricing of environmental and labour resources, and managed by less authoritarian governments.

Finally, is the Asian model dead? There are three parts to this answer. The currency collapse was, first and foremost, a crisis of global capitalism, generated in the financial markets by forces of excessive neo-liberalism with no concern for environmental and labour resources. In this respect, it was an 'imported' phenomenon and requires modification by means of effective made-at-home Asian rules based on international standards for better management of capital markets and banks and with the interests of Asian societies to the fore. Second, in the Asian model sharing is an important tenet and this remains as valid as ever. In the past, leaders in some Asia-Pacific economies have often ignored this ethic, or have chosen to ignore it for the sake of the blind pursuit of growth. They have chased 'enlargement of the GNP' at the cost of exploiting Asian workers (especially women and children) and environmental resources in order to create a new comparative advantage in export markets. In the process, while a few got rich, the masses suffered from a strategy of cheap labour and subsidized capital. Exploiting his people and Indonesia's vast resources is what finally brought Suharto down. Asian development in future should respect environmental quality and labour rights in accordance with international standards and it should pay attention to the equitable sharing of the fruits of growth. Third, and most profoundly, the major lesson emerging from the 1997–8 Asian currency collapse is the folly of authoritarian leaders seeking shelter behind discretionary definitions of 'Asian values' while colluding with the rich and powerful investors, domestic or foreign. Good governnance means always being accountable to the people, and development must benefit *all* the people, not the few who are powerful and privileged at the top.

6

THE LATEST STATE OF THE ART: ECONOMIC DEVELOPMENT THEORIZING SINCE 1980

In the last two decades of the twentieth century Eurocentricity has re-emerged as an explicit item on the agenda of development studies (Amin 1989) from three separate but reinforcing sources: (1) conditionality in debt, deficit and structural adjustment programmes; (2) sustainability and human rights issues in trade policy and (3) globalization and tripolarity in world trade and investment.

As far as narrow economic development theorizing is concerned, the Third World is now viewed within a general mood of pessimism. This is partly induced by foreign aid fatigue or ineffectiveness (Cassen and Associates 1986; Lipton and Toye 1990), partly as a result of the end of the Cold War, and partly due to fears about the sustainability of economic growth (World Commission on Environment and Development 1987; Goodland and Daly 1993). The earlier Western confidence in the trickle-down theory no longer commands widespread acceptance. After four UN development decades the income gap between the North and the South remains as wide as ever. In much of the South, crushing debts caused by economic mismanagement and reckless lending have brought about a *Fate Worse Than Debt* (George 1990; Darity and Horn 1988); whereas in the North, plagued by technological and ecological limits to growth, deskilling and the environment are emerging as the new preoccupation. The sudden end of the industrial-military complex did not generate a peace dividend. Instead, it has caused prolonged recession, joblessness and rising welfare costs for which neither monetarist nor Keynesian theorists have been able to offer effective prescriptions. Macroeconomics are truly being internationalized. Mainstream economists are in danger of losing their monopoly position: they have had to share their commanding heights over public policy with political and other social scientists and have been obliged to acknowledge the growing influence of new institutionalism (see below). Overall, for the foreseeable future, the Third World seems destined to remain at the bottom, even after the end of the Second World, owing to new investment opportunities in Eastern Europe.

Against this changing development agenda, the mainstream theorizing is now centred on the following main paradigms: (1) new institutionalism focused on the social efficiency of institutions, rights and contracts; (2) debts, deficits and structural adjustment relying on neoclassicism; (3) sustainable development; (4) endogenous growth based on human capital and (5) globalization and tripolarity in world trade. We shall now briefly discuss these frontiers of development studies.

THE NEW INSTITUTIONALISM

A critical presumption behind mainstream economic development theorizing was an optimistic view of the 'state'. It was accepted as a matter of faith that the 'state' would act as the modernizer and the developer acting as an unbiased actor, *with zero transaction costs*, in allocating scarce resources to promote national prosperity through economic growth along the path prescribed by neo-classical theory.

Only a handful observers, notably Myrdal in his massive *Asian Drama* (1968), dissented from the general presumption of a state equally competent everywhere to guide economic development. Myrdal classified states into 'soft' and 'hard', in order to reflect differing institutional capacities, and he took great pains to examine economic development in historical and interdisciplinary terms.

However, in the mainstream, the strong premise was that Western economic history lessons could be transferred to the developing countries, as if efficient states and the Protestant Ethic were indeed universal facts. It became apparent by the mid-1970s that the premise of ideal civil society was inappropriate, but only after the Western state itself came under attack not only from the ideological left (e.g. neo-Marxists) but also from the new neo-conservative school. At the same time, empirically speaking, economic development in post-independence countries proved to be more daunting and complex than the architects of modernization theory had ever imagined. Economic development could not be transplanted from outside as part of Westernization which was justified as 'becoming modern'. This simplistic view has now given way to the centrality of domestic politics and the social efficiency of institutions in explaining differentials in rates of economic development. Now mainstream development economists readily admit that the sources of underdevelopment may indeed lie outside economics, as Meier put it, based on a 'quarter century of development experience' it can be concluded that 'a country is poor because of poor politics' (Meier 1989: v).

Not surprisingly, therefore, 'a new political economy' of development focused on the politics of economic development, has become the new paradigm. From this perspective, 'government failure' (Bradhan *et al.* 1990) has been substituted for the earlier postwar 'market failure' argument and states are now classified explicitly according to the 'logic of developmental state' (Onis 1991). This is intended to differentiate statist ones from other kinds, depending on whether or not their policies and strategies enable or constrain economic development, especially on the emerging issues of democratization and human rights (Haggard and Mason 1990; Doner 1991; Islam 1992).

In this context, economic development is seen as a process induced by institutional efficiency; that is to say, a set of favourable legal and institutional environments, and not just accumulation or allocation of factors of production in markets. This new 'neo-classical political economy', as Srinivasan (1985) has termed it, is largely derived from the application of economic tools to explain the role of the state in terms of 'supply and demand of intervention' in markets by the inter-related public choice schools. According to a major pioneer of the paradigm, institutions are a set 'rules, enforcement characteristics of rules, and norms of behaviour that structure repeated human inter-actions. Hence, they limit and define the choice set of neo-classical theory' (North 1989: 1320). This school believes 'that *changing formal institutions can change political practice*' (Putnam 1993: 184, italics in original), which is a conclusion demonstrated in an exten-sive case study of Italy by Putnam, comparing political institutions in the more-developed North with the less-developed South.

There are several variants of new institutionalism. We can distin-guish three, with significant overlaps: the predatory state; property rights and rent-seeking behaviour.

The predatory state is pioneered by the economic historian Douglas North (1981), who regards the state as an organization with a comparative advantage in violence (North 1981: 21). Thanks to this comparative advantage, the state can trade services (e.g. protection or justice) for taxation revenue. The ruler is a wealth-maximizer who derives revenue from these services in the form of rents, taxes and fees. The ruler's wealth-maximization objective is limited by the threat of potential rivals and by the 'free-rider' problem whereby some of his subjects may avoid payments while still enjoying the services provided by the state. Therefore, the ruler needs a 'successful ideology' in order to sustain his rule and 'overcome the free-rider problem'. (North 1981: 53). Thus, he must innovate and induce institutional change to avoid his downfall. In an early extension of the predatory state, Niskanen (1971) conceptualized the bureaucrat as a utility-maximizer with a private objective function specified in terms of budget-maximization. Deepak Lal (1984) has applied the predatory state model to explain the rise and fall of several empires in the Indian subcontinent from the time of the Moguls.

The property rights school, an extension of North's theory, has been particularly illuminating in recent studies of agricultural development. Ruttan and Hayami (1984) have argued that successful agricultural development requires laws which regulate property rights based on clear titles. Bateman (1988) has applied this line of reasoning to the specific case of African agriculture and has linked its failure to a lack of proper institutional incentives and supporting state laws.

Both of the above variations of the new institutionalism can be regarded as by-products of the public choice theory which was pioneered by J.M. Buchanan (Buchanan *et al.* 1980). This theory regards the political process as a complex, competitive game with different actors pursuing conflicting interests. Thus, there are lobbies and special interest groups (for example tobacco, steel, agriculture, textiles, consumer groups) who are funded by supporting donors and staffed by professional fundraisers and technical experts who specialize in lobbying legislators and bureaucrats on behalf of their clients. Their objective is to secure laws which protect these special interests. Thus, tariff-seeking special interests may get tariff-protection against imports. Mancur Olson (1982) has gone furthest among the public choice theorists to explain the dynamics of special interest groups by means of the concept of 'distributional coalitions'. These cartel-like networks are dedicated to rent-seeking behaviour (a term originally coined by A. Krueger (1974)) which covers a wide range of corrupt practices and influence peddling. Rent-seeking not only biases income distribution in favour of powerful and well-connected groups, but also causes inflation due to higher transaction costs which are, ultimately, passed on to consumers.

The imperfect world of the developing countries, partly owing to market failure, but in part due to government failure, provides a fertile environment for the pursuit of rent-seeking and gate-keeping by domestic as well as foreign interests. The rent-seeking model has been utilized by a self-serving ruling elite in Malaysia ostensibly implementing an affirmative action strategy in aid of the majority ethnic group (Mehmet 1986). In Indonesia it has been institutionalized to shelter a culture of systemic corruption under Suharto's New Order (Mehmet 1994). More generally, in several Asian Tiger economies, rent-seeking, or *crony capitalism*, has been relied upon to channel high savings into speculative projects, typically in the private sector financed by the equity participation of foreign investors and resulting in untenably high debt–equity ratios which ultimately spilled into the financial crisis of 1997–8.

The other notable feature of the rent-seeking Asian authoritarian state was the elite-managed exploition of workers. The rationale for this unfair labour practice was that it would generate new forms of comparative advantage or increase global competitiveness. Consequently, a wide range of internal and external *enabling* policies were adopted: internally, capital imports were subsidized while worker rights and trade unions have been discriminated against (Hadiz 1997); indeed, Asian apologists have sought to justify unfair labour practices as being necessary conditions for global competitiveness in the name of 'Asian values' (Mendes 1997). Externally, Asian leaders such as Mahathir, have relied upon capitalist market forces and 'open regionalism' (Bergsten and Noland eds 1993) to attract foreign investment to finance growth, only to blame speculators and short-term investors when the latter decided to cash in their profits and abandon Southeast Asia economies to the whim of the same market forces.

DEBT, DEFICIT AND STRUCTURAL ADJUSTMENT

Starting in the late 1970s, state-led development in the Third World, based on the ideology of state capitalism, reached the limit of financial solvency. Short-term liquidity available under the emergency stand-by facilities of the International Monetary Fund (IMF), was no remedy for the chronic external imbalances in the balance of payments of numerous developing countries with inadequate foreign exchange earnings from traditional exports to pay for imports of oil and producer goods. However, from the OPEC October 1973 crisis on, external debt was not the only crisis facing Third World economies. They also had equally challenging internal budget deficits due to a multiplicity of contributing factors such as loss-making public enterprises, wasteful subsidy programmes which favoured influential elites linked to ISI industries, overvalued currencies, anti-rural strategies and inappropriate educational policies. As we have seen, these policies were based on faulty economic advice from donors and advisers from Eurocentric circles.

From 1980 on, structural adjustment and stabilization emerged as the new paradigm – the latest 'development counter-revolution' (Toye 1993: esp. chap. 4) – with the strong intellectual leadership of economists associated with the IMF and the World Bank (WB). This new paradigm reflected a major shift in the Bank's traditional lending policy from project lending to sector- or economy-wide lending. The Bank decided to place priority on energy and power, agriculture and rural development, education and health, as well as trade and industry. For its part, the IMF has abandoned its original mandate of providing international liquidity to countries experiencing temporary balance of payment disequilibria and emerged as a source of large-scale lending in aid of structural adjustment, typically preceded by a standard, one-fix deflationary stabilization package, consisting of currency devaluation, elimination of subsidies, tax hikes and financial liberalization, while also paying lip-service to greater 'transparency' and 'sound policy-making'. In terms of outcomes, however, the standard IMF package has seldom worked. Typically, the 'bail-out' package attached to IMF conditionalities benefited creditors (i.e. foreign banks) while ignoring the 'bread-and-butter' needs of the people in these countries. As a consequence, 'social conflict' (Rodrik 1998) has become the almost predictable outcome of the promise of long-term gain for short-term pain.

This is also true for structural adjustment programmes. But what exactly is structural adjustment? It is a programme of painful economy-wide restructuring expected to last some seven to ten years. More technically, Edwards and Wijnbergen (1988) have defined structural adjustment as a set of policy measures that attempt to bring about permanent change in the relative prices of tradable goods, and to reallocate resources in accordance with the new set of external and domestic economic circumstances.

The new orthodoxy was solidly neo-classical, based on free market ideology articulated by IMF–WB development economists (Little and Mirrlees 1974; Balassa and Associates 1982; Lal 1985) which espoused the notion of a competitive market as a 'level playing field'. Quickly endorsed by neo-conservatives as well as leading public choice theorists, the neo-classical revival took straight aim at 'government failures in development' (Krueger 1990; Bhagwati 1982). The neo-classical counter-revolution seeks to liberalize markets, promote exports, de-regulate trade and generally relies on the private sector as the engine of growth. As with previous Western ideologies, the latest one has its Eurocentric bias; it favours large, capital-intensive formal sectors, opens the door to Western equity ownership and control of capital, while discriminating against indigenous informal and subsistence sectors. It also suffers from the gender bias of conventional neo-classical economics, especially macroeconomics.

The latest neo-classical revival has a neo-conservative agenda; it began in the United States under Ronald Reagan and in the United Kingdom under Margaret Thatcher, and eventually found its way into the Third World for two principal reasons.

In the first place, in the early 1980s the World Bank adopted a rightward shift, especially following the appointment in 1981 of W.A. Claussen as its new president. From being a champion of basic needs and poverty-focused development (see pp. 92–94), the Bank and the Fund made drastic stabilization and economic restructuring a new 'conditionality' for structural adjustment lending (SAL) to Third World countries (Sachs 1987, 1989), typically as a condition for debt rescheduling under Paris or London rules. A good example of this is the 'Washington Consensus' (Williamson in Emerij ed. 1997), a neo-liberal macroeconomic manifesto specifying 'Washington-approved policies' (Stewart in Emeris ed. 1997: 63). However, these conditionalities have been primarily creditor or banker conditions, as articulated in the Baker or Brady Plans. More specifically, repayment of loans to foreign creditors has taken precedence over the social costs of removal of subsidies or the political risks of drastic economic disruption within developing countries. As a result, the 1980s has been labelled 'the lost and debt-ridden decade' (Kay 1993: 697). These made-in-the-West policies have intensified poverty in the Third World and have generated a wide range of social problems (Ghai 1992); in particular, women in poverty have now emerged as 'a new global underclass' (Buvinic 1997). (See Box 11.)

The terms and conditionalities under which the WB–IMF function have always had a Eurocentric bias, but it got worse under SALs. The IMF bears a particular responsibility for promoting this

---

Box 11

Stabilization and structural adjustment: the WB–IMF 'medicine'

Until 1980, state-led development was the norm for Western donors. Commencing with the appointment of A.W. Clausen to the presidency of the World Bank, an ideological shift towards the right has occurred, centred on the neo-classical 'recipe' of market-led development for LDCs. This 'recipe' rests on two pillars of *stabilization* and *structural adjustment*.

Stabilization, primarily managed by the IMF, is a deflationary (i.e. tight) monetary and foreign exchange policy designed to curtail consumption and spending in order to stabilize balance of payments and eliminate budget deficits. Currency devaluation, privatization of state enterprises, abolition of marketing boards and liberalization of banking and financial sectors for foreign investment are typical policy instruments.

Structural adjustment, by contrast, is a longer-term strategy of economic development managed by the Bank. Its aim is to rely on market forces, in particular through user fees, cost-recovery pricing and private-sector promotion.

SAL is development lending to support stabilization and structural adjustment in borrowing countries on condition that these countries agree to performance criteria in line with the above WB–IMF recipes or 'medicine.'

Successful performance will, no doubt, ensure the timely repayment by borrowing countries of foreign debt, but this may be at great social cost (since the burden of higher prices will fall disproportionately on the poorest) and/or political unrest, possibly even regime change due to riots and disturbances in protest at dramatic price increases. The immediate beneficiaries of SAL 'bail-outs' are foreign banks and creditors.

---

trend: while adopting a tough line with borrowing LDCs, the Fund effectively operated as a front for Western banks. It ignored reckless and excessive lending by Western banks when they were awash with petrodollars in the early 1970s, but, when, subsequently, financial conditions changed, the Fund quickly imposed strict new conditionalities on borrowers, and insisted, as in Indonesia in 1998, on closing down mismanaged domestic banks, while all along soft-handling Western banks. There are, of course, historical explanations for the Eurocentric bias of the Fund and the WB. These international financial institutions (IFIs), from their inception in the late 1940s, have been dependent on Wall Street and this has biased not only their traditional lending favouring capital-intensive over social projects (Kapur and Webb 1994: 3), but also the fact that, under SALs, the IFIs have become 'credit-rating' institutions assessing Third World countries for Western bankers. Formulated in Washington, Paris or London, such neo-classical recipes for the Third World have not worked. These Western remedies have paid inadequate attention to fundamental causes of external imbalances and budget deficits in the developing countries themselves, such as deteriorating terms of trade, supply shocks and rising protectionism in rich countries for exports of developing countries (Helleiner 1992), or to corruption and ineffiency due to elite mismanagement of budgets (Dornbusch 1986). But, as Susan George (1990) has argued, it is futile to place the blame on Third World countries when the Western banks prospered from a crisis of their own making. The fundamental cause of the Third World debt problem was reckless lending by Western banks shortly after the OPEC crisis of 1973 (Kindleberger 1989).

The second major reason for structural adjustment stemmed from the early apparent success story of the graduation of the Far Eastern Dragons as newly industrialized countries (NICs) due to export-oriented industrialization (Lee ed. 1981; Harris 1987). For neo-classical theorists, the NIC success story was practical proof of the validity of *laissez-faire* non-interventionism. Accordingly, for these theorists, the 'lessons' for African and Latin American countries finding themselves trapped with huge debt problems, mounting budget deficits and loss-making public enterprises, was clear enough: 'get prices right'. This, in policy terms, meant *laissez-faire* economics of deregulation, privatization and liberalization (Little in Lee ed. 1981; Lall 1985; Hicks 1989). These policy prescriptions were highlighted, in particular, in an influential study by the World Bank, *The East Asian Miracle*, (World Bank 1993). The optimism of this study concealed the seeds of destruction, such as excessive liberalization in an environment of corruption through rent-seeking and gate-keeping (Mehmet 1994), that drove these high-performing economies towards an inevitable collapse (see pp. 117–120 above).

But, how reliable is the neo-classical prescription of *laissez-faire* non-intervention? Not very, either on theoretical or empirical grounds. With regard to theory, the very logic of macro-economics favoured by the IMF and the WB rests squarely on intervention based on a standard package of stabilization and structural adjustment. Yet, as has been pointed out by Taylor (1988), based on empirical evidence from 18 LDCs, the situation of each country differs, implying that specific measures, rather than a common 'medicine', are required for each case. In practice, stabilization and structural adjustment requires a relatively long transitional period, normally three to ten years, with major human costs that inordinately burden the low-income groups. These costs did not enter IMF–WB SAL programmes until critical voices, such as UNICEF (Cornia *et al.* 1986) and others (Lewis *et al.* 1988) became loud and clear. Even then, when social funds have been set up, they have been inadequate relative to the task at hand.

In theory, the path of adjustment and stabilization is unclear and perilous. There are always numerous alternatives, with delicate problems of timing and turning-points, as well as the fact that the required information is rarely available. The policy-makers' dilemma is which path and policy menu to select, at what precise time, and

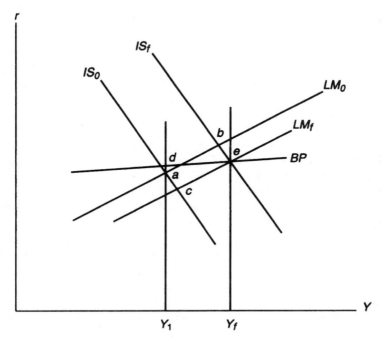

Figure 6.1 Alternative paths to full employment

how to monitor IMF–WB prescriptions. A fairly simple illustration using standard IS–LM–BP curves, is illustrated in Figure 6.1.

Suppose the economy happens to be at an initial point a where the IS_0 and LM_0 intersect. This point is well below the potential output of the economy designated by Y_f. Moreover, there is external deficit reflected by the PB curve below point a, and this fact alone may result in imported inflation, even though in theory unemployment and inflation cannot coexist simultaneously. Under these conditions, there are too many policy options to promote full employment output. Thus, transition to full employment equilibrium could be along a–b–e or a–c–e or a–d–e. Each path raises complex problems not only in terms of optimal timing, but also in packaging policies affecting the exchange rate, relative prices and interest rates.

Suppose, for example, that the first option, a–b–e, is initiated by fiscal policies, to achieve expansion and expenditure rationalization. The latter aims at reallocating public expenditures away from relatively unproductive towards more productive uses. If successful in practice, the strategy would generate growth in the markets for goods and services via an outward shift of the IS schedule to IS_f. The new macro-equilibrium at e is characterized by full employment at the higher aggregate income. But eliminating relatively unproductive expenditure programmes (for example, various subsidies) cannot be achieved instantaneously, since fiscal rationalization entails political losers and winners. Drastic measures along these lines can spill into violence, as has been demonstrated in numerous countries.

Alternatively, a monetarist intervention may be initiated via transition path along a–c–e. In this case, income growth would work through money markets via interest rate reduction or money expansion. This would lead to expansion of liquidity. Diagrammatically, it would shift the LM schedule to LM_f and income would rise from Y_1 to Y_f coinciding with macro-equilibrium at e. If, however, expectations or liquidity preferences do not match those of macro policy-makers, then the monetarist remedy would not work. Besides expectations, monetarism in developing countries would encounter additional institutional and structural obstacles (see pp. 105–106 above). Under a stabilization approach aimed at achieving external balance through devaluation and deflation, the transition path might be along a–d–e. Under this scenario, there would be austerity triggered by higher interest rates intended to achieve a net improvement in the capital account of the balance of payments; this measure would then be followed by devaluation and higher relative prices for imports in order to improve the trade balance. This complex austerity package, however, is no guarantee of success if export demand is inelastic or capital inflow is not forthcoming for reasons of strategic timing, political risk or other factors.

These textbook remedies may not exactly match IMF–WB policies. However, they do illustrate the fact that, analytically speaking, there are various alternative approaches to stabilization and structural adjustment, each with its own ambiguity, and none working smoothly or reliably as predicted. They all entail delicate balancing in terms of strategic timing and inter-policy shifts, and all of them give rise to social costs as the markets adjust. These social costs are real and fall disproportionately on the poor and vulnerable groups, such as women and children (Lele 1986; Lewis *et al.* 1988), necessitating costly programmes of social adjustment (Standing and Tokman 1991).

These social costs are highly burdensome, since typically the transition may take several years. Not surprisingly, the World Bank–IMF prescriptions have been roundly criticized for lacking a 'human face' (Cornia *et al.* 1986; Lipton 1990), especially in the case of Africa (Helleiner 1992). As a result, the Bank has moved to include poverty alleviation as part of its SAL strategy; for example, in Bolivia and Ghana (World Bank 1989: 18; World Bank 1990), though this has been too small a component in relation to the magnitude of social adjustment required. Also, more recently, the Bank has felt obliged to admit that the 'question remains open . . . whether an alternative adjustment path could have left the poor substantially better off than the actual path. Adequate information is not usually available to answer this question' (World Bank 1992a: 4).

In a more ideological sense, SAL lending has a Western, capitalist bias. It favours Western capital and technology, and tends to increase foreign control and ownership in developing countries. When Western banks are awash with funds, there is 'loan pushing' (Darity and Horn 1988: 3–4); but when there is belt-tightening, the borrowers are subjected to austerity through IMF–WB 'conditionality' (Killick 1984; Lipton 1990). The terms of 'conditionality' of SAL and debt rescheduling are determined in Washington, Paris or London in a manner which completely ignores the social and domestic policy constraints in borrowing countries. In more theoretical terms, it is also conveniently forgotten that it was Western theorizing which had built state capitalism and ISI industrialization in the Third World in the first place (see pp. 79–84 above). While theories and terms are simply reformulated in the West to ensure that foreign debts are repaid by borrowers, the true social costs, in the form of falling real wages and rising food prices, are borne by Third World victims. Ethnic violence and political instability, with food riots and civil wars, for example in Sri Lanka and several African and Latin American countries, are the pitiful manifestations of falling living standards for the sake of structural adjustment.

SUSTAINABLE DEVELOPMENT

Concern about falling living standards and diminishing food–population ratio in theories of economic development is nothing new; it goes back to Malthus (see pp. 38–43 above). This concern, along with related fears about limits to growth, the carrying capacity of the world's environment, conservation and ecology, began to gain renewed credibility in the 1970s. This movement was especially boosted as a result of the work of an influential group of Club of Rome scientists (Meadows *et al.* 1972; Tinbergen *et al.* 1976), who argued in favour of a zero growth rate for the sake of ecology. Schumacher (1973), another noted exponent, was an early advocate of low-cost, appropriate technology.

The turning-point in the emergence of sustainable development as a new paradigm occurred in mid-1980, specifically with the publication of the *Bruntland Report* (World Commission on Environment and Development 1987 – WCED).This report highlighted the conflicting nature of conventional economic growth and the environment, and popularized the concept of sustainable development (SD). While many, often conflicting, definitions have been offered of what exactly constitutes SD (South Commission 1990; World Resource Institute 1992; World Bank 1992; UNDP 1992), Western capitalist growth is increasingly recognized as the mainspring of unsustainability, destroying the rainforests, polluting lakes and rivers, and causing global warming. Externalizing ecology and the environment has amounted to treating Third World rainforests, waters and other natural resources as free goods. In other words, these natural resources have been under-priced, generating significant forms of global subsidies from the poor in the Third World to the affluent countries. These subsidies have been transmitted through trade and capitalization, developed and controlled in the West to finance a lifestyle of luxury for the privileged few at the top in the North, supported by mass poverty and deprivation in the South. The chief agents of this unequal exchange have been the MNCs, who, since colonial days, have undervalued assets to promote consumerism and wealth concentration in the North. Moreover. the trade–environment trade-off is acknowledged as a vehicle of unsustainability (French 1993), thus implying less trade and more self-reliant development in the developing countries in future (Daly 1993, 1993a).

In short, past economic growth and trade have been environmentally unfriendly, founded as they have been on inherently flawed Western economic axioms. Transition towards greater sustainability would require a more holistic approach to development, entailing inter-generational equity as well as harmonization of economic growth with other human needs and aspirations. In the words of the WCED: 'In essence, sustainable development is a process of change in which the exploitation of resources, the direction of investments, the orientation of technological development, and institutional change are all in harmony and enhance current and future potential to meet human needs and aspirations.'

Some new and encouraging signs of 'greener' development in the North are slowly emerging as demonstrated by greater sense of conservation and greater acceptance of 'social' and 'environmental labelling' (Hammelskamp and Brockman 1997). Most important of all, there are new and radical proposals that have been put forth to advance the cause of SD. Among these are ecotaxes on carbon emissions in high-income countries to finance ecobonuses to be distributed in the form of a monthly rent, on a per capita basis, in order to implement an active income policy that is environmentally friendly. These taxes amount to internationalizing fiscal policy, since pollution is a classic transboundary problem requiring international action. As such, international fiscal institutions and machinery would be required to administer such taxes and revenues, and to promote global sustainability. In particular, a major share of sustainability expenditures from ecotaxes in the North would have to be channelled to the South for investment in SD. Some proposals have been put forth before (Brandt Report 1980; Mehmet 1980) as autonomous transfers in place of official development aid, which has been declining since 1980, especially in terms of real resource flows (OECD 1990: 123) reflecting 'aid fatigue' (Toye 1993: 231). One such proposal is the Tobin Tax, originally put forward by Nobel Laureate James Tobin in the 1970s (See Box 12). Under this proposal, a 0.1 per cent tax would be imposed on all foreign exchange transactions which would yield a huge volume of revenue for investment in global sustainable development (ul Haq *et al*. 1996). In addition, the Environmental Financing Facility set up to

---

Box 12

The Tobin Tax proposal

In the 1970s, Nobel Laureate James Tobin put forward the intriguing idea of a small tax on all foreign-exchange transactions in order to limit speculative, short-term foreign exchange dealings. Such transactions do nothing for sustained, long-term development in host countries since the objective driving them is short-term capital gains. They are inherently destabilizing and, at least in theory, limits on such transactions make very good sense.

The main cause of the growth in speculative foreign exchange transactions is excessive and premature financial liberalization in global markets, vigorously promoted by the IMF. The most notable consequences of this strategy have been the 1994 Mexico peso crisis and the catastrophic Asian currency collapse of 1997–8.

A major merit of the Tobin Tax is its capacity to slow down speculative foreign exchange transactions while also generating huge amounts of revenue for global sustainable development. By 1997, the volume of foreign exchange transctions had reached US$1.3 trillion daily, and a 0.1 per cent Tobin Tax would yield enough autonomous revenue to put Third World development on a secure and sustainable footing without any 'strings-attached' aid.

Although the Tobin Tax proposal has been discussed at the Halifax G7 Summit, hosted by Canada, and though its technical feasibility is well established (Schmidt 1997), the proposal requires multilateral political agreement for any practical implementation.

---

implement Agenda 21 of the Rio Earth Summit is a potentially promising initiative (*Environmental Policy and Law* 1992: 265–7).

Without autonomous transfers attempts to promote monetization of ecology and the environment in the standard Western project-evaluation methodology ostensibly in aid of a green economy (Pearce *et al.* 1989) are dubious at best. Methodologically, monetization of ecological assets would be unreliable owing to the elusiveness of externalities, and hence it can be expected to be biased against future generations (van Pelt 1993). In pragmatic trade terms, monetization is more likely to facilitate the process of pro-Western capitalization of Third World resources, thus widening rather than narrowing global inequality and unsustainability.

The role of the World Bank in 'greening' economic development is of special importance. For one thing, the Bank has attempted to assume the mantle of environmental leadership (Conable 1990), and has endorsed the Global Environment Facility and the Montreal Protocol Fund intended to transfer funds to the South for environmental projects. It has also created administrative units inside the Bank, and has been recruiting ecologists and anthropologists for a more multidisciplinary approach. To date, however, its lending and decision-making remains in the hands of mainstream economists (Taylor 1993).

A fundamental issue in the SD debate is centred on how to prioritize the goals and objectives of a 'global partnership' for a sustainable world economy. As the Rio Earth Summit clearly exposed, Northern governments and agencies such as the World Bank (1992), view population growth in the developing countries as the top concern despite a strong counter-Malthusian position (Boserup 1981) derived from long-term trends of the impact of technology on food and demographic transition. Demographic pressures on the carrying capacity of the world are meaningless unless expressed in terms of consumption and income per capita. If and when this is done (Daly 1993a), then consumerism and income/wealth concentration in Northern countries emerge as the foremost policy target for action programmes to promote SD. Thus, in the former, average income per capita is over $12,000 compared with an average of just $800 in the South, implying that each consumer in the North is responsible for a multiple of 15 times the average depletion of resources by the average consumer in the South. Put differently, at this ratio, Northern consumption levels (e.g. each family owning two cars) would be utterly unsustainable if present economic development trends were to be replicated in the South. A truly 'global partnership' for SD would require an *internationally agreed upon constitution* for the global village, which would articulate goals, internationalize financing and define objective criteria for monitoring and enforcing sustainability rules.

In 1998, there was, sadly, little evidence of such a global partnership. In the Kyoto pact on global warming, whereby rich nations agreed to cut their collective gas emissions to about 5 per cent below the 1990 levels by early in the twenty-first century, the developing countries were notable by their absence. But, it is doubtful that even these minimal goals will be realized. And if 'rich nations do not control their emissions, poor ones will not even consider slowing theirs' (Jacoby *et al*. 1998: 61).

ENDOGENOUS DEVELOPMENT: HUMAN CAPITAL REVISITED

In the 1960s orthodox economics was shaken by the human capital revolution (Schultz 1961), which led to a 'generalized capital theory' (Johnson in OECD 1964) to solve the riddle of unexplained residual growth. At the same time the influential Chicago School pioneered by Schultz's disciples (Becker 1964; Mincer 1962) was instrumental in bringing about a significant expansion of investment in schooling, training and other forms of human capital formation in industrialized countries to raise labour productivity and enhance income equality. These initial expectations, however, were exaggerated both on theoretical (Weisbrod 1964; Jencks *et al*. 1972; Bowles and Gintis 1975; Blaug 1976) as well as on empirical grounds (Freeman 1976). Notwithstanding this, R&D policy and innovative, computer-based knowledge industry and entrepreneurship emerged as key sources of new comparative advantages in the First World, particularly in such new fields as electronics and telecommunications.

The human capital revolution had little impact on educational theory and policy in developing countries. There Eurocentric schooling remained very strong and dedicated to emulating colonial models and alien curricula irrelevant to post-independence requirements (Bacchus 1980: 259–64). Typically, the education system resembled an old tree with 'twisted roots' (Altbach 1989). Except in the case of the Far Eastern Dragons (see below), there was little adaptation of curricula to national requirements, and the dominant Oxbridge model of education ruled supreme in the Third World, producing relatively few 'loyal' graduates for the civil service. With 'rising expectations', enrolments exploded, but budgetary resources, especially in terms of real per capita allocations, declined, causing systemic underfunding and severe deterioration of quality, especially for underprivileged rural populations (UNESCO 1990, 1991). As part of SAPs, the adoption of user fees and other forms of privatization of education costs after the 1980s further limited accessibility and eroded the quality and efficiency of schooling in low- and middle-income countries. This resulted in further damaging the state of the children (UNICEF 1990) as reflected, for example, in higher drop-out and repetition rates as well as lower achievement levels in primary education – especially for students from disadvantaged status and family background (Fuller 1986: 493; Lockheed and Verspoor 1991).

The one significant educational innovation in the postwar period was in the case of the Far Eastern Dragons where the Eurocentric education model was quitely dismantled by modernizing ruling elites in favour of the Japanese or Confucian model (Weiss 1986; Mehmet 1988: chap. 2). Education was harmonized with the labour market through curriculum design and other made-at-home reforms, to fit national manpower requirements for rapid economic development; entrepreneurship was recognized as a key development resource. For example, in South Korea and Taiwan, education was utilized as an instrument of entrepreneurial development, both in industrial and agrarian sectors. In early phases of development, rural education was stressed to raise farmers' productivity through modern farm technology as part of agrarian reform (Lee 1979; Woo 1991); later, in these and other NICs, such as Singapore and Hong Kong, industrial and vocational (but not university) education was expanded and encouraged as part of 'learning-by-doing' industrial strategy to promote small enterprises as a basis for export-led industrialization (Mehmet 1988; Selvaratnam 1994).

The NIC approach to human capital formation matched what has now been recognized as 'total factor productivity' or endogenous technical change; here, human capital, particularly productivity-augmenting innovation and entrepreneurship, determine the rate of growth of an economy and its ability for integration in world markets. In neo-classical growth models, initial endowments of capital, labour and land, and their respective productivities, determine differences in growth rates or income per capita amongst nations; in endogenous models, by contrast, international growth and income differences are shown to depend on initial human and physical capital endowments (Lucas 1988; Romer 1990).

The new view of economic growth is presented by Scott (1989, 1991) who simply argues that growth is 'entirely due to investment . . . [which] by changing the world, both creates and reveals new investment opportunities' (1991: 5). Whereas Lucas and Romer rely on production functions and specify human capital capital/knowledge as a separate factor and as the key to economic growth, Scott abandons production functions and residual growth. Instead, he explains growth in terms of gross investment, defined in general terms to include both 'material' and 'quality-adjusted employment' inclusive of the effects of human capital investments (Scott 1991: 19–28).

Yet, all this sudden attention in mainstream theory to human capital is nothing new: It is re-visiting Schultz (1961) and Denison *et al.* in the 1960s (OECD 1962, 1964). In retrospect, the sad reality is that the developing countries, save for the Far Eastern NICs, had chosen to rely on the advice of Lewis, Harrod and Domar rather than Schultz and Denison. As a result they had missed the lesson of the first human capital revolution to invest in education for skill and entrepreneurial development, and to opt for R&D investments in innovation and technology generation at home. They missed this lesson because mainstream (Eurocentric) development economists dismissed the human capital revolution, banking instead on Big Push, two-sector and ISI theories of industrialization, believing to the end in the trickle-down process; however, in reality, MNCs emerged as the agents of inappropriate technology transfers from the West. Thus, the new view of growth is significant in one respect at least: it confirms the flawed theorizing of the 1960s and 1970s when investment in education for skills and entrepreneurship should have been given top priority, but was not. In short, the Far Eastern NICs' experience, a look-East model is the one to learn from, especially in terms of promoting 'shared growth' (Campos and Root 1996) through public investment in skills training and vocational education in the early stages of development.

SOCIAL CAPITAL

There is, however, one significant new contribution in the human capital field, namely, *social capital*, closely associated with Putnam (1993) and his collaborators, which extends neo-institutionalism to emphasize the importance of social networks and values such as trust in fostering development (See Box 13).

Social capital can be a positive factor in development through the acquisition of desirable values amongst households, communities and networks which bind societies in solidarity and promote cohesion and stability. As such, social capital can play an essential role in promoting 'good governance' and civil society (World Bank 1997). Alternatively, its absence can cause 'undesirable outcomes' ultimately leading to social disharmony and national disintegration as when the Mafia in Southern Italy or drug cartels in Colombia take

---

Box 13

Social capital

Originated by Robert Putnam, based on his work in Italy, in particular on the Mafia, social capital consists of social networks, such as the extended family, civic associations of all sorts, including at community and village level. The norms and values that bond these networks affect productivity and the outcomes of economic transactions. In particular, the quality of trust, the depth of reciprocity and obligations influence vitally contracts and their enforceability.

Social capital, which clearly goes beyond the conventional concept of 'human capital' can, to some extent at least, be acquired or shaped by investment in education. This is especially true in the case of the education of young girls, who, as future wives and mothers of the next generation, can be expected to play a crucial role in the quality of future human resources necessary for sustainable development.

---

control and rely on violence. Most recently, the concept of social capital has been linked to the idea of sustainable development and environmental management, including social forestry, better wildlife management and well-functioning village water associations (World Bank 1997a: chap. 6).

GLOBALIZATION OR TRIPOLARITY?

Globally, however, the world economy is at a turning-point. It is undergoing a multi-dimensional restructuring called 'globalization'. This has two major dimensions: political and economic. In political theory, globalization is the transition to one world or a global village; in economics, it is the emergence of an integrated world economy. The former is lagging; the latter is already evolving as a result of internationalizing production, consumption and trade patterns by creating global assembly lines, global supermarkets and by integrating the world economy into larger and newer forms. In this *de facto* sense, globalization empowers MNCs relative to nation-states, since, like oligopolies, they not only dominate markets, research and development, and investment and trade; they also undermine conventional public policy as tax laws, full employment policies and environmental protection regulations increasingly become 'obsolete, unenforceable, or irrelevant' (Barnet and Cavanagh 1994: 19). National policies are increasingly inadequate to overcome trans-boundary problems. Sovereignty has to be traded for international policy solutions to these problems.

De facto globalization, under existing capitalist rules of the game, favours capital and rewards owners of capital relative to labour. Thus, on the assembly lines in labour-surplus countries, job losses follow rising capital-output ratios as a result of such new strategies as 'flexibilization' of technologies and 'just-in-time' sourcing (UN Centre on Transnational Corporations 1988, 1993). Also, in high-income countries there is growth without employment due to technological deskilling; for example, the fastest-growing sectors, services, are being rapidly capitalized as offices become computerized and decision-makers join the electronic highways. Overall, there is swelling of technological unemployment (Liemt 1992; Barnet 1993). By 1993, a record 35 million workers were unemployed in the OECD countries alone (ILO 1994: 20), where a new 'underclass' is emerging, labelled the 'socially excluded'.

In product markets, there has long been globalization of consumer habits and advertising in the worldwide supermarket (Barnet and Muller 1974). In factor markets, computer-communication technol-ogies have already globalized capital and stock exchanges, while a cosmopolitan top-level manpower market is slowly emerging for the highly skilled in demand by MNCs (Fortune 1992). As dealers in technology and capital, MNCs are no longer kept 'at bay' (Vernon 1985, 1993); on the contrary, in the new world economy the MNCs are 'in' and the nation-state is 'out' as sovereignty is increasingly eroded by the forces of globalization (Rugman 1993). While 'social clauses' are entering trade agreements, MNC codes of conduct leave much to be desired (ILO 1993) in labour-surplus economies; here wages are not only low, but have been declining under structural adjustment and deregulation policies since 1980.

Mainstream economic theory has much to say about globalization, but, as with postwar development theorizing, is quite at variance with the practice of international business dominated by oligopolies without any effective rules or regulations. The principal theoretical construct is the factor payment equalization theorem (FPET) which predicts that, given perfect competition and unimpeded

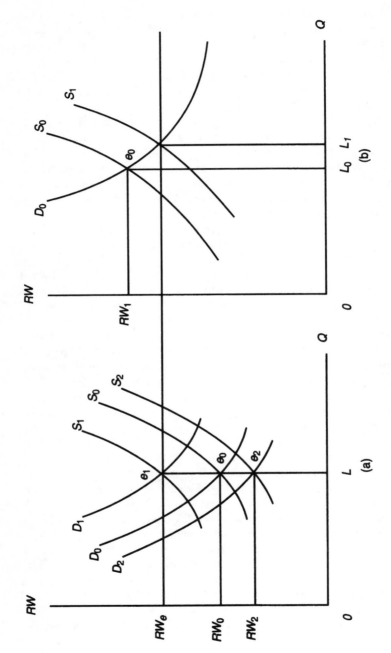

Figure 6.2 Factor equalization theorem: (a) low-income country; (b) high-income country

global factor mobility, in particular, market forces will ultimately equalize income levels.

FPET is illustrated in Figure 6.2 where panel (a) refers to a low-income country, and panel (b) to a high-income country. RW_e is the global equilibrium real wage (RW). Initially real wages in the low-income country are RW_0, while in the high-income country they are RW_1 determined by the interaction of supply–demand relationships in the respective labour markets. Under competitive assumptions, these markets clear at the intersection of supply and demand schedules at e_0, resulting in a global wage differential equalling $(RW_1 - RW_0)$. Since, by assumption, there is free and un-impeded international mobility of jobseekers, the wage differential generates outmigration from the low-wage to the high-wage country. As a result, supply is reduced in the former, and increased in the latter, shown by the shift from S_0 to S_1. To give more realism to the analysis (bearing in mind trends in the postwar period), it is assumed that in panel (a), demand for labour increases as result of economic growth, so that the volume of outmigration is actually less than it would otherwise be. Consequently, real wages are equalized, as predicted by FPET, with L volume of employment in panel (a) and a higher volume of employment in panel (b) indicated by L_1 relative to L_0.

But FPET has not worked as predicted. It has been invalidated by several causal factors in reality. First, although capital may move internationally with relative ease, there are passport and visa regulations which prevent international labour mobility. Second, technology transfers to the low-income country have been too capital-intensive, so that the labour absorption capacity of the economy in the low-income countries has actually shrunk, towards D_2 in panel (a). Third, structural adjustment programmes calling for downward wage flexibility in order to clear the market at e_2, have actually worsened real wages, reducing them to RW_2, which is often below subsistence levels for the sake of debt repayment (Dornbusch 1985).

What the above analysis demonstrates is that globalization, in the sense of equalizing incomes and economic welfare, is *not* working in accordance with the predictions of mainstream theory, as manifested by waves of ever-increasing refugees and mass-scale violence in many developing countries. Indeed, prospects in the foreseeable future are more pessimistic than optimistic. Before any global village emerges, there may be trade wars due to 'aggressive unilateralism' (Bhagwati 1991) and economic rivalry between new trade blocs. The signs of a post-Cold War tripolar world, or triadic blocs (Rugman 1993) are already evident, centred on the European Union (EU), the North American Free Trade Area (NAFTA) and the Pacific. If each bloc became inward-looking, as in Fortress Europe and Fortress North America, 'managed trade' might replace multilateralism generating trade wars between blocs as well as with the rest of the world. The most likely causes of trade wars would be 'old' irritants such as subsidies, dumping, tariffs and non-tariff barriers as well as 'new' conditionalities over human rights. At the grassroots level, too, globalization of capital-intensive technology can be expected to encounter resistance from peasants (for example, the case of Chiappas in Mexico) threatened by multinational and agri-business enterprises, aggressively pursuing profits at the expense of local peoples and ecology (Campbell in ILO 1993).

In the mainstream school there are always optimists. This is true for every generation. For example, reference may be made to John Stuart Mill who, writing about a hundred and fifty years ago, was convinced that a competitive market 'would be the nearest approach to social justice and the most beneficial ordering of industrial affairs for the universal good which it is now possible to foresee.' (Mill 1917: 792). Mill's optimism, like the presentday mainstream economists', derived from his deep-seated confidence in *laissez-faire* economics (Mill 1917: Book V, chap. XI). Significantly, Mill's confidence in the competitive market mechanism was so great that he believed it would also provide gender equality (ibid.: 757–60). Surely that is long enough to prove any theory!

Nevertheless, a more optimistic scenario cannot be ruled out. Such a scenario would likely be based on open regionalism, equitable multilateralism, and a more cooperative MNC–state relations (Eden and Potter eds 1993). This is, of course, provided there is appropriate, enabling international institution-building to promote such objectives. There are, to be sure, early signs of this from Southeast Asia, where members of the Association of Southeast Asian Nations (ASEAN), prompted by policy pragmatism above all else, are moving towards the ASEAN Free Trade Area (AFTA). It is possible that NAFTA countries may, in future, be linked with members in the NAFTA, to form a kind of Pacific Basin OECD (English and Smith in Bergsten and Noland eds 1993) based on shared prosperity and cooperation. Similarly, the new World Trade Organization may be able to utilize multilateralism, instead of unilateralism, to solve transboundary problems in support of environmental and social standards, thereby building on the work of the Uruguay Round of

GATT negotiations and emerging as the voice of reform in world trade.

Reforming the present world trading system is an imperative which can no longer be avoided. The system is outmoded since its institutional and legal bases were designed in the early 1940s by the victorious allies, well before the unprecedented growth and expansion in world trade in the postwar period. More fundamentally, as we have seen in the pages above, the system has strong Eurocentric roots which still promote neo-mercantilism.

A new international consensus is required as soon as possible for a rule-based regulation of world trade reflecting the ethics of global equity and sustainability, as well as the emergence of Japan, the NICs, China and the new economic integration movements in the pipeline. According to a recent estimate, there were no less than 34 regional integration arrangements in 1992 with a further 17 in prospect (Whalley and Young in Bergsten and Noland eds 1993). If world trade is to be harmonized with sustainability and equity, there should be non-discrimination in trade access, and its legal and institutional foundations should be updated based on truly global consensus. Such updating has to acknowledge openly, and seek to remedy adequately, the fact that past trade practice has gone largely unregulated and without rules of best practice. As a result, oligopolies and unfair trade practices have promoted global inequity, which has concentrated wealth in the North while impoverishing the South.

TOWARDS A RULE-BASED GLOBAL TRADE SYSTEM

Although there has been much discussion of human rights in recent years, to date globalization has so far meant freedom of movement for capital and technology, primarily empowering Western MNCs and capitalists. There has been only lip-service paid to freedom of labour in the global marketplace. Without parallel freedoms for people and workers to move across national and regional boundaries, the global trade system is in peril of degenerating towards a new age of slavery, systematically exploiting the weak and unorganized (such as women and children). The International Labour Office estimates that child labour is a growing global problem with at least 120 million working children between the ages of 5 and 14 (ILO 1996: 3). In India, the country with the highest incidence of child workers, it is estimated that there are 15 million child labourers in human bondage, typically as a result of failure to discharge a family debt, often transmitted from one generation to the next (Tucker 1997: 573). However, the problem is part of a much larger global challenge, intricately embedded within the globalizing capitalist system. Exploitation is rapidly emerging as the basis of global trade as countries compete with one another in a 'race to the bottom' to create new forms of comparative advantage risking social conflict and environmental degradation in the process.

Only a rule-based system of international regulation, based on global partnership, can prevent 'free trade' leading to new forms of slavery along the global assembly line. The essential ingredients of these global rules must be a universal floor of 'core' labour standards (Mehmet et al. 1999), administered by the ILO in collaboration with the WTO, and implemented by all international development agencies, in particular by the international financial institutions as part of their lending policies. Worker rights, as a specific form of human rights, must be harmonized in the global workplace in order to safeguard a level global marketplace. The way to start doing this is through universal declaration of a new charter of worker rights enshrined in 'core' international labour standards to serve as 'best-practice' for national policy. The Declaration of Fundamental Rights adopted by the International Labour Organization (ILO 1998) is a promising initiative in this direction.

7

CONCLUSION AND FUTURE AGENDA

In the postwar period, global inequality widened sharply; the rich countries got richer while the poor ones got poorer. Thus, according to the United Nations Human Development Report 1992, between 1960 and 1989, the countries with the richest 20 per cent of the world population saw their share of global GNP rise from 70.2 per cent to 82.7 per cent. During the same period, the share of countries with the poorest 20 per cent of the world population shrunk from 2.3 per cent to 1.4 per cent. As a result, '[the] consequences for income inequalities have been dramatic. In 1960, the top 20 per cent received 30 times more than the bottom 20 per cent, but by 1989 they were receiving 60 times more.' (UNDP 1992: 34). In the recent past, these trends have continued to worsen. Thus, during the period from 1985 to 1995, no less than 47 countries, mostly in Africa and the former Soviet Union, registered negative growth, while rich countries achieved positive growth (World Bank 1997: Table 1, pp. 215–16).

These results are as bitter as they are ironic. They reflect the fact that mainstream economics, the major theoretical yardstick which has guided the design of economic growth in developing countries, has failed to deliver what it promised – prosperity via economic expansion. Tricklism did not work, except in the case of the Far Eastern NICs where pragmatism and endogenous factors, (including domestic cultural values based on family and community), played the key role, as shown above (see pp. 114–117).

The economists' failure is, first of all, a technical one. It was originally perceived as a case of 'market failure'; but more recently the perception has shifted to 'government failure'. In reality it was a combination of both types. Second, and even more profoundly the economists' failure is also a moral failure because, like the nineteenth-century missionaries bent on saving souls of natives, it masks a dramatic change in the lives of masses of people for the promotion of economic growth. Regrettably, this change has generally been for the worse: increased poverty, joblessness, environmental degradation and, recently, waves of refugees trying to enter the privileged First World!

Mainstream development economics failed because economics is not a neutral, objective science. Indeed, far from being value-free (as claimed by those who believe in 'positive economics'), it has been too Eurocentric, too 'rationalist', dismissing alternative reasoning or worldviews as 'mistakes' or 'irrational' (Sen 1987: 69). Accordingly, it has always attempted to transplant Western norms and solutions into non-Western environments. This transplantation has extolled the technocratic method; it has been too divorced from ethics and history to be appropriate to the postwar development challenge of developing countries. According to Eurocentric theories, development has sought to capitalise Third World resources and has benefited Western interests at the expense of the welfare of the great majority of Third World populations. In many communities, people have become victims of capitalization or what was in fact 'anti-development' (Goulet 1992).

This study has sought to explore the deeper roots of Eurocentricity in positive (i.e. mainstream) economic development theorizing. At this deeper level of analysis the fundamental flaws are identified as the behavioural and subjective assumptions on which rest mainstream economics. In static terms, this ensures that the market forces of supply and demand clear. Market clearance is no more than a fleeting moment; it may be efficient at the point of equilibrium ensuring profit-maximizing output. But in the more normal state of disequilibrium, neither efficiency nor equity conditions hold in income distribution. Putting efficiency first, as mainstream growth economics does, effectively ignores equity; it rewards capital and marginalizes labour in the dynamic growth process. The typical efficiency argument by mainstream economists who object to people-focused basic needs (Streeten et al. 1981) or community development (Cernea ed. 1991) is that these are welfare schemes which reduce the growth rate. This is a voice endorsing capitalist growth. But when capitalism dominates market forces, all resources including ecology are gradually monetized and capitalized; while the market rewards capitalists concentrated in capital-rich countries of the First World, globally impoverishing the rest of the world.

Eurocentric economics presents a further problem: it is necessary to question the assumption of rational, self-interested economic man, narrowly defined within an objective function as a utility maximizer subject only to his own taste and budgetary constraints. Such behaviour encourages selfishness and rejects the ethics of altru-ism or reciprocity, i.e. interdependent utilities in a family or community. In the Walrasian equilibrium system, rational behaviour is no more than a mechanical self-satisfaction process of choice that is revealed in markets in which participation is strictly determined by an individual's ability to pay, regardless of how that ability is acquired. Honesty, virtue and justice are irrelevant in this market process, as is the question, for example, of how money may end up in secret Swiss bank accounts (was Marcos a rational utility maximizer?). The sole significant fact is that individualism clears the market. The Western market ennobles 'the selfish gene' (Dawkins 1989), and it does this in unsustainable, anthropomorphic terms.

Self-interested utility maximization looks like a fair competition; a game played on 'a level playing field', in which market forces objectively determine not only resource allocation, but distribution of rewards according to productivity. However, distribution and productivity are, in fact, subjectively determined by initial inequalities which the Pareto Optimality theorem ignores. In pragmatic policy terms, Western capitalism does not have an objective theory of distribution; it merely rewards the stronger. The inner logic of the system (which drives capitalism) is the extraction of supernormal profits by capitalists, captured as an additional return on capital. Hence, the capitalist has a single- purpose aim of continually expanding the capital base. Accordingly, under capitalism, all things that are potentially productive are converted into capital, sooner or later, replenishing and augmenting over time the return of the capitalist. 'Things' here include not only natural resources, but knowledge and technology as well as individuals themselves. Everything else which cannot be priced and marketed is externalized and ignored in the market process. Poverty is, then, attributed to 'irrationality', the fault of the poor, for the Eurocentric mind seems incapable of perceiving others' impoverishment as a systemic outcome, namely the converse of its own greed.

These Eurocentric biases of Western economics have resulted in the ennoblement of financial markets, and banks atop these markets, at the expense of the welfare of ordinary people. In its latest manifestation, capitalism has emerged as *financial capitalism*. Rewards are no longer based on thrift and hard work, but on 'playing the market', i.e. speculative transactions in global stock markets by portfolio managers of huge sums of finance pooled in banks and hedge funds

---

Box 14

Financial capitalism and 'social exclusion'

In its most recent phase, Western capitalism is evolving into *financial capitalism,* which empowers banks and financial asset owners whose portfolios are increasingly being internationalized. Against this wealth concentration, there is systemic disregard of social justice. Indeed, currently fashionable neo-liberal prescriptions (such as de-regulation, privatization, and user-pay principles) entail concentrated attacks on the welfare state and social safety net programmes.

Financial capitalism is now being globalized as a result of free capital mobility with increasing wealth concentration in the world. In this pro-capital globalization, it is important to observe that there is no effort to promote higher mobility for labour and worker rights. Consequently, a critical capital–labour asymmetry is emerging, with mounting social costs. The victims are migrants, refugees, displaced persons as well as vulnerable social groups such as women and children.

While these groups are mostly in the Third World, there is also a rising volume of the 'socially excluded' in the First World too.

---

relying on programme trading in financial (as opposed to real) assets, including derivatives and junk-bonds (See Box 14).

The social costs of the new global financial capitalism fall disproportionately on the poor and vulnerable groups such as migrants, women and children. While some of these groups reside in the First World and are now labelled as the 'socially excluded' (de Haan 1998), the bulk are in the Third World, victims of a new phenomenon of capital–labour asymetry in global markets (Mehmet *et al.* 1999). Under this asymmetry, there is free mobility of capital across national boundaries, but not of labour. Indeed, migrants, refugees and displaced persons are subjected to increasing mobility restrictions. As a result, an underground and illegal trafficking in human beings is being created by unscrupulous agents and middlemen in a new form of slavery (ibid., chap. 2).

Under this new financial capitalism, no currency or economy is safe. Fortunes can rise and fall unpredictably. The Indonesian débâcle, in the summer of 1998 in the wake of the Asian currency collapse ushering the downfall of Suharto, offers perhaps the clearest example of what can go wrong when people's welfare is sacrificed systematically and persistently by a regime blindly following neo-classical economic prescriptions modelled on Eurocentric premises. For two decades, Suharto's new regime was regarded as a success story within the context of the 'Asian miracle' (World Bank 1993). But Suharto's economics, built on Eurocentric economic advice, put finance and profit ahead of the welfare of the ordinary Indonesians. While building toll-roads, luxury buildings and supermarkets, all functioning to concentrate wealth at the top, Suharto ignored employment and the basic needs of the masses, relying on the military to suppress workers and peasants. When the banking system collapsed under the weight of the Asian currency crisis, the poor and unemployed ran onto the streets, staging an Indonesian variant of 'people power', and suddenly bringing down the oldest and most corrupt dictatorship in Asia.

The 'lesson' here is that Third World leaders and regimes which rely on Eurocentric economics are like the captain of the *Titanic*: they risk all on market forces. Capitalist economics is founded on inequality, and ultimately it must explode because its inner logic, profit, depends, as explained in Chapter 1, on market fluctuations; that is, what goes up must come down. While these fluctuations reward capitalists and speculators, the capitalist economy ignores social justice because it is a system working to reward Eurocentric interests. In particular, the big winners are the Western banks and financial houses situated atop the system, now rapidly globalizing. In this system, the IMF, in theory mandated to stabilize the world financial system, has become a 'curse rather than a cure' (Kapur 1998) precisely because it has allowed itself to emerge as a front for creditors even risking social conflict in borrowing countries.

In the age of globalization, Western economics is fundamentally flawed (Rodrik 1998). Since the time of Adam Smith, as we have seen in the first part of this study, Western capitalism has steadily been globalizing. This has been capitalism's 'great ascent' (Heilbroner 1963), although, as noted above, for the great majority of humankind, victims of pro-capital growth, it has been more aptly a case of *great descent*. In the postwar period, colonialism gave way to the Third Worldism, and development economics emerged as a field of study, an offshoot of positive economics. In the international economy, MNCs have been empowered, initially under the protectionist ISI strategy which introduced branch-plant manufacturing in enclave economies. Slowly but surely, exploitation of Third World resources via monetization and capitalization for consumerism and wealth concentration in the First World accelerated, with little regard for environmental sustainability. In time, neo-Marxist and revisionist branches of development economics evolved to provide alternative paradigms to mainstream theorizing. But, mainstream development economists have dominated the commanding heights, both in the 'ivory tower' and in the policy field, especially in such important donor agencies as the IMF and the World Bank. Even with best intentions and good faith in development, mainstream economists, nevertheless facilitated the evolution of an increasingly unsustainable and inequitable world economy.

Much of the blame for this unfair outcome must be attributed to the subjective and cultural biases hidden behind Western positive economics. Thus, mainstream development economics has been Euro-US-centric; it is formulated by Westerners for Western interests, often through the instrumentality of donor agencies. Western aid has promoted the economic developmentalism of outsiders looking in to acquire a 'bird's-eye' view of an economy to be developed or modernized, in accordance with predetermined models and modes of Eurocentric thinking. The ahistorical, engineering approach to economic development has succeeded, to an astonishing degree, in rationalizing and justifying the globalization of capitalism in a grand logic of exploitation of non-European resources and peoples, for the concentration of wealth and income in the West.

But the limit has already been reached, unfolding in the First World itself no less than elsewhere. The ideology of Third Worldism (Harris 1987) is vanishing under the weight of new realities. Sustainability and the greening of high-income economies is leading to a more conservationist society, putting new restraints on consumer sovereignty. The end of the Cold War is testing the capacity of capitalism to convert from an industrial–military basis to a more peaceful production basis. The new hi-technology and communications (the latest form of capitalization) have dramatically altered the skill mix in the demand for labour, causing flexibilization in the labour market (Kaplinsky 1988) and creating deskilling and technological unemployment (Liemt 1992). This is productivity growth without jobs. A new generation X is growing up as the 'socially excluded' with uncertain career prospects and a shrinking social safety net! Meanwhile, the Western nation-state is declining in efficiency, in large measure due to poor leadership at the top. Indeed, political leadership has become captive to TV ratings of popularity with little or no concern for democracy at home or to the challenges of globalization and internationalism.

Under the cumulative impact of these challenges, Western capitalism is reaching the limit of exhaustion of goods and services for profitable exploitation. There are powerful voices of dissent from environmentalists worried about an increasing conflict between economic growth and sustainable development (Daly and Cobb 1994; Ayres 1997) and there are philosophical challenges to the rationalist foundations of Western civilization (Saul 1992; Gray 1998). In the meatime, a 'crime pays' mentality is emerging as gambling, drugs, pornography and other 'evils' are becoming the new frontiers of corporate capitalism. There is erosion in American cultural values (Harrison 1992); while neo-conservative pop-philosophers blame decadence and moral decay within, drawing parallels with the final days of Rome. It is said that America is being frayed in a divisive 'culture of complaint' (Hughes 1993). There are growing signs of 'racial polarity, educational dysfunction, social fragmentaton of many and various kinds' (Kaplan 1994: 76) contributing to a declining US economy similar to England about a hundred years earlier (Kennedy 1993: chap. 13; Porter 1990). In response, American trade policy-makers are adopting aggressive unilateralism (Bhagwati 1991: 48), relying on article 301 and super 301 of the US trade law and other legislative means to extract concessions and impose its will on others, while risking trade wars in the process.

This 'zero-sum' view of international trading is neo-mercantilism, as inward-looking trade blocs such as the EU attempt to assume a dominating position in the world economy. In the Asia-Pacific, the once-confident Japan and the new Tigers in Southeast Asia have seen their enviable GNP growth rates of 7–8 per cent p.a. evaporate suddenly in the wake of 1997–8 Asian currency collapse. As we saw (pp. 117–120 above), much of this growth performance was artificial, owing to government policies that deliberately under-priced environmental and labour resources in a misguided attempt to manufacture comparative advantage. In reality, however, these inappropriate pricing policies merely facilitated the process of capitalization (see chap. 1, esp. Appendix).

But all is not lost. The idea of a 'Third World', like colonialism, is effectively dead. In the developing world there are dramatic new realities emerging. There is fatigue with foreign aid, and increasing resentment of new 'conditionalities' in trade/aid relations. In an age of chronic debts, deficits and declining budgets, the economic and political destinies of nations now increasingly rest on indigenous sectors and on domestic actors themselves. That accountability begins and may end at home is being increasingly acknowledged. In some of the poorest countries, people are empowering themselves through self-help projects in the slums and in the informal sectors to solve their own problems. Thus, in Bangladesh there is a new banking system, the Grameen Bank, in which character-lending takes the place of conventional (Western) asset-lending; in Karachi, Pakistan, the poor slum dwellers have organized themselves to form the Orangi sewerage project to clean up their environment (World Bank 1992: 109). These made-at-home solutions are admittedly small projects in the totality of world poverty, but they are indicative of future paths and the possibilities ahead for development. The last 50 years painfully show that not only are there no 'quick fixes' for modernization, but also that Eurocentric blueprints imported from the West for economic growth do not work.

Developing countries are not homogeneous, notwithstanding such labels as 'the Third World'. The narrow, reductionist assumption of the self-interested maximizer (which rationalist economics claims to be 'universal') clashes with the realities found in different countries, where ethics, history and economics are interwoven into more distinct, yet holistic, conceptions of the individual, state and nature. Culture-specificity abounds everywhere, as people seek or reassert their identities. In this sense, Western economics has caused immense damage in that it has destroyed group values and local cultures for an unfilled promise of mass prosperity. The blind pursuit of self-centred individualism was a global attempt at Westernizing the Third World through successive paradigms, documented above, that facilitated massive inflows of inappropriate technology, skill transfers and conditional aid, followed by mass-scale deprivation, debt and destruction.

Institutional and structural changes are also unfolding in the world economy. The Pacific rim, until recently confidently surging ahead with dynamism, is now facing recession in the face of the Asian currency crisis. This downturn however, may have some salutary effects both on politics and the economy, resulting in essential reforms for civil society and greater economic self-reliance based on higher environmental and labour standards. The earlier predictions about the twenty-first century being the 'Pacific century' (Inoguchi 1994), may still turn out to be accurate, once the Japanese economy recovers and China keeps growing and gains WTO membership. On this basis, China's economy would surpass the USA's as early as 2002

(Kristof 1993: 61); according to Japanese projections, the size of the East Asian economies early in the next century will be more than twice that of the USA (Furukawa 1993: 49). Also, in other regions of the developing world, the next century will witness the emergence of new powers reflecting newly acquired comparative advantages. Some notable candidates on this list include Indonesia in South-east Asia, given its riches in natural resources and a large market; a secular and emerging economic power in the Middle East, Turkey, with surplus water in a region running dry; Brazil in South America controlling the vast resources of Amazonia; and, possibly Nigeria in West Africa, if it can peacefully return to civilian rule and channel its oil wealth into national development. The path of progress, however, is seldom straight ahead; more likely it will be marked with instability arising from regime changes or regional conflicts, as demonstrated by the sudden collapse of the Suharto regime in Indonesia in 1998, where things will most likely get worse before getting better in the next century.

Meanwhile in the West, serious structural and societal change is under way. The European Union is pushing ahead with a single currency and eastward expansion and Germany is emerging as the dominant power. US influence in this new Europe is declining. Across the Atlantic, while the North American Free Trade Area and free trade with the Americas are increasing, within the USA and Canada there is rising inequality and social polarization, with a serious decline in public education and in such institutions as family. Consumerism is the new religion, but it is being financed by an unprecedented expansion of credit and personal indebtedness. Western liberal democracies are facing new threats from within and without, their privilege as an island of affluence in a world of poverty challenged by waves of refugees and economic migrants flooding in. Europe, in particular, seems unsure of its destiny and borders and is haunted by new threats from 'the East' (Hobsbawm 1993), perhaps awaiting the uncertain outcome of Yeltsin's Russian experiment. In fanciful grand designs, Eurocentric prophets see Western civilization in peril along its 'fault-lines', due to the threat from an imaginary Islamic–Confucian coalition (Huntington 1993). With a growing army of unemployed, Europe is experiencing a new wave of fascism, ethnic cleansing and racism. As a result, the West is losing those very credentials it claimed in the age of Eurocentric developmentalism. In the future, 'civilizations' or cultures may indeed become more significant as cultural reassertion signals the decline of the Western invention of the nation-state based on a territorially-juridically bounded sovereignty (Gottlieb 1993). Yet, more likely than *inter*-civilizational clashes as predicted by Huntington, would be civil wars and regional or *intra*-civilizational conflicts in the transitional state marked by chaos, anarchy and disorder especially in Africa where the colonial legacy is undergoing deconstruction (Kaplan 1994).

What, then, is likely to be the agenda of economic development for a post-US–Eurocentric world (i.e. less manifest destiny and whiteman's burden) that features a declining Western role and influence in international development? Western international relations theory, conventionally focused obsessively on East–West relations (Neuman ed. 1998), is certain to become increasingly irrelevant to developing nations as they take increasing control of their economic and social development. While Western powers may attempt to impose their visions and definitions of human rights and labour codes on the developing countries, unilateral and bilateral 'conditionalities' will be resisted, especially if, as expected, foreign aid flows continue to diminish. Instead of unilateral or made-in-the-West prescriptions, it is more likely that in future human rights and labour standards will evolve out of multilateralism based on inter-cultural dialogue and multi-cultural consent. Similarly, 'environmental trade measures' (ETMs), if imposed from outside as part of Western unilateralism, are likely to be perceived, and opposed in the South as neo-mercantilist strategies. Multilateralism, on the other hand, is likely to prove more effective, especially if Northern countries seriously dedicate themselves to promoting fair global trade and greater social justice in the international workplace, by supporting North–South dialogue on these issues and working in a less paternalistic and more equal basis in the spirit of global partnership through the new World Trade Organization and the International Labour Organization. For their part, the international financial institutions need to update and reform their mandates to become more effective funding agencies for sustainable development in the South rather than as instruments of Western capitalism.

At the same time, and generally speaking, it can be expected that as new economic orders are slowly reconstructed from within, socioeconomic development will become more pro-labour and less capital-biased. The new development priorities would place more weight on community values and less weight on individualism when compared to the past; more developing countries would assert their own domestic needs and requirements in tandem with an increasing responsiveness to domestic demands for a better quality of life. This could only empower and enrich local cultures and institutions, thus creating a more self-reliant, and hence more natural and organic, relationship between the rulers and the masses.

Also, as part of the same process, extensive deconstruction in Euro-centric theorizing can be expected in order to acknowledge and reverse the damaging legacy of Westernization as development: This is especially true of its pro-capital (i.e. anti-labour) growth strategies that have favoured capital-rich countries. Generalizing from the above survey, it can be concluded that mainstream economic theories of Third World development have worked, even when unintended by the theorists themselves, as tools of Western capitalism. This has created global inequity and an unsustainable culture of Northern consumerism at the expense of mass impoverishment in the South.

Five distinct phases in theory construction can be identified, each revealing a strong, period-specific Eurocentric slant:

1   In the classical (pre-1914) period, when Eurocentric theorizing derived from a strong presumption of Victorian cultural superiority over others was taken for granted, the idea of 'development' did not mean the welfare of colonial populations. It openly and unashamedly meant exploiting and capitalizing natural resources, trading in slavery or human labour as a commodity, encroaching on tribal or native land, investing in plantations, mines and railways, all for profits and dividends transmitted to the mother country. Classical growth theory, defined as capital accumulation, was anti-labour, regarding population as the antithesis of growth.

2   During the second (post-1914) period, the Eurocentric order was gradually replaced by the Euro-American order which was reconstructed on Three Worlds. Economic growthmanship emerged as the new gospel going out from the First World to save the Third World, against a perceived communist threat from the Second. Under increasing American intellectualism, neo-classical growth theories, collectively termed 'tricklism', aspired to win the 'hearts and minds' of the people of the Third World as part of the global containment policy aimed at the Second World. Regrettably, however, the neo-classical growth theories retained their pro-capital, anti-labour biases, promoting capitalization with renewed vigour. The Third World, or more aptly selected countries therein, became favoured recipients of large inflows of foreign aid and Western technology and skill transfers in a

top-down process of state-led industrialization to become 'modern' – in short, to promote the Westernization or Americanization of the Third World. In the process, MNCs have been empowered (initially thanks to ISI policies), and they emerged as agents for the transfer of inappropriate technologies to the Third World. This contributed to financial as well as ecological unsustainability.

3   During the third phase, starting after the mid-1960s, economic growthmanship began to give way to growth-with-equity (GwE) theories which were still based on the conventional Eurocentric biases of 'made in the West' prescriptions. Somewhat surprisingly, the World Bank under McNamara assumed a leading role in GwE theorizing. However, this was half-hearted and short-lived, and was soon replaced by a new WB–IMF neo-classical orthodoxy and counter-revolution (Toye 1993); this was typically a case of adjustment with heavy social costs and without a 'human face'.

4   During the 1980s, against the backdrop of crushing foreign debt and budget deficits (reflecting the ultimate failure of past theorizing), restructuring and stabilization emerged as the new medicines to cure the errors of the past. Positive economists lost their monopoly of commanding heights; development studies became broader and increasingly multi-disciplinary, more gender-neutral and less Eurocentric. By the end of the decade, even the WB–IMF structural adjustment lending began to take a more human face to address the emerging issues of the social costs of adjustment and increasingly unsustainable development. However, the weight of the social costs mounted, measured not only by growing labour market imbalance, but in terms of violence, riots and social conflict (Rodrik 1998).

5   Recently, Western theorizing on Third World development has sought to come to terms with the dilemmas of post-modern realities with the end of a bipolar world and the new NIC challenge from East and Southeast Asia. This new political economy of development, especially with renewed interest in institutionalism, has put into question the social efficiency of institutions, contracts and rights, and even of the state itself. But the most intriguing trend has been the emergence of the Far Eastern endogenous development model (Mahbubani 1992; Kausikan 1993) which has resulted in other developing countries looking East rather than West for the acquisition of new comparative advantages. To be sure, the Asian Model had its intrinsic

weaknesses (see pp. 117–120), which ultimately resulted in the currency collapse of 1997–8, but this is not a permanent failure, merely a temporary setback necessitating political and economic reforms for greater self-reliance.

In all these phases, there is no denying the great intellectual achievements of development economics as a field which has produced an impressive crop of Nobel Laureates. At the same, it would be a linear projection to claim that 'development economics continues to be alive and well' (Ranis and Schultz eds 1988: 1); this would ignore the serious analytical, empirical and ethical dilemmas of economic development.

This study has attempted to demonstrate that increased global inequality is not accidental. Rather, it stems from Eurocentricity – the deep-seated Western propensity to ignore the inherent flaws in neo-classical market theory by deductive, rationalist idealization at the expense of realistic analysis. These flaws, cumulatively and progessively contributing to capitalization, have been pro-capital and have favoured owners of capital and capital-rich First World countries; simultaneously, and as part of the same process, they have been anti-labour, thereby impoverishing the masses of the Third World. This study points in particular to the following three conclusions.

The Eurocentric mindset

The most remarkable aspect of mainstream economic development theories was the us–them mindset of the Western theorists; the former being the 'rational' and ideal, and the latter being the 'irrational' and inferior. In this context, to develop was simply a transitive verb – the subject 'us' doing it (namely, development) for the objectivized 'them'. Intertwinted with these normative motives was the classical and neo-classical orthodoxy justifying the search for capitalist profits and surpluses. These theories promoted a kind of religion of the marketplace in which, behind the myths of helping outsiders, the reality was an unlevel playing field the rules of which always favoured 'us'. The Western presumption of superiority embedded in the idealized, abstract theory also acted as a cultural escape route for Westernized local elites; it facilitated their endorsement, with appropriate incentives, of plans and strategies to deplete and transfer asset values out of a Third World rich in natural resources, but, nevertheless, mythologized and stereotyped as irrational, inferior and, above all, underdeveloped.

Abstraction was an essential part of the Western myth of technocratic tricklism. The theories surveyed above have all been *a priori*, deductive constructions of outsiders looking in, without adequate historical, cultural or institutional knowledge. This has led to the implementation of technocratic prescriptions and strategies lacking realistic grounding. None of the theories surveyed above has been constructed inductively and with an open mind from actual realities within the developing countries themselves; as a result, critical empirically based voices, went unheeded. The sole case of successful economic take-off in the Third World, namely, the case of the Far Eastern NICs, was achieved independently and out of policy pragmatism. It was shaped by indigenous or national necessity reflecting internal cultural values and choices, despite, rather than because of, Western mainstream theorizing; although some, as we have seen, it has sought to fit this case, *ex post facto*, into the neo-classical theoretical mould.

Reductionism: economic rationality versus ethics

Eurocentric theories of economic development are distanced from ethics in order to formulate an 'engineering' view of economics (Sen 1987). As a result, mainstream theories of economic development are not only rationalist, but also reductionist constructions; human relations are reduced to market relations, assumptions are substituted for reality, and wisdom is confused with rational behaviour expressed in a cash-based ability to pay. Individuals with needs but no cash are ignored as 'losers'; those with cash are empowered as successful 'winners'. This accounting, explicitly or implicitly, marginalizes group preferences or entitlements (Sen 1987: 71–3).

In the reductionist view, economic development is synonymous with economic growth requiring functional inequality as a condition of the pro-capital bias of growth. This is then justified on efficiency grounds or by vague appeals to borrowed political ideologies. For example, Arndt, an exponent of economic reductionism, concludes his book, *Economic Development: The History of an Idea* (1989: 177), by justifying economic growth for promoting individual 'human choice'. He says: 'The advantage of economic growth is . . . that it increases the range of human choice. The case for economic growth is that it gives man greater control over his environment, and thereby increases his freedom.'

But what exactly these key terms (e.g. choice, freedom) mean is never explicitly stated. In fact, 'choice' is often limited by ability to pay; this means that the poor are disenfranchised as if they have no willingness to buy, merely because they lack cash-based ability. Similarly, 'freedom' is, once again, something proportional to one's net worth! The appropriateness of terms like 'man' (i.e. the individualistic decision-maker) or 'environment', needs to be re-evaluated. For example, in the light of the sustainable development debate, quite the opposite to what Arndt suggests would appear to be closer to sustainability.

The engineering view of economic development loses sight of the ethics of the process, ignoring such human virtues as reciprocity, sharing and cooperation. Therefore, abandoning reductionism would re-integrate ends and means in a more holistic framework going beyond Eurocentric rationalism, and would recognize the relevance of group, as opposed to private, benefits and costs. That would broaden the boundaries of development studies to include non-economic topics such as ethnicity and ethnic conflict (Horowitz 1985) as determinants of resource allocation in economic development. This is all the more essential as it is now evident that social conflict in the Third World has emerged as a significant part of development studies. Regrettably, this conflict is often caused by inappropriate economic policies such as structural adjustment and IMF-imposed 'conditionalities' imported from the West (Rodrik 1998). For example, a banking system which is designed exclusively according to IMF 'conditionalities' is likely to work more as an agency of foreign investors and as a facilitator of foreign debt repayment rather than as an instrument of socio-economic development at home. For genuine sustainable development, there can be no alternative to made-at-home solutions based on a realistic appraisal of domestic capacities and potential that often depend on cultural and institutional determinants. In other words, development studies must become more interdisciplinary and far broader in scope than conventional (Western) economics. A broader agenda like this would incorporate indigenous cultures and institutions within an endogenous development theorizing.

Endogenous development and pro-labour development

The main challenge facing development economists is how to shift towards a more holistic field of study, to dynamize and harness endogenous sources of growth for sustainable, human development. A pro-labour, people-focused development that empowers local cultures and places the individual in a community (not as some isolated, egoistic utility maximizer) is the path for sustainable development. Education and human resource development policies must be relevant to local environments in order to mobilize and utilize local-level energies, especially in indigenous sectors and microenterprises (Levitsky ed. 1989).

Pro-labour development does not mean the rejection of technical change or capital; indeed, capital goods and new technologies are essential and desirable for generating value-added. But, there must be a balance in the distribution of such value-added to ensure that local people benefit no less than outsiders; these people must also be involved in technology choices, and in assessing and articulating needs and the means to achieve them. Grassroots voices and reasoning should be respected and, indeed, actively sought out as a basis for problem-solving strategies. As such, local cultures need to be empowered, and not dismissed as barriers or obstacles. Improvement in the quality and capacity of local institutions to solve human problems (an essentially technical task) is where the economist, along with the engineer, may assist the most; however, the social and cultural appropriateness of the economist in this process must be determined, partly in a multi-disciplinary framework, but ultimately with reference to the actual developmental impact on the lives of the community as a whole.

Pro-labour development enhances human beings as creative agents, while employment creation dignifies the individual as a worker and expands the labour share of income. To these ends, labour standards and the legal protection of workers are essential through clear and enforceable legal codes to ensure adequate wages and healthy working conditions. But laws, *per se*, are not enough; there must be effective implementation to promote economic justice in the labour market. Likewise, improving the social efficiency of local institutions to solve community problems as a necessary pre-condition for endogenous development to benefit present and future generations must evolve out of grassroots democracy, as a result of direct participation and dialogue with the affected peoples and communities.

'TRADE IS NOT ENOUGH'

In this sense, economic growth is far more than the naive neo-classical belief that 'trade will do the job', i.e. that specialization and exchange according to Ricardian trade theory can work as a proxy for low savings and inadequate domestic demand capable of leading a low-income economy willing to rely on international trade to achieve mass prosperity through 'tricklism'. We have learnt that such pre-scriptions are subject to (1) 'export pessimism' due to the expanding number of exporting countries all competing for a share of markets in high-income countries and (2) external vulnerability with rising foreign debt and control.

Put in positive terms, Third World development needs to be more pro-labour and less pro-capital. Labour and environmental resources in developing countries must be priced more realistically to stop (indirect) subsidization of capital. It must be noted that pro-labour development is not anti-trade. It is anti-mercantilist, whereby trade is seen as a 'zero-sum' game in a 'cowboy–Indian' mentality, enriching the rich and powerful by impoverishing the poor and the weak. Future trade policy needs to shaped by a genuine effort to distribute the gains of trade equitably amongst trading partners, with prices and terms ensuring sustainability for the sake of present and future generations.

But these are only necessary and not sufficient conditions. They are means towards the higher end of human development, which, of course, cannot be divorced from such ethical values as social justice, cooperation, harmony and global equity at the international level. Outsiders do have a role in this bottom-up, evolutionary and holistic approach; however, this role must be conditioned and shaped by an open mind, ready first and foremost to learn and appreciate local environments and cultures before prescribing remedies or reforms. Transplantations or impositions must be avoided.

Endogenous development implies that in the future development economists would shift from *a priori*, deductive theorizing formu-lated as blueprints from outside, towards a more inductive, factual research agenda formulated internally and grounded on actual social reality and articulated bottom-up. Careful study and evalua-tion of internal institutions and cultural norms are essential, and should be based on hard evidence. Consistent with realistic social science, corruption and injustice, as cases of waste and inefficiency, must be exposed; visiting academics and researchers in the field need to utilize local authors and experts in diverse disciplines, in order for coherent and reliable images of internal reality to emerge. In the words of Douglas North (1990: 140): 'We need to know much more about culturally derived norms of behavior and how they interact with formal rules to get better answers to such issues. We are just beginning the serious study of institutions.' Thus, economic growth to serve sustainable development requires deep structural transformation in social, economic and political institutions within developing economies. Central in this transformation must be respect for basic human rights, and policies which enable the empowerment, not destruction, of local initiatives and agencies for development.

This is 'good governance', a subject which has now emerged as a key precondition of world development (World Bank 1997). The credibility of the state is now seen as an essential ingredient to lay the foundations of development. There must be clear and enforceable rules, not only for purposes of investment, but also for ensuring trust and confidence in contracts and in the capacity of institutions to foster and enable development. In brief, development requires 'civil society' and 'social capital' (Putnam *et al.* 1993) because 'human capital is not enough' (Adelman and Taft 1997: 832). Rather, it is a long-term, historical process that is increasingly multi-disciplinary as opposed to technocratic prescriptions such as the notorious 'capital-is-everything' theory.

REFORMING INTERNATIONAL RELATIONS

Western international theory has always rested on hegemonic premises, dividing the world into abstract us–them categories. The exploitation of Third World peoples and resources, before, during and after the age of colonialism, has been justified not only on biased economic theorizing, but in literature, culture and religion whereby the 'other' has been presented as inferior. This inferiority in Western theories of international relations matches the ethnic/ nationalistic premises of capitalist economics as exposed in the pages above. Western leaders, educated on these faulty theories, end up lacking the necessary internationalist vision (which briefly prevailed immediately after World War II) to contribute to the emergence of a truly global village based on 'one global family'.

As a result of an inadequate commitment to internationalism in Western economic and political circles, the existing international organizations, constructed by Western architects, continue to linger on the sidelines, still burdened by the patronizing Eurocentric assumptions that gave rise to them in the first place. Their mandate and functions are still shaped by Western interests. The voices of developing countries are marginalized. International fora, from the Vienna Human Rights Summit to the Copenhagen World Summit for Social Development, while laudable in terms of their scope and aims, nevertheless, tend to remain as lofty ideals on paper (UN 1995).

Development economics, which emerged as a discipline in the postwar period, has operated within this unequal structure of Western international relations theory. From the earliest forms of foreign aid and technical assistance in the 1950s to the latest programmes of structural adjustment and IMF stabilization, developing countries have been regarded as passive recipients of Western advice and prescriptions, typically on patronizing terms. As demonstrated in the preceding pages, these have been fundamentally flawed, resting as they have on Eurocentric premises, and, thefore, they have failed to generate the promise of mass prosperity. The Marshall Plan in postwar Europe worked because Europeans, even in defeated countries, were not patronized into marginality; they were left to run their own affairs. The US Lend–Lease programmes of aid supplemented and reinforced European recovery plans made at home. These aid programmes worked because they were based on sound (European) social grounding, restoring and repairing European institutions; they did not aspire to convert Europeans into Americans!

Western aid to the Third World in the postwar period lacked social grounding. Instead of building and reinforcing local institutions, Western aid attempted to transfer Western values and institutions to developing countries. In overcoming the current 'aid crisis' the joint responsibilities of donors and receipients must be acknowledged, perhaps within a new 'development contract' emphasizing ownership rather than conditionality (Killick 1998).

But the cultural and social grounding of development economics, in relevant local environments, would not be enough. A new, reformed system of international relations is required to achieve global equity. Existing bilateral and multilateral institutions are in need of radical reform for greater internal efficiency and actual developmental effectiveness. The postwar foreign aid system is too dysfunctional and should be reformed in the context of broader reforms of international relations.

Three categories of reforms in international relations are called for. First, at the global level, agreed international ethical codes and enforcement rules are essential to transcend Eurocentricity; in particular, neo-mercantilism in trade relations, towards greater global equity. This may well require 'one more revolution' (O'Manique 1994), a cultural one leading to global partnership in order to replace unilateralism with multilateralism in trade, aid, the environment and human rights. An essential precondition of such a global partnership has to be effective curbs on consumerism in the North, with appropriate taxes and higher prices for Third World resources, to pay for ecological and developmental expenditures in the South.

Second, macroeconomic policies need to be coordinated internationally through summitry and closer and effective North–South dialogue over transnational boundary problems in the fields of environment, technology, trade and development. Western economics has risen, and is now declining, with the Western idea of a sovereign nation-state, as the latter erodes under the pressure of globalization and transboundary problems that demand internationally agreed actions and remedies. New communication technology is inching humankind towards the global village, although racism, injustice and violence, in rich and poor societies alike, make the road ahead far from peaceful and straight. More realistically, financial markets have already been largely internationalized, although without minimal international regulation, a pattern of instability is likely to be the order of the day. International regulation must be comprehensive in at least two respects. First, participation in rule-making should be comprehensive, i.e. involve developing as well as developed countries. Second, it should cover all markets, not just capital, but labour markets. On both of these counts, the ill-fated Multinational Agreement on Investment (MAI) proposed by the 29 richest countries at the OECD was a failure. At a minimum, MAI must be complemented by a parallel multilateral agreement on labour mobility and worker rights and implemented effectively by coordination between the ILO, WTO and the IFIs.

In future, monetary and macroeconomic policies should evolve into multilateralism, by increasingly being harmonized through summit meetings of major political leaders. This multilateralism aim would be greatly facilitated if summitry were truly internationalized, for example, if the G7 countries in the North and G15 or similar groupings in the South were to enter into productive dialogue and promote coordinated macroeconomic policy management for a just global order based on international regulation.

Third, international fiscal policies are essential to finance global equity. Ecotaxes in the North and development levies on MNCs or Tobin Taxes are the means to generate autonomous tax revenues for investment in environmental and developmental projects in the South towards global partnership and equity. In this context, it would be necessary to effect urgently needed radical reform for greater efficiency of the UN and international organizations, going beyond the World War II mindset of victors and vanquished. However, new and largely non-governmental channels, are needed as well for fiscal transfers from the North to the South in order to reach the needy target groups in the South directly for maximum effectiveness.

DEVELOPMENT ETHICS

Conventional development studies is slowly giving way to a relatively new field of study, namely, development ethics, a programme of study seeking to develop a 'counter-movement to protect the rights of all the people from the global trends that threaten to destroy the very fabric of society' (Pierre Sane quoted in Drydyck and Penz eds 1997: 1). Leading voices in this field, such as the philosopher-economist A.K. Sen, the 1998 Nobel Prizewinner (1987, 1998), are reconstructing an internationalist ethics based on fairness and egalitarian values rather than on economic inequality. In Sen's 'entitlement' approach, every individual is entitled, by virtue of his or her membership of humanity, to a fair share of global wealth.

Development ethics recognizes the fact of multiplicity of cultures within the global family, and adopts a more holistic view of development studies. Ultimately, it is to be hoped, it will replace Eurocentric economics and contribute towards a new global code of ethics and greater committment to international stewardship of global commons (UN Commission on Global Governance 1995). Such stewardship needs to be founded on the legitimacy of multicultural consent and implemented multilaterally for effective regulation of international trade and sustainable development for global equity. The primary requirement for implementing such global stewardship, however, is dedicated leadership in the West and elsewhere, with the necessary internationalist vision, to lead the global family past the nation-state for a world built on justice and fairness, not exploitation.

Development economics should contribute to this goal of internationalism. To be relevant in the future, economic development theories will need to deconstruct their ethnocentricity, and mercantilist roots, and actually serve global equity towards the ultimate aim of a sustainable world in which wealth distribution more closely approximates population distribution. More specifically, an objective development economist must be able to transcend mercantilist national interests back home, and to promote *de facto* shared prosperity for all stakeholders in a one world/global village built on tolerance, cooperation and cultural diversity.

BIBLIOGRAPHY

Abbot, L.D., ed., 1946, *Masterworks of Economics, Digests of Great Classics*, Doubleday & Co: New York

Adelman, I. and C.T. Morris, 1973, *Economic Growth with Social Equity in Developing Countries*, California University Press: Stanford

Adelman, I. and Cynthia F. Taft, 1997, 'Editorial: Development History and Its Implications for Development Theory', *World Development*, vol. 25, no. 6

Agarwal, Bina, ed., 1988, *Structures of Patriarchy, State, Community and Household in Modernizing Asia*, Zed Books: London

Agarwala, A.N. and S.P. Singh, eds, 1963, *The Economics of Underdevelopment*, Oxford University Press: New York

Ahluwalia, M.S., 1976, 'Income Distribution and Development: Some Stylized Facts', *American Economic Review*, vol. 66, no. 2, May

Alatas, Syed Hussein, 1977, *The Myth of the Lazy Native*, Frank Cass: London

Alavi, H. and T. Shanin, eds, 1982, *Introduction to the Sociology of 'Developing Societies'*, Monthly Review Press: New York

Altbach, P.G. 1989, 'Twisted Roots: The Western Impact on Asian Higher Education', *Higher Education*, vol. 18, no. 1

Amin, Samir, 1976, *Unequal Development*, Monthly Review Press: New York

——, 1979, *Imperialism and Unequal Development*, Monthly Review Press: New York

——, 1989, *Eurocentrism*, Monthly Review Press: New York

Arndt, H.W., 1981, 'Economic Development: A Semantic History', *Economic Development and Cultural Change*, April

——, 1983, 'The 'Trickle-down Myth', *Economic Development and Cultural Change*, October

——, 1987, *Economic Development: The History of an Idea*, University of Chicago Press: Chicago

——, 1988, 'Market Failure and Underdevelopment', *World Development*, vol. 16, no. 2

Arrow, Kenneth J., 1951, *Social Choice and Individual Values*, John Wiley: New York

Ayres, Robert U., 1997, *The Turning Point: The End of the Growth Paradigm*, Earthscan: London

Bacchus, M.K., 1980, *Education for Development or Underdevelopment: Guyana's Educational System and its Implications for the Third World*, Wilfred Laurier University Press: Waterloo, Ont.

Baer, Werner and Michel Herve, 1966, 'Employment and Industrialization in Developing Countries', *Quarterly Journal of Economics*, vol. 80, no. 1, February

Balassa, Bela, *et al.*, 1980, *The Process of Industrial Development and Alternative Development Strategies*, Princeton Essays in International Finance no. 141, December

—— and Associates, 1982, *Development Strategies in Semi-Industrial Economies*, World Bank: Washington

Baran, Paul, 1957, *The Political Economy of Growth*, New York: Modern Reader Paperbacks

Barnet, Richard, 1993, 'The End of Jobs', *Harper's*, September

Barnet, Richard and Ronald Muller, 1974, *Global Reach*, Simon & Schuster: New York

Barnet, Richard and John Cavanagh, 1994, *Global Dreams*, Simon & Schuster: New York

Bateman, Robert H., ed., 1988, *Toward a Political Economy of Development: A Rational Choice Perspective*, University of California Press: Berkeley

Bator, F.M., 1957, 'The Simple Analytics of Welfare Maximization', *American Economic Review*, vol. 47, March

Bauer, P.T., 1948, *The Rubber Industry*, Longman: London

—— 1971, *Dissent on Development*, Weidenfeld & Nicolson: London

Bauer, P.T. and Yamey, 1957, *The Economics of Underdeveloped Countries*, London: Cambridge University Press

Becker, Gary, 1964, *Human Capital: A Theoretical and Empirical Analysis*, NBER: New York

Beckford, George, 1972, *Persistent Poverty: Underdevelopment in Plantation Economies of the Third World*, New York: Oxford University Press

Berg, E.J., 1961, 'Backward Sloping Labor Supply Functions in Dual Economies: The Africa Case', *Quarterly Journal of Economics*, vol. 75, August

Berger, P. and H.H.M. Hsiao, eds, 1988, *In Search of an East Asian Development Model*, Transaction Publications: New Brunswick

Bergsten, F.C., 1975, *Toward a New International Economic Order*, DC. Heath: Lexington, Mass.

——, 1976, 'International Trade in Raw Materials: Myths and Realities', *Science*, February

Bergsten, F.C. and L.B. Krause, eds, 1975, *World Politics and International Economics*, Brookings Institution: Washington, DC

Bergsten, F.C. and Marcus Noland, eds, 1993, *Pacific Dynamism and the International Economic System*, Institute of International Economics: Washington, DC

Berry, A. and R.H. Sobot, 1978, 'Labor Market Performance in Developing Countries: A Survey', *World Development*, November–December

Bettleheim, C., 1959, *Studies in the Theory of Planning*, Asia Publishing House: New York

Bhagwati, J., 1958, 'Immiserizing Growth', *Review of Economic Studies*, June

——, 1962 'The Theory of Comparative Advantage in the Context of Underdevelopment and Growth', *Pakistan Development Review*, Autumn

——, ed., 1970, *Economics and World Order from the 1970s to the 1990s*, Free Press: New York

——, 1982, 'Directly Unproductive, Rent-Seeking Activities', *Journal of Political Economy*, vol. 90, October

——, 1984, 'Development Economics: What Have We Learnt?', *Asian Development Review*, vol. 2, no. 1

——, 1991, *The World Trading System at Risk*, Princeton University Press: Princeton

——, 1993, 'The Case for Free Trade', *Scientific American*, November

Bird, Richard, 1981, 'Exercising Policy Leverage Through Aid: A Critical Survey', *Canadian Journal of Development Studies*, vol. 2, no. 2

Birkhaeuser, D.R. and G. Feder, 1991, 'The Economic Impact of Agricultural Extension: A Review', *Economic Development and Cultural Change*, vol. 39, no. 3

Blaug, Mark, 1976, 'Human Capital Theory: A Slightly Jaundiced Survey', *Journal of Economic Literature*, vol. 14, no. 3, September

Blitzer, Charles, Peter B. Clark and Lance Taylor, eds, 1975, *Economy-wide Models and Development Planning*, Oxford University Press: London

Boeke, J.H., 1953, *Economics and Economic Policy in Dual Societies*, Jjeenk Willink: Haarlem

Boserup, Esther, 1970, *Women's Role in Development*, Allen & Unwin: London

——, 1981, *Population and Technological Change, A Study of Long-term Trends*, University of Chicago Press: Chicago

Bowles, S. and H. Gintis, 1975, 'The Problem with the Human Capital Theory: A Marxist Critique', *American Economic Review Supplement*, vol. 65, no. 2, May

Bradhan *et al.*, 1990, 'Symposium on the State and Economic Development', *Journal of Economic Perspectives*, vol. 4, no. 3, Summer

Brandt Report, 1980, *North–South: A Programme for Survival*. The Report of the Independent Comission on International Development Issues under the Chairmanship of Willy Brandt, Pan Books: London

Braudel, Fernand, 1994, *A History of Civilizations* (translated by Richard Mayne), Penguin Books: New York

Brown, Judith M., 1985, *Modern India: The Origins of Asian Democracy*, Oxford University Press, New York

Buchanan J. M. *et al.*, eds, 1980, *Toward a Theory of Rent-seeking Society*, Texas A&M University: College Station

Buvinic, Mayra, 1997, 'Women in Poverty: A New Global Underclass', *Foreign Policy*, no. 108, Fall

Byrne, Francis C., 1966, 'Role Shock: An Occupational Hazard of American Technical Assistants Abroad', *Annals of the American Academy of Political and Social Science*, November

Campos, Jose E. and Hilton L. Root, 1996, *The Key to the Asian Miracle: Making Shared Growth Credible*, Brookings Institution: Washington, DC

Cassen, R. and Associates, 1986, *Does Aid Work?* Report to an Intergovernmental Task Force, Clarendon Press: Oxford

Cernia, M., ed., 1991, *Putting People First*, Oxford University Press: New York

Chandler, A.D., 1962, *Strategy and Structure: Chapters in the History of American Industrial Enterprise*, MIT Press: Cambridge, Mass.

Chant, Sylvia, ed., 1992, *Gender and Migration in Developing Countries*, Bellhaven Press: London

Chen, E.K.Y., 1979, *Hyper-growth in Asian Economies: A Comparative Study of Hong Kong, Japan, Korea, Singapore and Taiwan*, Holmes & Mei: New York

Chenery, Hollis, *et al.* 1974, *Redistribution with Growth*, Oxford University Press for the World Bank

Chenery, Hollis and P.G. Clark, 1959, *Interindustry Economics*, J. Wiley: New York

Chenery, Hollis and M. Bruno, 1962, 'Development Alternatives in an Open Economy: The Case of Israel', *Economic Journal*, vol. 72

Chenery, Hollis and A.M. Strout, 1966, 'Foreign Assistance and Economic Development', *American Economic Review*, September

Chenery, Hollis and T.N. Srinivasan, eds, 1988, *Handbook of Development Economics*, Elsevier: New York

Clark, Colin, 1940, *The Conditions of Economic Progress*, St Martin's Press: New York

Cline, W.R., 1982, 'Can the East Asian Model of Development be Generalized?', *World Development*, vol. 10, no. 2

Clower, Robert, *et al.*, 1966, *Growth without Development: An Economic Survey of Liberia*, Northwestern University Press: Evanston

Conable, Barber B., 1990, 'Development and the Environment: A Global Balance', *International Environmental Affairs*, vol. 2, no. 1, Winter

Coombs, Philip, with Manzoor Ahmed, 1974, *Attacking Rural Poverty, How Nonformal Education Can Help*, Johns Hopkins University Press: Baltimore

Corbo, V., *et al.*, eds, 1987, *Growth-Oriented Adjustment Programs*, IMF and World Bank: Washington, DC

Corner, Lorraine, 1992, 'Women, Men and Macroeconomics, the Gender Differentiated Impact of Macro-Economics with Special Reference to Asia and Pacific', UNIFEM Workshop, Bali, 27–8 August

Cornia, A., R. Jolly and F. Stewart, 1986, *Adjustment with a Human Face, Protecting the Vulnerable and Promoting Growth (A Study by Unicef)*, vol. I, Clarendon Press: Oxford

Culpeper, Roy, 1998, 'Systemic Instability or Global Growing Pains? Implications of the Asian Financial Crisis', *Briefing B-41*, The North–South Institute: Ottawa, Ont.

Cutter, Susan L., 1995, 'The Forgotten Casualties: Women, Children and Environmental Change', *Global Environmental Change*, vol. 5, no. 3, June

Dahlman, C.J. *et al.* 1987, 'Managing Technological Development', *World Development*, June

Daly, Herman E., 1993, 'The Perils of Free Trade', *Scientific American*, November

——, 1993a, 'Why Northern Income Growth is Not the Solution to Southern Poverty', *Ecological Economics*, vol. 8

Daly, Herman E. and J.B. Cobb Jr, 1994, *For the Common Good: Redirecting the. Economy towards Community, the Environment and a Sustainable Future*, Beacon Press: Boston

Darity, William, 1985, 'Review', *of Friedrich List, The National System of Political Economy, 1837, History of Political Economy*, vol. 17, no. 3

Darity, William and Bobbie L. Horn, 1988, *The Loan Pushers: The Role of Commercial Banks in the International Debt Crisis*, Ballinger: Cambridge, Mass.

Dawkins, Richard, 1989, *The Selfish Gene*, Oxford University Press: Oxford

de Haan, Arjan, 1998, '"Social Exclusion": An Alternative Concept for the Study of Deprivation', *IDS Bulletin*, vol. 29, no. 1, January

de Melo, J., 1988, 'SAM-based Models: An Introduction', *Journal of Policy Modelling*, vol. 10, no. 3

Denison, Edward, 1962, *The Sources of Economic Growth in the US and the Alternatives before Us*, Committee for Economic Development: New York

de Soto, Hernando, 1989, *The Other Path*, Harper & Row: New York

Dobbs, M.M., 1960, *An Essay on Economic Growth and Planning*, Routledge & Kegan Paul: London

Domar, E.D., 1946, 'Capital Expansion, Rate of Growth and Employment', *Econometrica*, April

——, 1947, 'The Problem of Capital Accumulation', *American Economic Review*, March

Doner, R.F., 1991, 'Approaches to the Politics of Economic Growth in Southeast Asia', *Journal of Asian Studies*, vol. 50, no. 4

Dornbusch, R., 1985, 'Dealing with Debt in the 1980's', *Third World Quarterly*, vol. 7

——, 1986, *Dollars, Debts and Deficits*, MIT Press: Cambridge

Drake, P.J., 1961, *Financial Development in Malaya and Singapore*, Australian National University: Canberra

Drydyck, J. and Peter Penz, eds 1997, *Global Justice, Global Democracy*, Society for Socialist Studies/Fernwood Publishing: Winnipeg/Halifax

Dunning, John H., 1992, *Multinational Enterprises and the Global Economy*, Addison-Wesley: Don Mills, Ont.

Eckaus, R., 1955, 'The Factor Proportions Problem in Underdeveloped Areas', *American Economic Review*, September

ECLA, 1950, *The Economic Development of Latin America and Its Principal Problems*, UN Department of Economic Affairs, New York

——, 1957, *Economic Survey for Latin America for 1956*, UN: New York

Eden, Lorraine and Evan H. Potter, eds, 1993, *Multinationals in Global Political Economy*, St Martin's Press: New York

Edgell, Alvin G., 1973/4, 'Aid Encounter in Iboland', *International Development Review/Focus*, vol. 15

Edwards, E.O., ed., 1974, *Employment in Developing Countries*, Columbia University Press: New York

Edwards, E.O. and S. van Wijnbergen, 1988, 'Disequilibrium and Structural Adjustment', in Chenery and Srinivasan, eds

Eisenstadt, S. N., 1987, *Patterns of Modernity*, Pinter: London

Elegant, Robert, 1991, *Pacific Destiny, Inside Asia Today*, Avon: New York

Ellis, H.S., 1958, 'Accelerated Investment as a Force in Economic Development', *Quarterly Journal of Economics*, November

Eltis, Walter, 1987, *The Classical Theory of Economic Growth*, Macmillan: London

Emeris, L., ed., 1997, *Economic and Social Development in the XXIst Century*, Inter-American Development Bank: Washington, DC

Emerson, Rupert, 1964, *Malaysia, A Study of Direct and Indirect Rule*, University of Malaya Press: Kuala Lumpur

Enos, J.L., 1989, 'Transfer of Technology', *Asia-Pacific Economic Literature*, vol. 3, no. 1, March

Enos, J.L. and W.H. Park, 1988, *The Adoption and Diffusion of Imported Technology: The Case of Korea*, Croom Helm: London

Environmental Policy and Law, 1992, 'Tokyo Declaration on Financing Environment and Development', vol. 23, no. 4

Esman, J., 1978 'Development Administration and Constituency Organization', *Public Administration Review*, March–April

Evers, H. Deiter and Ozay Mehmet, 1994 'The Management of Risk: Informal Sector Trade in Indonesia', *World Development*, vol. 22, no. 1, January

Faber, M. and D. Seers, eds, 1972, *The Crisis in Planning*, vol. 1: *Issues*, Chatto & Windus: London

Fallows, James, 1994, *Looking at the Sun*, Pantheon: New York

Fei, John C.H. and Gustav Ranis, 1961, 'A Theory of Economic Development', *American Economic Review*, September

Fei, John C.H. and S.W.Y. Kuo, 1979, *Growth and Equity: The Taiwan Case*, Oxford University Press: New York

Ferguson, C. E and J.P. Gould, 1975, *Microeconomic Theory*, 4th edn, Irwin: Homewood

Fortune, 1992, 'The New Global Work Force', no. 26, 14 December

Frankel, F.R., 1969, 'India's New Strategy of Agricultural Development: Political Costs of Agrarian Modernization', *Journal of Asian Studies*, vol. 28, no. 4

Freeman, R., 1976, *The Overeducated American*, New York: Academic Press

French, Hilary, 1993, *Costly Tradeoffs, Reconciling Trade and Environment*, Worldwatch Paper 113, Washington, DC

Friedman, Milton, 1958, 'Foreign Economic Aid; Means and Objectives', *The Yale Economic Review*, Summer

Fry, M.J., 1982, 'Models of Financially Repressed Development Economies', *World Development*, September

Fukuyama, F., 1989, 'The End of History?', *The National Interest*, Summer

———, 1992, *The End of History and the Last Man*, Hamish Hamilton: London

Fuller, Bruce, 1986, 'Is Primary School Quality Eroding in the Third World?', *Comparative Education Review*, vol. 30, no. 4, 1986

Furukawa Eiichi, 1993, 'Changes in Southeast Asian Views of Japan', *Japan Echo*, vol. 20, no. 3, Autumn

George, Susan, 1990, *A Fate Worse than Debt*, Penguin: London

Ghai, Dharam, 1992, *Structural Adjustment, Global Integration and Social Democracy*, United Nations Research Institute for Social Development: Geneva, Discussion Paper 37, October

Gillis, M., D.H. Perkins, M. Roemer and D.R. Snodgrass, 1992, *Economics of Development*, W.W. Norton: New York

Gilpin, Robert, 1987, *The Political Economy of International Relations*, Princeton University Press: Princeton

Gladwin, Christina, ed., 1991, *Structural Adjustment and African Women Farmers*, University of Florida Press: Gainesville

Goode, Ricard, 1984, *Government Finance in Developing Countries*, Brookings Institution: Washington, DC

Goodland, Robert and Herman Daly, 1993, 'Why Northern Income Growth is Not the Solution to Southern Poverty', *Ecological Economics*, vol. 8

Gordon, R.G., 1982, 'Why US Wage and Employment Behaviour Differs from that in Britain and Japan', *Economic Journal*, March

Gottlieb, G., 1993, *Nation against State: A New Approach to Conflicts and the Decline of Sovereignty*, Council on Foreign Relations Press: New York

Goulet, Denis, 1992, 'Development: Creator and Destroyer of Values', *World Development*, vol. 20, no. 3

Gray, John, 1998, *False Dawn: The Delusions of Global Capitalism*, Granta Books: London

Griffin, Keith, 1974, *The Political Economy of Agrarian Change*, Macmillan: London

———, 1976, *Land Concentration and Rural Poverty*, Macmillan: London

———, ed., 1987, World Hunger and the World Economy, Macmillan: London:

Griffin, Keith and J.L. Enos, 1970, 'Foreign Assistance: Objectives and Consequences', *Economic Development and Cultural Change*, April

Griffin, Keith and A.K. Ghose, 1979, 'Growth and Impoverishment in the Rural Areas of Asia', *World Development*, vol. 7, nos 4/5

Hadiz, Vedi R., 1997, *Workers and the State in New Order Indonesia*, Routledge: London and New York

Hagen, E.E., 1958, 'An Economic Justification for Protection', *Quarterly Journal of Economics*, November

Haggard, S. and E. Kim, 1997, 'The Sources of East Asia's Economic Growth', *Access Asia Review*, vol.1, no. 1

Haggard, S. and C. Mason, 1990, 'Institutions and Economic Policy: Theory and a Korean Case Study', *World Politics*, 42, January

Hahn, F.H. and R.C.O. Matthews, 1964, 'Growth and Technical Progress: A Survey', *Economic Journal*, vol. 74

Hamilton, Clive, 1983, 'Capitalist Industrialization in East Asia's Four Little Tigers', *Journal of Contemporary Asia*, vol. 13, no. 1

——, 1987, 'Can the Rest of Asia Emulate the NICs?', *Third World Quarterly*, vol. 9, no. 4, October

Hammelskamp, J. and K.L. Brockman, 1997, 'Environmental Labels: The German "Blue Angel"', *Future*, vol. 29, no. 1

Harbison, F. H. and C.A. Myers, 1973, *Human Resources as the Wealth of Nations*, Oxford University Press: New York

Harris, J.R. and M. Todaro, 1970, 'Migration, Unemployment and Development: A Two-Sector Model', *American Economic Review*, March

Harris, M., 1968, *The Rise of Anthropological Theory: A History of Culture*, Crowell: New York

Harris, Nigel, 1987, *The End of the Third World: Newly Industrializing Countries and the Decline of an Ideology*, Penguin: Harmondsworth

Harrison, Lawrence E., 1992, *Who Prospers: How Cultural Values Shape Economic and Political Success*, Basic Books: New York

Harrod, R.F., 1939, 'An Essay in Dynamic Theory', *Economic Journal*, vol. 49

——, 1948, *Toward a Dynamic Economics*, St Martin's Press: New York

——, 1963, *The Life of John Maynard Keynes*, Macmillan: London

Hart, Gillian, 1992, 'Household Production Reconsidered: Gender, Labor Conflict, and Technological Change in Malaysia's Muda Region', *World Development*, vol. 20, no. 6

Hart, Keith, 1973, 'Informal Income Opportunities and Urban Unemployment in Ghana', *Journal of Modern African Studies*, March

Healey, Derek T, 1972, 'Development Policy: New Thinking about an Interpretation', *Journal of Economic Literature*, September

Hecksher, Eli, 1919, 'The Effects of Foreign Trade on the Distribution of Income', *Economise Tidskrift*

Heilbroner, Robert, 1961, *The Worldly Philosophers: The Lives, Times and Ideas of the Great Economic Thinkers*, rev. edn, Simon & Schuster: New York

——, 1963, *The Great Ascent: The Struggle for Economic Development in our Time*, Harper & Row: New York

——, 1973, 'Economics as a "Value-Free", Science', *Social Research*, vol. 40, Spring

Helleiner, G.K., ed., 1976, *A World Divided: The Less Developed Countries in the International Economy*, Cambridge University Press: New York

———, ed., 1986, *Africa and the International Monetary Fund*, IMF: Washington, DC

Helleiner, G.K., 1992, 'The IMF, the World Bank and Africa's Adjustment and External Debt Problems: An Unofficial View', *World Development*, vol. 20, no. 6

Heller, H. Robert, 1968, *International Trade Theory and Empirical Evidence*, Prentice-Hall: Englewood Cliffs, New Jersey

Henderson, James M. and Richard E. Quandt, 1958, *Microeconomic Theory: A Mathematical Approach*, McGraw Hill: New York

Herrick, Bruce and Charles P. Kindleberger, 1988, *Economic Development*, international 4th edn, McGraw-Hill: Singapore

Hettne, Bjorn., 1990, *Development Theory and the Three Worlds*, Longman: London

Hicks, G., 1989, 'The Four Little Dragons: An Enthusiast's Reading Guide', *Asia-Pacific Economic Literature*, vol. 3, no. 2

Hicks, J.R., 1965, *Value and Capital: An Inquiry into Some Fundamental Principles of Economic Theory*, 2nd edn, Clarendon: Oxford

Higgins, Benjamin, 1956, 'The Dualistic Theory of Underdeveloped Areas', *Economic Development and Cultural Change*, January

———, 1968, *Economic Development, Principles, Problems, and Policies*, revised edn, Norton & Co., New York

Higgot, Richard A., 1983, *Political Development Theory*, Croom Helm: London

Himawan, Charles, 1980, *The Foreign Investment Process in Indonesia*, Gunung Agung: Jakarta

Hirschman, Albert, 1958, *The Strategy of Economic Development*, Yale University Press: New Haven

———, 1977, *The Passions and the Interests: The Political Arguments for Capitalism before Its Triumph*, Princeton University Press: Princeton

———, 1981, 'The Rise and Decline of Development Economics', in A.O. Hirschman, *Essays in Trespassing: Economics to Politics and Beyond*, Cambridge University Press: Cambridge

———, 1984, 'A Dissenter's Confession: 'The Strategy of Development Revisited', in Meier and Seers, eds

———, 1986, 'The Rise and Decline of Development Economics', *Development: Seeds of Change*, Society for International Development (Rome), vol. 3, no. 3

Hobsbawm, Eric, 1992, *Nations and Nationalism since 1780: Programme, Myth, Reality*, Cambridge University Press: New York

———, 1993 'The New Threat to History', *The New York Review of Books*, 16 December

Horowitz, Donald L., 1985, *Ethnic Groups in Conflict*, University of California Press: Berkeley

Hughes, H., ed., 1985, *Explaining the Success of East Asian Industrialisation*, Cambridge University Press: Cambridge

Hughes, H., ed., 1988, *Achieving Industrialization in East Asia*, Cambridge University Press: Cambridge

Hughes, Robert, 1993, *Culture of Complaint, the Fraying of America*, Oxford University Press: New York

Huntington, S., 1993, 'The Clash of Civilizations?', *Foreign Affairs*, Summer

——, 1996, *The Clash of Civilizations and the Remaking of World Order*, Simon & Schuster: New York

Hymer, Stephen, 1970, 'The Efficiency (Contradictions) of Multinational Corporations', *American Economic Review*, May

ILO, 1972, *Employment, Incomes and Equality* (the Kenya Report), ILO: Geneva

——, 1976, Employment, *Growth and Basic Needs: A One World Problem*, ILO: Geneva

——, 1993, *Multinationals and Employment: The Global Economy of the 1990's*, ILO: Geneva

——, 1994, *Defending Values, Promoting Change: Social Justice in a Global Economy, An ILO Agenda*, Report of the Director-Genetral to the 81st Session 1994, ILO: Geneva

——, 1996, *Child Labour: Targetting the Intolerable*, ILO: Geneva

—— 1998, *ILO Declaration on Fundamental Principles and Rights at Work*, International Labour Conference, 86th Session, Geneva, June (http: //www.ilo.org/public/english/iloilc/ilc86/com-dtxt.htm)

Inkeles, Alex and David M. Smith, 1974, *Becoming Modern: Individual Change in Six Developing Countries*, Harvard University Press: Cambridge

Inoguchi, Takashi, 1994, 'The Coming Pacific Century?', *Current History*, January

Islam, Iyanatul, 1992, 'Political Economy and East Asian Economic Development', *Asian-Pacific Economic Literature*, vol. 6, no. 2

Jackson, J.C. 1968, *Planters and Speculators*, University of Malaya Press: Kuala Lumpur

Jackson, J.C. and C. Kirkpatrick, 1986, 'Export-led Development, Labour-market Policy Conditions and the Distribution of Income: The Case of Singapore', *Cambridge Journal of Economics*, vol. 10, no. 2, June

Jacoby, Henry, D., Ronald G. Prinn, and Richard Schmalense, 1998, 'Kyoto's Unfinished Business', *Foreign Affairs*, July–August

Jacoby, N.H, 1966, *US Aid to Taiwan*, Praeger: New York

Jencks, Christopher, *et al.*, 1972, *Inequality: A Reassessment of the Effects of Family and Schooling in America*, Basic Books: New York

Johnson, C., 1982, *MITI and the Japanese Miracle: The Growth of Industrial Policy, 1925–1975*, Stanford University Press: Stanford, Calif.

Johnson, Paul, 1997, *A History of the American People*, HarperCollins: New York

Johnson, W.L. and D.R. Kamerschen, eds, 1972, *Readings in Economic Development*, South-Western Publishing Co.: Cincinnati, Ohio

Johnston, B.F. and William Clark, 1982, *Redesigning Rural Development: A Strategic Perspective*, Johns Hopkins University Press: Baltimore

Johnston, B.F. *et al.*, 1972, 'Criteria for the Design of Agricultural Development Studies', *Food Research Institute Studies*, vol. 11, no. 1

Jolly, Richard, 1976, 'The World Employment Conference: The Enthronement of Basic Needs', *ODI Review*, no. 2

Kaldor, Nicholas, 1955–6, 'Alternative Theories of Distribution', *Review of Economic Studies*, vol. 23, no. 2

Kaldor, Nicholas, 1957, 'A Model of Economic Growth', *Economic Journal*, December

——, 1967, *Strategic Factors in Economic Development*, New York State School of Industrial and Labor Relations, Cornell University: Ithaca, New York

——, 1985, *Economics Without Equilibrium*, Sharpe: New York

Kaplan, R.D., 1994, 'The Coming Anarchy', *The Atlantic*, February

Kaplinsky, R., 1988, 'Restructuring the Capitalist Labour Process: Implications for Administrative Reform', *IDS Bulletin*, October

Kapur, Devesh, 1998, 'The IMF: A Cure or a Curse?', *Foreign Policy*, Summer

Kapur, Devesh and Richard Webb, 1994, 'The Evolution of the Multilateral Development Banks' (Paper prepared for a conference sponsored by the Group of 24 on the occasion of the 50th Anniversary of Bretton Woods, Cartagena, Colombia, 18–20 April 1994)

Kausikan, B., 1993, 'Asia's Different Standard', *Foreign Policy*, Fall

Kay, Christobal, 1993, 'For a Renewal of Development Studies: Latin American Theories and Neoliberalism in the era of Structural Adjustment', *Third World Quarterly*, vol. 14, no. 4

Kedourie, E., 1966, *Nationalism*, Hutchinson: London

Kennedy, Paul, 1993, *Preparing for the Twenty-first Century*, HarperCollins: Toronto

Keynes, John M., 1936, *The General Theory of Employment, Interest and Money*, Papermac 12, Macmillan: London

Killick, T., 1976, 'The Possibilities of Development Planning', *Oxford Economic Papers*, vol. 41, no. 4, October

——, 1981, *Policy Economics: A Textbook of Applied Economics on Developing Countries*, Heinemann: London

——, ed., 1984, *The Quest for Economic Stabilisation: The IMF and the Third World*, Heinemann: London

——, 1998, *Conditionality: Donors and the Political-Economy of Policy Reform in Developing Countries*, Routledge, London.

Kindleberger, Charles, 1958, *Economic Development*, 2nd edn, McGraw-Hill: New York

——, 1989, *Manias, Panics and Crashes: A History of Financial Crises*, Basic Books: New York

Kindleberger, Charles and P. Lindert, 1982, *International Economics*, Irwin: Homewood, Ill.

Krishna, Raj, 1973 'Unemployment in India', *Economic and Political Weekly*, 3 March

Kristof, Nicholas, 1993 'China's Rise', *Foreign Affairs*, November–December

Krueger, Anne, 1974, 'The Political Economy of Rent-seeking Society', *American Economic Review*, June

——, 1990, 'Government Failures in Development', *Journal of Economic Perspectives*, vol. 4, no. 3, Summer

Krugman, Paul, 1994, 'The Myth of Asia's Mircale', *Foreign Affairs*, vol. 73, no. 6.

Kuznets, Simon, 1955, 'Economic Growth and Income Inequality', *American Economic Review*, March

Kuznets, Simon, 1959, 'Quantitative Aspects of the Economic Growth of Nations: Part 4. Distribution of National Income By Factor Shares', *Economic Development and Cultural Change*, vol. 7, (supplement), April

——, 1965, *Economic Growth and Structure*, Heinemann: London

——, 1966, *Modern Economic Growth: Rate, Structure and Spread*, Yale University Press: New Haven, Conn.

——, 1971, *Economic Growth of Nations: Total Output and Production Structure*, Cambridge University Press: Cambridge, Mass.

Lal, Deepak, 1984, *The Political Economy of the Predatory State*, World Bank Discussion Paper DRD 105, Washington, DC

——, 1985, *The Poverty of Development Economics*, Harvard University Press: Cambridge, Mass.

Lall, S., 1978, 'Transnationals, Domestic Enterprises, and Industrial Structure in Host LDCs: A Survey', *Oxford Economic Papers*, July

Lall, S. and F. Stewart, eds, 1986, *Theory and Reality in Development*, Macmillan: London

Lange, Oscar and Fred M. Taylor, 1938, *On the Economic Theory of Socialism*, University of Minnesota Press: Minneapolis

Lee, Eddy, 1979, 'Egalitarian Peasant Farming and Rural Development: The Case of South Korea', *World Development*, vol. 7

——, ed., 1981, *Export-led Industrialization and Development*, ILO: Geneva

Leibenstein, Harvey, 1978, *X-Efficiency Theory and Economic Development*, Oxford University Press: New York

Lele, U., 1979, *The Design of Rural Development: Lessons from Africa*, Johns Hopkins University Press: Baltimore

——, 1986, 'Women and Structural Transformation', *Economic Development and Cultural Change*, vol. 34

Leontieff, W., 1953, 'Domestic Production and Foreign Trade: The American Position Re-examined', *Proceedings of the American Philosophical Society*, September

Lerner, Abba P., 1946, *The Economics of Control*, Macmillan: New York

Lerner, Daniel, 1958, *The Passing of Traditional Society*, 2nd edn, Oxford University Press, London

Levitsky, Jacob, ed., 1989, *Microenterprises in Developing Countries*, Intermediate Technology Publications: London

Lewis, Arthur, 1954, 'Economic Development with Unlimited Supplies of Labour', *Manchester School*, May

——, 1955, *The Theory of Economic Growth*, Unwin: London

——, 1966, *Development Planning: The Essentials of Economic Policy*, Allan & Unwin: London

Lewis, John P., *et al.*, 1988, *Strengthening the Poor: What Have We Learnt?*, Overseas Development Council: Washington, DC

Liemt, G. van, 1992, 'Economic Globalisation: Labour Options and Business Strategies in High Labour Cost Countries', *International Labour Review*, vol. 131, nos. 4–5

Lim, L.Y.C., 1983, 'Singapore's Success: The Myth of the Free Market Economy', *Asian Survey*, vol. 23. no. 6, June

——, 1998, 'Whose "Model", Failed? Implications of the Asian Economic Crisis', *The Washington Quarterly*, vol. 21, no. 3

Lindblom, Charles E., 1977, *Politics and Markets: The World's Political-Economic Systems*, Basic Books: USA

Lipsey, R.G and K. Lancaster, 1957, 'The General Theory of the Second Best', *Review of Economic Studies*, no. 1

Lipton, Michael, 1968, 'The Theory of Optimising Peasant', *Journal of Development Studies*, vol. 4, no. 3

——, 1977, *Why People Stay Poor*, Temple Smith: London

——, 1990, 'Requiem for Adjustment Lending', *Development Policy Review*, vol. 8, no. 4

Lipton, Michael and J. Toye, 1990, *Does Aid Work in India? A Country Study of the Impact of Official Development Assistance*, Routledge: London

List, Frederich, 1885, *The National System of Political Economy* (translated by Sampson S. Lloyd), Longmans, Green & Co.: London

Little, I.M.D., 1957, *A Critique of Welfare Economics*, Oxford University Press: New York

Little, I.M.D., T. Scitovsky and M. Scott, 1970, *Industry and Trade in Some Developing Countries: A Comparative Study*, Oxford University Press: London

Little, I.M.D. and Mirrlees, James A., 1974, *Project Appraisal and Planning for Developing Countries*, Basic Books: New York

Lockheed, M. E and A. M. Verspoor *et al.*, 1991, *Improving Primary Education in Developing Countries*, Oxford University Press: New York

Lofchie, Michael F. and Stephen K. Cummins, 1981 'Food Deficits and Agricultural Policies in Tropical Africa', *Journal of Modern African Studies*, vol. 20, no. 1, March

Lubbel, Harold, 1991, *The Informal Sector in the 1980s and 1990s*, OECD: Paris

Lucas, Robert E., 1988, 'On the Mechanics of Economic Development', *Journal of Monetary Economics*, vol. 22, July

Mahbubani, K., 1992, 'The West and the Rest', *The National Interest*, Summer

Malthus, Robert, 1803, *An Essay on the Principle of Population*, Bensley, London (ed. D. Winch 1992)

Mamdani, M., 1972, *The Myth of Population Control: Family, Caste and Class in an Indian Village*, Monthly Review Press: New York

Manne, A.S., 1974, 'Multi-sector Models for Development Planning: A Survey', *Journal of Development Economics*, vol. 1, no. 1, June

Manning, C. and P. E. Fong, 1990, 'Labour Market Trends and Structures in ASEAN and the East Asian NIEs', *Asian Pacific Economic Literature*, vol. 4, September

Marchand, M. and J. Pappart, eds, 1995, *Feminism/Postmodernism/Developmen*, Routledge: London

Marshall, Alfred, 1962, *The Principles of Economics*, 8th edn, papermac 16, Macmillan: Toronto

Marx, Karl, 1972, *Capital*, 2 vols, Everyman Paperback, Dent: London

Mason, E.S. *et al.*, 1980, *The Economic and Social Modernisation of the Republic of Korea*, Council on East Asian Studies, Harvard University: Cambridge, Mass.

Mathieu, Karl-Heinz, 1993, 'Bioeconomics and Post-Keynesian Economics: A Search for a Common Ground', *Ecological Economics*, vol. 8

Mazumdar, Dipak, 1976, 'The Urban Informal Sector', *World Development*, August

Meade, J.E., 1962, *A Neo-classical Theory of Economic Growth*, 2nd edn, Unwin: London

Meadows, D. *et al.*, 1972, *The Limits to Growth*, Universe Books: London

Mehmet, Ozay, 1971, 'Manpower Planning and Labour Markets in Developing Countries: A Case Study of West Malaysia', *Journal of Development Studies*, vol. 8, no. 2

——, 1978, *Economic Planning and Social Justice in Developing Countries*, Croom Helm: London

——, 1980, 'An International Development Levy on Multinational Corporations', *International Interactions*, vol. 7, no. 2

——, 1983, 'Growth with Impoverishment in a Dual Economy with Capital Imports', *Australian Economic Papers*, June

——, 1986, *Development in Malaysia: Poverty, Wealth and Trusteeship*, Croom Helm: London

——, 1988, *Human Resource Development in the Third World: Cases of Success and Failure*, R.F. Frye & Co: Kingston, Ont.

——, 1990, *Islamic Identity and Development: Studies of the Islamic Periphery*, Routledge: London

——, 1992, 'Eurocentricity of A.R. Wallace', *PRISMA* (Jakarta), vol. 6

——, 1994, 'Rent-seeking and Gate-keeping in Indonesia: A Cultural and Economic Analysis', *Labour, Capital and Society*, vol. 27, no. 1, April

——, 1997, 'Tigers, Asian Values and Labour Standards: Promoting a Fairer Global Trade', in *Canada Among Nations 1997: Asia Pacific Face-Off*, edited by F.O. Hampson, M.A. Molot and M. Rudner, Carleton University Press: Ottawa, Ont.

Mehmet, Ozay, E.P. Mendes and R. Sinding, 1999, *Towards a Fair Global Labour Market: Avoiding a New Slave Trade*, Routledge: London and New York

Meier, Gerald M., ed., 1976, *Leading Issues in Economic Development*, 3rd edn, Oxford University Press: New York

——, 1984, *Leading Issues in Economic Development*, 4th edn, Oxford University Press: New York

——, 1989, *Leading Issues in Economic Development*, 5th edn, Oxford University Press: New York

Meier, Gerald M. and D. Seers, eds, 1984, *Pioneers in Development*, Oxford University Press: New York

Mendes, E.P., 1997, 'Canada, Asian Values and Human Rights: Helping the Tigers Set Themselves Free', in *Canada Among Nations 1997: Asia Pacific Face-Off*, edited by F.O. Hampson, M.A. Molot and M. Rudner, Carleton University Press: Ottawa, Ont.

Mies, Maria, 1986, *Patriarchy and Accumulation on a World Scene*, Zed Books: London

Mill, John Stuart, 1917, *Principles of Political Economy* (Ashley edition), Longmans, Green & Co.: London

Mincer, J., 1962, 'On-the-job Training: Costs, Returns and Some Implications', *Journal of Political Economy*, vol. 70

Mishan, E.J., 1960 'Survey of Welfare Economics 1939–59', *Economic Journal*, vol. 70, no. 278

Moffat, L. *et al.* 1991, *Two Halves Make a Whole*, OCCIC: Ottawa

Morawetz, David, 1977, *Twenty-five Years of Economic Development*, World Bank: Washington

Morgan, Dan, 1980, *Merchants of Grain*, Penguin: Harmondsworth

Mumford, Lewis, 1934, *Technics and Civilization*, London: Routledge

Murray, Colin, 1980, 'Migrant Labour and Changing Family Structure in the Rural Periphery of Southern Africa', *Journal of Southern African Studies*, vol. 6, no. 2

Myint, Hla, 1958, 'The Classical Theory of International Trade and Underdeveloped Countries', *Economic Journal*, vol. 68

——, 1971, *Economic Theory and the Underdeveloped Countries*, Oxford University Press: New York

——, 1977, 'Adam Smith's Theory of International Trade in the Perspective of Economic Development', *Economica*, vol. 44

Myrdal, Gunnar, 1968, *Asian Drama*, Pantheon: New York

——, 1972, *Rich Land and Poor Land*, Harper: New York

Nakane, C., 1970, *Japanese Society*, University of California Press: Berkeley

Nash, June and Maria P. Fernandez-Kelley, eds, 1983, *Women, Men and the International Division of Labor*, State University of New York: Albany

Neuman, Stephanie, ed., 1998, *International Relations Theory and the Third World*, St Martin's Press: New York

Niskanen, W.A., 1971, *Bureaucracy and Representative Government*, New York: Aldine

North, Douglas C., 1981, *Structure and Change in Economic History*, Norton: New York

——, 1989, 'Institutions and Economic Growth: An Historical Introduction', *World Development*, vol. 17, no. 9

——, 1990, *Institutions, Institutional Change and Economic Performance*, Cambridge University Press: New York

Nurske, R., 1952, 'Some International Aspects of the Problem of Economic Development', *American Economic Review*, May (reprinted in Agarwala and Singh eds, 1963)

——, 1953, *Problems of Capital Formation in Underdeveloped Countries*, Blackwell: Oxford

OECD, 1962, *Forecasting Educational Needs for Economic and Social Development*, edited by H.S. Parnes, OECD: Paris

——, 1964, *The Residual Factor and Economic Growth*, OECD: Paris

——, 1982, *The Industrial Policy of Japan*, OECD: Paris

——, 1990, *Development Cooperation. Efforts and Policies of the Members of the Development Assistance Committee*, OECD: Paris

Ohlin, Bertil, 1929, 'The Reparation Problem: A Discussion', *Economic Journal*, June

O'Leary, A. and L. Lemmott, eds, 1995, *Women at Risk: Issues in the Primary Prevention of AIDS*, Plenum Press: New York

Olson, Mancur, 1982, *The Rise and Decline of Nations*, Yale University Press: New Haven

O'Manique, John, 1994, 'One More Revolution' (Paper presented at York University Conference on New Imperatives in International Development), February

Onis, Z., 1991, 'The Logic of the Developmental State', *Comparative Politics*, October

Paauw, Douglas S, and John C. Fei, 1973, *The Transition in Open Dualistic Economies: Theory and Southeast Asian Experience*, Yale University Press: New Haven, Conn.

Pack, H., 1974, 'The Employment–Output Trade-Offs in LDCs: A Microeconomic Approach', *Oxford Economic Papers*, vol. 26, no. 3, November

Papanek, Gustav, 1967, *Pakistan's Development: Social Goals and Private Incentives*, Harvard University Press: Cambridge, Mass.

——, 1988, 'The New Asian Capitalism: An Economic Portrait', in P. Berger and H.H.M. Hsiao, eds, *In Search of an East Asian Development Model*, Transaction Publications: New Brunswick

Papanek, Gustav and Kyn O, 1986, 'The Effect on Income Distribution of Development, the Growth Rate and Economic Strategy', *Journal of Development Economics*, vol. 23

Parmer, Norman, 1960, *Colonial Labor Policy and Administration: A History of Labor in the Rubber Plantation Industry of Malaya, c. 1910–1941*, J.J. Augustin: New York

Pasinetti, L., 1961–2, 'Rate of Profit and Income Distribution in Relation to the Rate of Economic Growth', *Review of Economic Studies*, vol. 29

Pearce D. *et al.*, 1989, *A Blueprint for a Green Economy*, Earthscan Publications: London

Polanyi, Karl, 1944, *The Great Transformation*, Rinehart & Co: New York

Porter, Michael, 1990, *The Competitive Advantage of Nations*, Free Press:

Prebisch, Raoul, 1959, 'Commercial Policy in the Underdeveloped Countries', *American Economic Review Papers and Proceedings*, May

Psacharopoulos, George, 1973, *Return to Education: An International Comparison*, Elsevier: San Francisco

Putnam, Robert D. *et al.* 1993, *Making Democracy Work, Civic Traditions in Modern Italy*, Princeton University Press: Princeton

Pyatt, F.G., 1988, 'A SAM Approach to Modelling', *Journal of Policy Modelling*, vol. 10, no. 3

Ranis, G., ed., 1972, *The Gap Between Rich and Poor Nations*, London: Macmillan

——, 1978, 'Equity with Growth in Taiwan: How "Special" is the "Special Case"?', *World Development*, vol. 13, April

——, 1985, 'Can the East Asian Model of Development be Generalised? A Comment', *World Development*, vol. 13, April

Ranis, G. and T. Paul Schultz, eds, 1988, *The State of Development Economics*, Oxford: Blackwell

Redding, S.G., 1993, *The Spirit of Chinese Capitalism*, de Gruyter: Berlin & New York

Rhode, D.L., ed., 1990, *Theoretical Perspectives on Sexual Difference*, Yale University Press: New Haven

Ricardo, David, 1911, *The Principles of Political Economy and Taxation*, (Everyman Library), Dent: London

Riedel, 1988, 'Economic Development in East Asia: Doing What Comes Naturally', in Hughes, ed.

Robinson, Joan, 1936, 'Disguised Unemployment', *Economic Journal*, June

——, 1956, *The Accumulation of Capital*, Macmillan: London

——, 1962, *Economic Philosophy*, Penguin: Harmondsworth

——, 1970, 'A Model of Accumulation', in Sen, ed.

Rodgers, Gary, ed., 1989, *Urban Poverty and the Labour Market: Access to Jobs and Income in Asian and Latin American Cities*, ILO: Geneva

Rodrik, Dani, 1998, 'Globalisation, Social Conflict and Economic Growth', *The World Economy*, vol. 21, no. 2, March

Romer, Paul, 1990 'Endogenous Technological Change', *Journal of Political Economy*, vol. 98, no. 5, Part 2, October

Rondinelli, Dennis, 1983, *Development Projects as Policy Experiments*, Routledge: London & New York

Rosenstein-Rodan, P.N., 1943, 'Problems of Industrialization of East and South-Eastern Europe', *Economic Journal*, June–September

Rostow, W.W., 1956, 'The Take-off into Self-Sustaining Growth', *Economic Journal*, March

——, 1960, *The Stages of Economic Growth, A Non-Communist Manifesto*, Cambridge University Press: Cambridge

——, 1975, *How it All Began: Origins of Modern Economy*, Methuen: London

Rugman, Alan M., 1993, 'Drawing the Border for a Multinational Enterprise and a Nation-State', in Eden and Potter, eds

Ruttan, V.W and Y. Hayami, 1984, 'Toward a Theory of Induced Institutional Innovation', *Journal of Development Studies*, July

Sachs, J.D., 1987, 'Trade and Exchange Rate Policies in Growth-oriented Adjustment Programs', in Corbo *et al.*, eds

——, ed., 1989, *Developing Country Debt and Economic Performance*, University of Chicago Press: Chicago

Said, Edward, 1978, *Orientalism*, Random House: New York

——, 1993, *Culture and Imperialism*, Knopf: New York

Saul, John R., 1992, *Voltaire's Bastards: The Dictatorship of Reason in the West*, Viking, Toronto

—— 1995, *The Unconscious Civilization*, Anansi: Concord, Ont.

Schmidt, Rodney, 1997, 'A Feasible Foreign Exchange Transactions Tax' (mimeo.), North–South Institute: Ottawa, Ont., September

Schultz, T., 1961, 'Investment in Human Capital', *American Economic Review*, March

——, 1964, *Transforming Traditional Agriculture*, Yale University Pess: New Haven

Schumacher, E.F., 1973, *Small is Beautiful: A Study of Economics as if People Mattered*, Blond & Briggs: London

Scitovsky, Tibor, 1952, *Welfare and Competition, the Economics of a Fully Employed Economy*, Unwin: London

Scott, J.C., 1976, *The Moral Economy of the Peasant, Rebellion and Subsistence in Southeast Asia*, Yale University Press: New Haven

——, 1985, *Weapons of the Weak: Everyday Forms of Peasant Resistance*, Yale University Press: New Haven

Scott, M.F.G., 1989, *A New View of Economic Growth*, Oxford University Press: Oxford

——, 1991, *A New View of Economic Growth, Four Lectures*, World Bank Discussion Papers 131, Washington, DC

Seabrook, Jeremy, 1993, *Victims of Development*, Verso: London

Seers, Dudley, 1962, 'Why Visiting Economists Fail', *Journal of Political Economy*, August

——, 1963, 'Limitations of the Special Case', *Bulletin of the Oxford Institute of Economics and Statistics*, May

Selvaratnam, V., 1994, *Innovations in Higher Education: Singapore at the Competitive Edge*, World Bank Technical Paper no. 222, World Bank: Washington, DC

Sen, Amartya, ed., 1970, *Growth Economics*, Penguin: Harmondsworth

——, 1973, *On Economic Inequality*, Oxford University Press: New York

——, 1987, *On Ethics and Economics*, Blackwell: Oxford

——, 1998, 'Human Development and Financial Conservatism', *World Development*, vol. 26, no. 4

Sen, Gita and Caren Grown, 1987, *Development Crises and Alternative Visions: Third World Women's Perspectives*, Monthly Review Press: New York

Sethuraman, S.V., 1976, *Jakarta: Urban Development and Employment*, ILO: Geneva

Shiva Vandana, 1989, *Staying Alive*, Zed Books: London

Shonfield, A., 1961, *The Attack on World Poverty*, London: Chatto & Windus

Singer, Hans W., 1950, 'The Distribution of Gains Between Investing and Borrowing Countries', *American Economic Review*, May

——, 1975, 'The Distribution of Gains from Trade and Investment, Revisited', *Journal of Development Studies*, vol. 11, no. 6, July

——, 1988, 'Food Aid: Development Tool or Obstacle to Development', *Development Policy Review*, vol. 5, no. 4

——, 1989, 'Lessons of Postwar Development Experience, 1945–99', Discussion Paper 210, IDS, University of Sussex

Smith, Adam, 1776, *The Wealth of Nations*, 2 vols, Cannan 5th edn, Methuen & Co: London

Solow, Robert, 1956, 'A Contribution to the Theory of Growth', *Quarterly Journal of Economics*, February

——, 1970, *Growth Theory: An Exposition*, Oxford University Press: New York

South Commission, 1990, *The Challenge to the South*, Oxford University Press: Oxford

Southward, Herman M. and Bruce F. Johnston, eds, 1967, *Agricultural Development and Economic Growth*, Cornell University Press: Ithaca, New York

Sraffa, P., 1960, *Production of Commodities by Commodities*, Cambridge University Press: Cambridge

Srinivasan, T., 1977, 'Development, Poverty and Basic Human Needs: Some Issues', *Food Research Institute Studies*, no. 2

——, 1985, 'Neo-classical Political Economy, the State and Economic Development', *Asian Development Review*, vol. 3, no. 2

Standing, G. and V. Tokman, eds, 1991, *Toward Social Adjustment: Labour Market Issues in Structural Adjustment*, ILO: Geneva

Stavrianos, L. S., 1981, *Global Rift: The Third World Comes of Age*, Marrow: New York

Stern, N., 1989, 'The Economics of Development: A Survey', *Economic Journal*, vol. 99, September

Stolper, W., 1967, *Planning Without Facts*, Harvard University Press: Cambridge, Mass.

Streeten, Paul P., 1963, 'Balanced Versus Unbalanced Growth', *Economic Weekly* (April 20), reprinted in Johnson and Kamerschen, eds

——, 1972, *Frontiers of Development Studies*, Macmillan: London

——,1979, 'Basic Needs: Premises and Promises', *Journal for Policy Modeling*, vol. 1

Streeten, Paul P. and Stewart, F., 1971, *Conflicts Between Output and Employment Objectives in Developing Countries*, Oxford: Queen Elizabeth House, July

Streeten, Paul P., S.Burki, M. ul Haq, N. Hicks and F. Stewart, 1981, *First Things First: Meeting Basic Needs in Developing Countries*, Oxford University Press: New York

Sunkel, O., 1972, 'Big Business and "Dependencia"', *Foreign Affairs*, April

Tan, Gerald, 1992, *The Newly Industrializing Countries of Asia*, Times Academic Press, Singapore

——, 1993, 'The next NICs of Asia', *Third World Quarterly*, vol. 14, no. 1

Taylor, L., 1979, *Macro Models for Developing Countries*, McGraw-Hill, New York

——, 1983, *Structuralist Macroeconomics: Applicable Models for the Third World*, Basic Books: New York

——, 1988, *Varieties of Stabilization Experience*, Clarendon: Oxford

——, 1993, 'The World Bank and the Environment: The World Development Report 1992', *World Development*, vol. 21, no. 5

Thurow, Lester, 1996, *The Future of Capitalism: How Today's Forces Shape Tomorrow's World*, Morrow: New York

Tickner, J.A., 1992, *Gender in International Relations*, Columbia University Press: New York

Timmer, Peter C., 1988, 'The Agricultural Transformation', in *Handbook of Development Economics* in Chenery and Srinivasan, eds

Tinbergen, J., 1964, *Central Planning*, Yale University Press: New Haven, Conn.

——, 1967, *Development Planning*, Weidenfeld & Nicolson: London

Tinbergen, J. *et al.*, 1976, *Reshaping the International Order*, Dutton & Co: New York

Tinker, Irene, ed., 1990, *Persistent Inequalities, Women and World Development*, Oxford University Press: New York

Todaro, M., 1969, 'A Model of Labor Migration and Urban Unemployment in Less Developed Countries', *American Economic Review*, vol. 59, no.1, March

——, 1971, *Development Planning: Models and Methods*, Oxford University Press, New York

——, 1977, *Economics for a Developing World*, Longman: London

——, 1981, *Economic Development in the Third World*, 2nd edn, Longman: New York

——, 1994, *Economics of Development*, Longman: London

Tokman, V., 1978, 'An Exploration into the Nature of Informal–Formal Sector Relationships', *World Development*, vol. 6, September–October

Tolbert, W.C. and S.M. Baum, 1985, *Investing in Development: Lessons of World Bank Experience*, Oxford University Press: Washington, DC

Toye, J.F.J, ed., 1979 *Taxation and Economic Development*, Frank Cass: London

——, 1993, *Dilemmas of Development*, 2nd edn, Blackwell: Oxford

Tsuru, S., 1976, *The Mainsprings of Japanese Growth: A Turning Point?*, Atlantic Institute for International Affairs: Paris

Tucker, Lee, 1997, 'Child Slaves in Modern India: The Bonded Labor Problem', *Human Rights Quarterly*, vol. 19: 572–629

Turnham, David and I. Jaeger, 1971, *The Employment Problem in Less Developed Countries: A Review of Evidence*, Paris: OECD

ul Haq, Mahbub, 1981, 'Beyond the Slogan of South-South Cooperation', in *Dialogue for a New Order*, edited by Khadija Haq, Pergamon: New York

ul Haq, Mahbub, Inge Kaul and I. Grunberg, eds, 1996, *The Tobin Tax, Coping with Financial Volatility*, Oxford University Press: New York

UN, 1989, *Elements of an International Development Strategy for the 1990's*, UN Department of International Economic and Social Affairs: New York

——, 1995, *World Summit for Social Development: The Copenhagen Declaration and Programme for Action*, New York, 6–12 March

UN Centre on Transnational Corporations, 1988, *Transnational Corporations in World Development: Trends and Prospects*, United Nations: New York

——, 1993, *World Investment Report: Transnational Corporations and Integrated International Production*, UNCTC: New York

UN Commission on Global Governance, 1995, *Our Global Neighbourhood: The Report of the Commission for Global Governance*, Oxford University Press: New York

UNCTAD, 1976, *Economic Cooperation and Integration Among Developing Countries*, UNCTAD: Geneva

UNDP, 1992, *Human Development Report*, Oxford University Press: New York

——, 1993, *Human Development Report*, Oxford University Press: New York

UN ECAFE, 1955, 'Economic Development and Planning in Asia and the Far East', *Economic Bulletin for Asia and the Far East*, vol. 6, no. 5

——, 1960, *Programming Techniques for Development Planning*, Bangkok

UNESCO, 1990, *Statistical Yearbook 1990*, UNESCO: Paris

UN High Commissioner for Refugees, 1995, *The State of the World's Refugees: In Search of Solutions*, Oxford University Press: New York

UNICEF, 1990, *The State of the World's Children*, Oxford University Press: NY

——, 1991, 'Improving Primary Education', Conference on Education for All Report, Paris

Uphoff, J. *et al.*, 1979, *Feasibility and Application of Rural Development Participation: A State-of-the-Art Paper*, Monograph Series no. 3, Rural Development Committee, Cornell University, Ithaca, New York, January

Uppal, J., 1969, 'Work Habits and Disguised Unemployment in Under-developed Countries: A Theoretical Analysis', *Oxford Economic Papers*, vol. 21, no. 3, November

——, 1973, *Disguised Unemployment in an Underdeveloped Economy: Its Nature and Measurement*, New York: Asia Publishing House

Vaitsos, C.V., 1978, 'Crisis in Regional Cooperation among Developing Countries: A Survey', *World Development*, vol. 6

van Pelt, Michael, 1993, 'Ecologically Sustainable Development and Project Evaluation', *Ecological Economics*, vol. 7

Vernon, R., 1966, 'Comprehensive Model Building in the Planning Process: The Case of Less Developed Countries', *Economic Journal*, March

——, 1971, *Sovereignty at Bay*, Basic Books: New York

——, 1985, *Exploring the Global Economy: Emerging Issues in Trade and Investment*, University Press of America: MD

——, 1993, 'Sovereignty at Bay: Twenty Years After', in Eden and Potter, eds

Vickers, Jeanne, 1990, *Women and the World Crisis*, Zed Books: London

Vogel, Ezra F., 1991, *The Four Little Dragons*, Harvard University Press: Cambridge, Mass.

Wade, R. , 1988, 'The Role of Government in Overcoming Market Failure: Taiwan, Republic of Korea and Japan', in Hughes, ed.

——, 1990, *Governing the Market, Economic Theory and the Role of Government in East Asian Industrialisation*, Princeton University Press: Princeton

Wallace, A.R., 1989, *The Malay Archipelago: The land of the Orang-Utan, and the Bird of Paradise*, (with an introduction by John Bastin), Oxford University Press: Singapore

Walters, Robert S., 1973, 'UNCTAD: Intervener Between Poor and Rich States', *Journal of World Trade Law*, September–October

Warinner, Doreen, 1969, *Land Reform in Principle and Practice*, Clarendon Press: Oxford

Watkins, M., 1963, 'A Staple Theory of Economic Growth', *Canadian Journal of Economics and Political Science*, vol. 29, no. 2

Watson, Andrew and Jeel Dirlam, 1965, 'The Impact of Underdevelopment on Economic Planning', *Quarterly Journal of Economics*, vol. 79, May

Weeks, J., 1975, 'Policies for Expanding Employment in the Informal Urban Sectors of Developing Countries', *International Labour Review*, January

Weisbrod, B.A., 1964, *External Benefits of Public Education: An Economic Analysis*, Princeton University, Industrial Relations Section: Princeton

Weiss, J., 1986, 'Japan's Postwar Protection Policy: Some Implications for Less Developed Countries', *Journal of Development Studies*, January

Westphal, L.E., 1978, 'The Republic of Korea's Experience with Export-Led Development', *World Development*, March

——, 1990, 'Industrial Policy in an Export-Propelled Economy: Lessons from South Korea's Experience', *Journal of Economic Perspectives*, vol. 4, no. 1, Summer

Wharton, C.R., 1962, 'Marketing, Merchandising and Moneylending', *Malayan Economic Review*, vol. 7, no. 2, October

Wilber, Charles, ed., 1984, *The Political Economy of Development and Underdevelopment*, 3rd edn, Random House: New York

Williams, Eric, 1972, ' The Purpose of Planning', in *The Crisis of Planning*, vol. 1, in Faber and Seers, eds

Williamson, J., 1997, 'The Washington Consensus Revisited', in Emerij, ed.

Winch, Donald, 1992, *Malthus, An Essay on the Principle of Population*, Cambridge University Press: New York

Woo, Jennie H., 1991, 'Education and Economic Growth in Taiwan: A Case of Successful Planning', *World Development*, vol. 19, no. 8

Woolley, F.R., 1993, 'The Feminist Challenge to Neoclassical Economics', *Cambridge Journal of Economics*, vol. 17

World Commission on Environment and Development, 1987, *Our Common Future*, Oxford University Press: New York

World Bank, 1984, *World Development Report*, Oxford University Press: Washington, DC

——, 1989, *Adjustment Programs and Social Welfare*, WB Discussion Paper 44, WB: Washington, DC,

——, 1990, *World Development Report*, Oxford University Press: Washington, DC

——, 1992, *World Development Report*, Oxford University Press: Washington, DC

——, 1992a, *Adjustment Lending and Mobilization of Private and Public Resources for Growth*, WB: Washington, DC

——, 1993, *The East Asian Miracle*, Oxford University Press: New York

World Council on Development and Environment (Brundtland Report), 1987, *Our Common Future*, Oxford University Press: Oxford

——, 1997, *World Development Report 1997*, Washington, DC

——, 1997a, *Expanding the Measure of Wealth, Indicators of Environmentally Sustainable Development*, CSD Edition, Washington, DC, April

World Resource Institute, 1992, *World Resources 1992–3, A Guide for the Global Resources: Toward Sustainable Development*, Oxford University Press: New York

Yergin, D., 1993, *The Prize: The Epic Quest for Oil, Money and Power*, Simon & Schuster: New York

Young, Allyn, 1928, 'Increasing Return and Economic Progress', *Economic Journal*, vol. 38

Yunis, M., 1988, 'The Poor as the Engine of Growth', *Economic Impact*, no. 63

Yutopoulos, Pan A. and Jeffrey B. Nugent, 1976, *Economics of Development: Empirical Investigations*, Harper & Row: New York

Zuvekas, Clarence, Jr, 1979, *Economic Development: An Introduction*, St Martin's Press: New York

INDEX

Abbot, L.D. 37
absolute advantage principle 46–8, 47, 49
accumulation of capital *see* capital accumulation
Adelman, I. 3, 14, 89, 164
Africa: anarchy and disorder 156; debt problems 129; decline in food production and resulting mass hunger 98; decline in real incomes 2; ethnic conflict 113; failure of agricultural development 124; negative growth 147; plantation economies 38; political instability 133; post-independence planning failure 62; World Bank–IMF prescriptions 132; *see also* East Africa; South Africa
Africans: racism of colonials 11; slave labour mobilized by colonials 43; Westernization of 60
Agarwal, Bina 91
Agarwala, A.N. 63, 69, 72, 76, 80
aggregate disequilibrium: Keynesian macro-model 103, 106
aggressive unilateralism 143–4, 153
agriculture: capital-intensive mechanization 97–8; failures of development 97; large-scale 26; modernization in Far Eastern NICs 77–9, 98, 114, 138; neo-classical structuralism 96; regulation of property rights 124; relegation in Rostowian theory 72; seasonality 105; subsistence production 75;

successful development in Taiwan and South Korea 98; transition to industry 36; viewed as primitive or underdeveloped 74, 76
Ahluwalia, M.S. 115
aid 103; American programmes 62, 67, 89, 114; need to reform system 166; and trade 153; Western projects 83, 97, 165; *see also* food aid; foreign aid
AIDS *see* HIV/AIDS
Alatas, Syed Hussein 12
Algiers Conference (1973) 111
Altbach, P.G. 137
Amazonia: resources 155
America: slavery in Southern states 4; *see also* Central America; Latin America; North America; United States of America
Americanization 157–8; and Westernization 58, 59, 67, 74, 95, 101
Amin, Samir 10–11, 57, 96, 113, 121
anthropologists 136
anti-labour views: colonial administrators 38, 40; Malthusian theory 40, 43; Western theories 95, 148, 157, 159
anti-rural strategies 64, 75, 76, 77, 79, 81, 83, 126
aristocracy: displacement by captains of industry 37
Aristotelian logic 54, 55
Arndt, H.W. 13, 33, 38, 56, 87, 88, 160–1

DATE DUE

SEP 1 2 2001			
JAN 2 1 2003			